Under Pallor, Under Shadow

Bill Felber

UNDER PALLOR,

UNDER SHADOW

The 1920 American League Pennant Race That Rattled and Rebuilt Baseball

UNIVERSITY OF NEBRASKA PRESS | LINCOLN & LONDON

Library of Congress
Cataloging-in-Publication Data

Felber, Bill.
Under pallor, under shadow: the
1920 American league pennant
race that rattled and rebuilt
baseball / Bill Felber.
p. cm.
Includes bibliographical
references and index.
ISBN 978-0-8032-3471-0
(cloth: alk. paper)
1. American League of
Professional Baseball
Clubs—History. 2. Baseball—
United States—History.
3. Cleveland Indians (Baseball
team)—History. 4. Chicago
White Sox (Baseball team)—
History. 5. New York Yankees
(Baseball team)—History.
I. Title.
GV875.A15F45 2011
796.357'640973—dc22
2010033685

Set in Iowan Old Style
by Bob Reitz.
Designed by R. W. Boeche.

If baseball is to continue to exist as our National game . . . it must be with the recognition on the part of club owners and players, that the game itself belongs to the American people, and not to either owners or players. — *Albert Lasker, October 1920, from his plan to reform the game's administrative structure*

Contents

Acknowledgments ix

1. Ralph Young's Big Moment 1

2. A Babe in the City 12

3. Winter of Their Discontent 28

4. The Honeymoon 48

5. Reactive Revolutionary 61

6. The Record 69

7. The Last Three Weeks of Innocence and Purity in the History of Baseball 93

8. Under Pallor 117

9. Under Shadow 133

10. A Chigger in Conspiracy with Gamblers 153

11. A Phosphate at the Edelweiss 170

12. Eddie Chews, Chicago Stews 195

13. Losers Laugh, Winners Cry 214

14. Aftermath 236

15. Damon and Ring at the Series 246

Notes 261

Index 273

Acknowledgments

I want to acknowledge the assistance of several people in the preparation of this story. That list begins with my agent, Robert Wilson, who believed in *Under Pallor, Under Shadow* when times were rough. I also want to recognize Walt Wilson, a fine Chicago-based researcher who was a tremendous help combing the files of the Chicago History Museum for documents that turned broad-brush intimations into specific, attributable assertions. Similarly, George Rugg, curator of special collections at Notre Dame, facilitated access to the Ritter tapes, which effectively enabled me to interview eyewitnesses who have been dead for two decades concerning events that took place in their youth.

Finally, a word of appreciation goes to my family. The process of writing a book necessarily is a lonely one, and family members put up with a lot. My wife and son are understanding in ways that many would not be.

1. Ralph Young's Big Moment

Ralph Young was a second baseman of unremarkable talent for nine Major League seasons during the first quarter of the twentieth century. He never hit better than .300, and his career .247 batting and .959 fielding averages failed to gain much notice among contemporaries.

Yet for one moment on an August afternoon in 1920, Ralph Young symbolically controlled the future of both a star-crossed Major League season and a starstruck game. On August 23 at New York's Polo Grounds, Young, acting in concert with his Detroit Tigers teammates, determined whether the American League pennant race continued or halted in place. And because the pennant race not only was compelling on its own merits but also was the engine of a broader force for change, Young's decision held consequences well beyond the outcome of a single game.

Big league baseball stood at the cusp of crisis and change that summer. The focal point was the alleged fixing by gamblers of the previous year's World Series between the Chicago White Sox and the Cincinnati Reds. In August 1920 there was no such thing as an investigation into the honesty of the 1919 World Series, but that would soon change. Within two weeks rumors of another fix—this time an obscure game between noncontenders in the other league—would trigger legal action . . . if games continued to be played.

Given the prevalence of such talk that summer, the lack of an investigation reflected the decrepit state of the American League management. The feuding principals were a once-powerful but tottering league executive whose commands increasingly went ignored and a self-possessed club owner. Once a feared dictator, American League (AL) president Ban Johnson by 1920 lacked the power within his own ranks to pursue rot. Chicago White Sox owner Charles Comiskey simply lacked motivation. Beyond that, since the two men hated each other, they refused to cooperate. So the matter of the game's integrity simmered toward combustibility.

The stakes were high because baseball, mirroring American society in general, was a growth industry after World War I. In 1920 attendance rose in six of the eight American League cities. Part of the increase could be explained by postwar exuberance, and part by the 10 percent increase in schedule length, from 140 games to 154. But the attendance gains were uniformly far steeper than 10 percent—a 70 percent increase in Cleveland, 33 percent in Chicago, and 53 percent in Washington. The Athletics drew 20 percent more fans despite finishing last for the sixth consecutive season. Leaguewide the average increase approached 40 percent.[1]

The main reason for this increase in baseball passion was Babe Ruth. Since coming to the New York Yankees from Boston the previous January, the Babe had hit home runs at an unheard-of pace. By mid-July he already stood at the brink of the all-time single-season home run record. At a time when an average big league gate was about 6,500, his appearance routinely brought out two or three times that many fans, even to midweek afternoon games. Yankees dates generated more than one-third of the season's total seventy-seven-game attendance in several visiting cities.

Nowhere was Ruth's impact at the turnstiles more powerful than at his home field, the Polo Grounds. In 1920 the Yankees became the first team in baseball history to draw more than 1 million fans, setting a season attendance record (1,289,422) that more than doubled their turnout in 1919. It took twenty-six years for any team to surpass 1.289 million, far and away the longest duration of an attendance record in the history of the Major Leagues.[2]

Ordinarily interest in the league's tense three-way pennant race involving New York, Cleveland, and Chicago could have been expected to build through the summer, especially with Ruth as a special attraction. But in August 1920 two circumstances were at work. First, on August 16 a ballplayer had been killed during a game. Ray Chapman died on that very field, the Polo Grounds, in New York, struck down by the man poised to take the mound against Ralph Young. In the intervening week players around the league debated the extent of Carl Mays's guilt for throwing the beanball that felled Chapman.

Because of his reputation for throwing at hitters, Mays was not a sympathetic figure. When he learned the morning after the game that Chapman had died of his injuries, first baseman Doc Johnston said Mays should "be strung up." Outfielder Jack Graney wouldn't go that far, but he did say that the team was "unanimous in not wanting ever to bat against Carl Mays again."[3] That same afternoon Cleveland manager Tris Speaker released a statement that was presented as absolving Mays of malicious intent, although it actually only acknowledged the impossibility of knowing what the pitcher's intentions were. But decades later, with neither ramifications nor reprisals to be feared, several of the Indians admitted that they believed Mays had tried to bean Chapman because both his batting prowess and his experience were viewed as indispensable to his team's prospects.

"This dirty louse of a Carl Mays," Joe Wood would tell author Lawrence Ritter in 1963, even at that date insisting his remarks be kept "off the record." "I understand he made the crack before the game that he was going to take Chappie out of there that day." Ritter honored Wood's request and did not use any of the revealing material in *The Glory of Their Times*, his 1966 oral history of the game's early days. But he kept the tapes for posterity, ensuring that although Wood has been dead for a quarter of a century, his assessment of Mays's motives would survive.[4]

The Indians may have lacked the damning evidence to mount an action against Mays, but others were not so reticent. In Boston the Red Sox and the Tigers held an unusual joint team meeting designed to create momentum behind a boycott of the pitcher. A similar discussion involved the Senators and the Browns in Washington.

As the American League's founder and only president, Johnson could have been expected to crush such an insurrection by threatening to suspend rebels. Formally, the league president went on record as declaring Mays innocent of any malevolent intent in the Chapman beaning, although he added his expectation that Mays would not pitch anymore that year. In other words he presumed Mays would suspend himself. But Johnson's position in part also spoke to the second unique circumstance: it was not at all clear that Johnson could have rallied the league behind any position he took. Biographer Eugene Murdock has described Johnson as "a man of numerous hates . . . whose nature it was to demand subservience."[5]

The conflicts created by that dictatorial approach eroded Johnson's control more or less continuously for five years, accelerating in 1919 during a tumultuous fight that involved the services of Mays himself. In 1920 Johnson knew that any effort by him to halt a work action aimed at Mays might easily trigger a wider-scale revolt. It was no certainty that he could prevail against such an insurrection.

Johnson's relationship with some of the AL owners—particularly Comiskey—had always blown hot and cold. The two men, once loyal friends and hunting buddies, had fallen out over causes so musty and long-standing that by the middle of the century's second decade they could hardly be recalled. One version placed the responsibility on Johnson's decision fifteen years earlier to suspend Sox manager Fielder Jones, also the team's star center fielder, following a run-in with an umpire during a particularly sensitive moment in a heated pennant race. Coincidentally Johnson had sent Comiskey some freshly caught bass from one of his frequent fishing excursions. "Does Ban want me to play the fish in the outfield?" Comiskey is said to have remarked bitterly.[6]

The Johnson-Comiskey relationship waxed and waned so frequently that the split could have had half a dozen causes, both profound and trivial. There is no question, however, that by 1919 the two viewed each other as entirely expendable. A 1918 incident involving Jack Quinn precipitated the final break. Quinn was a journeyman pitcher with years of big league experience but laboring at the time in a small Minor League that had collapsed due to the war. The National Commission had ruled that such players were free agents, and Comiskey signed Quinn, who won five of his six decisions. At virtually the same time, however, Quinn's old Minor League team sold his 1919 contract to the Yankees. "The controversy is rather unfortunate," a sheepish commission said in awarding Quinn to the Yankees.[7] Comiskey blamed Johnson.

It also did not take the dictatorial Johnson long, following purchase of the Yankees by the team of Col. Tillinghast Huston and Col. Jacob Ruppert, to make enemies of the league's richest owners. Again the precise cause is obscure, although the Ruppert-Huston perception that what was good for the Yankees was necessarily good for the American League almost certainly clashed with Johnson's vision of himself as chief policy-setter. By 1920 Ruppert and Huston viewed Johnson (probably correctly) as the vindictive, behind-the-scenes force pushing the Giants to terminate the Yanks' lease on the Polo Grounds. Ironically this action, which the New York franchise owners saw as openly hostile to their financial futures, forced the construction of Yankee Stadium, probably the second most vital step (behind the signing of Ruth) in the formation of the Yankees dynasty.

The rift between Johnson and the Red Sox and the Yankees reached insolubility during the summer of 1919, with Mays as the focal point. Known around the league for his temper, Mays had left the Red Sox that July during a game in Chicago, bemoaning what he viewed as the absence of support from his Boston teammates and vowing not to pitch for Boston again. He particularly singled out infielder Jack Barry, asserting in print that the thirty-two-year-old middle infielder, a veteran of five world's championship teams, should be benched. It was not Mays's first dustup with management or fans. A few weeks earlier he had become enraged when he concluded that a spectator named Bryan Hayes was banging too loudly on the tin roof of the visitors' dugout in Philadelphia. Mays had reacted by throwing a ball at Hayes, striking the fan's straw hat. Despite pleas not to do so by Connie Mack himself, Hayes filed assault charges against Mays.

When Mays abandoned the Red Sox, Johnson berated Red Sox owner Harry Frazee and team manager Ed Barrow for not suspending their star pitcher. But Frazee and Barrow had other ideas. Frazee's team was going nowhere, and he needed money. If Mays would no longer play for the Red Sox, he remained a reliable starter and therefore a marketable asset to a contender. Frazee's allies, Comiskey and Ruppert and Huston, all fit that description. Frazee announced the trade of Mays to the Yanks in exchange for two journeyman pitchers and seventy-five thousand dollars.

Johnson reacted by suspending Mays himself, concurrently threatening to hold up New York postseason shares if his order was ignored. Following Mack's lead of two years earlier, Ruppert sought and received a court order that summer enjoining Johnson from preventing Mays's participation in games. Then, to make sure his defiance of Johnson was registered, Ruppert gave Mays a raise. The pitcher, whose record in Boston had been 5-11 at the time of his trade, responded by winning nine of his thirteen New York starts and posting a 1.65 earned run average. The Yankees finished third, a game and a half ahead of Detroit. When Johnson made good on his threat to hold up Yankees winnings, players asked the court to order Johnson to release their shares.

Mays's departure from Boston was only one step in the cash-strapped Frazee's ongoing process of reducing costs, which had the by-product of seeding former Mays teammates—and therefore enemies—around the league. By August 1920 several clubs had what amounted to anti-Mays factions, and those factions bubbled up naturally after Chapman's death. Former teammates known to strongly dislike Mays included Amos Strunk (A's–White Sox), Dutch Leonard (Tigers), Tris Speaker (Indians), as well as Sam Jones, Stuffy McInnis, Harry Hooper, and Wally Schang, all still with the Red Sox.

Also Mays's "don't give a damn" pitching style, which featured high and tight fastballs from a submarine delivery, provoked strong emotions even among players who had never suited up with him. Ty Cobb, for one, hated Mays more than he did any other pitcher, which given Cobb's distaste for pitchers in general says a lot. Cobb was the playing face of Detroit, and on the afternoon of August 23, 1920, in New York, everyone believed the Tigers collectively would follow Cobb's directive.

But if Mays was the immediate polarizing force behind the events of the summer of 1920, gambling created its own longer-term impacts on the game. Although today there is no precise list of the baseball games that were fixed, it is likely that several players in both leagues had already been corrupted prior to 1920 by their associations with gamblers. The evidence, while not prosecutable, has long been considered strong against such prominent stars of the era as Hal Chase, Lee Magee, Rube Benton, Heinie Zimmerman, Jean Dubuc, Bill James, Gene Paulette, and Buck Herzog. In the case of Chase, some of that evidence dated back as much as a decade prior to the 1919 World Series. In recent years evidence has begun to accumulate casting suspicion on the 1918 World Series, in which the Boston Red Sox defeated the Chicago Cubs.[8]

In the summer of 1920, the public record consisted of nothing more than talk, and lessening amounts of that in print as the Series faded from memory. On the field and in the clubhouse, however, circumstances differed. The White Sox operated for most of the 1920 season more as two clans than one team. The seven suspects who remained following ringleader Chick Gandil's retirement constituted one clique. They included pitchers Eddie Cicotte and Lefty Williams, third baseman Buck Weaver, shortstop Swede Risberg, outfielders Joe Jackson and Happy Felsch, and reserve Fred McMullin. The so-called Clean Sox—catcher Ray Schalk, pitchers Red Faber and Dickie Kerr, second baseman Eddie Collins, first baseman Shano Collins, outfielder Nemo Leibold, and a handful of reserves—represented the other faction. It was said that the only time the two groups got together was to fight, and although clubhouse diaries have not survived, the accounts of games of that era contain more than one reference to the White Sox battling one another in their own dugout or on the playing field.

The honest players may well have considered themselves to have ongoing reason for hostility, since rumors were rife that the Black Sox remained on the take throughout 1920. Gamblers supposedly manipulated their wins and losses to maximize betting interest in the race. Whether such rumors were true or not, the Sox—who had combined generally strong performances with occasional game-costing lapses all season—held first place by two games over Cleveland and by three and one-half over the Yanks that Monday afternoon. It was a gambler's dream scenario.

But that scenario had not envisioned the fatal beaning of Chapman by Mays. When Chapman's death became known, the Tigers and the Red Sox—who considered Mays a pariah for his betrayal the previous season—held their joint clubhouse meeting in Boston at which a boycott designed to force Johnson's hand on Mays was informally agreed to. The only condition was that Speaker sign off on the idea. The Indians manager—away from his team at the time for the Chapman funeral and preoccupied with those arrangements—took no position on the boycott. The Browns and the Senators added their support, but only in an abstract, "okay by us" sort of way.

The United Press quoted Cobb as calling for Mays's banishment, an assertion that inflamed New Yorkers. When the Tigers arrived for the opening game of their series with the Yankees on Friday, the New York fans met Cobb with boos and some threats. He responded by vigorously denying those published reports. But neither he nor manager Hughie Jennings went as far as to declare that the Tigers either would or would not take the field against Mays.

W. O. McGeehan, columnist for the New York Tribune, took the anti-Mays talk sufficiently seriously to publicly call out Cobb and the Tigers that morning. "There is a disposition in a small part of the baseball world to be cruelly unfair to Carl Mays," McGeehan wrote. "When certain players declare that they will not play unless Mays is put out of the game, they apparently wish it inferred that the killing of Ray Chapman was not an accident." Those players, McGeehan asserted, "are showing how petty they can be." The columnist called on Johnson to see that Mays got "a square deal for the sake of the game," in other words, to stand firm against Cobb if the Tigers walked out.[9]

The New York public rallied behind Mays, who was, after all, an eighteen-game winner. Yankees fans greeted his appearance for warmups with a resonant ovation. We know now that by the morning of the opening game, boycott momentum had already died out. But the fans on the scene did not know that.

The boycott might have materialized had the White Sox chosen to add their voices. At that point only Chicago and Connie Mack's last-place Athletics had not expressed at least some level of sentiment against the pitcher. The Sox had every reason to do so. The Yankees' pennant hopes would have been lost without the services of their best pitcher, effectively reducing the race to the Sox and the crippled Indians. Comiskey had an additional motive. Were Johnson cornered over the Mays matter, he may have lacked the support to enforce his desire to leave Mays alone. That in turn might have forced Johnson's resignation.

But Comiskey hated many of his players for what he believed they had done the previous autumn as much as they hated one another. White Sox players remained mum, the cliques too busy not talking to each other to take an action that was in their mutual interest.

So as the first pitch approached, the question of a response to Mays—with its various implications for the broader game—remained to all appearances an open one. The entire complex issue appeared to depend on Ralph Young. Would he hit, or would he touch off a boycott? And if the latter, what would happen then?

Young emerged from the dugout, took his place in the batter's box, and awaited Carl Mays's first pitch. It was a called strike.

The New York crowd cheered wildly. The game—and the game's reshaping—was on.

2. A Babe in the City

Baseball began when Babe Ruth came to New York.

Not literally, of course. Major League professional baseball had been played in this country for a half century before the Yankees laid out $125,000 to buy Ruth from the Boston Red Sox on January 5, 1920. Ruth himself was by that time an established star. Approaching his twenty-fifth birthday, he had pitched nearly ninety regular season victories (plus three in the World Series.) The American League earned run average (ERA) leader in 1916, he had a career 2.19 ERA at a time when the league standard ranged from 2.70 to 3.20.

The Babe wasn't just a great pitcher; he could do things with the baseball that no other pitcher could hope to achieve. He could hit it, frequently and long. While winning that ERA title in 1916, he also batted a respectable .272 with fifteen runs batted in (RBI). The following season he raised his average to .325, a performance that would have ranked him fourth in the league behind only Ty Cobb, Tris Speaker, and Bobby Veach if he had gotten enough plate appearances to qualify.

So profuse were Ruth's offensive talents that they posed a problem for the new Boston manager, Ed Barrow, entering the 1918 season. If Barrow moved Ruth to the outfield, he would lose the Red Sox's best pitcher. If Barrow didn't, he would lose the Red Sox's best hitter three days out of every four. Barrow tried to finesse the dilemma. In 1918 the Babe started nineteen games on the mound, just half his total of the previous season, and made one additional relief appearance. He also played fifty-nine other games in the outfield. The results were good and good. He completed eighteen of those nineteen starts with a record of 13-7 and a 2.22 ERA. It was his highest in three seasons, yet still among the league's ten best. He also tripled his at bats and hit .300. More notably, for the first time Babe Ruth ranked atop American League home run hitters with eleven. That equaled the number hit by Philadelphia's Tilly Walker, although Walker had nearly one hundred more at bats. During spring training prior to the 1919 season, Ruth drove a pitch out of the ballpark, through a fairground, and into a hospital yard. A group of reporters later measured the distance to where the ball landed: 579 feet.

Barrow responded in logical fashion, by pushing the Babe more and more frequently into the heart of Boston's lineup. In 1919 he started just 15 games on the mound, but 111 in the outfield. By the standards of the time, his season was a marvel. He scored 103 runs and drove in 114, both league-leading totals. His .456 on-base average also led the league; in fact, it was the league's highest in four years. He hit .322, broke the league home run record in early August, and in September passed the all-time record of twenty-seven, finishing with twenty-nine. With seventy-five extra base hits, Ruth's slugging average for 1919 stood at .555, also a league-leading total.

So much of an offensive force had the Babe become that opposing pitchers did something for which there was no parallel in baseball history to that time: they consistently pitched around him. In 1919 Ruth was walked 101 times, or about 20 percent of his plate appearances. Compare that to Ty Cobb, the game's most feared hitter and by 1919 an eleven-time batting champion. Only once in his entire career did Cobb walk more than eighty times. In 1911, at the height of his glory, Cobb batted .420 with 127 RBIs, yet pitchers walked him just forty-four times. They did not fear Cobb. They did fear the Babe.

In one sense Red Sox owner Harry Frazee also feared the Babe. Frazee feared the escalating cost of signing him. "A player is worth all he can get," Ruth told the *Sporting News* in November 1919.[1] Beyond that, though, Ruth's remarkable season had made him something unique in American team sports at the time: his own drawing card. The Babe barnstormed through California that winter and mused openly about his options outside baseball: the movies, for example, or perhaps a heavyweight title fight against Jack Dempsey. It was Ruth's way of telling Frazee that he was going to make a lot more money, either from the Red Sox or from somebody else. The Red Sox owner set about identifying a market for his prize. There was one obvious market, the largest and richest of all: New York.

Frazee was no stranger to Yankees owners Jacob Ruppert and Tillinghast L'Hommideau Huston. He had dealt with them often over the past few seasons, generally for the same reason that he thought they'd be interested in Ruth. The Yankees owners had money, and they were unafraid to spend it. Three times in the past two years alone, Frazee had dealt with Ruppert and Huston, swapping ten players and more than fifty-five thousand dollars, most of the latter coming Frazee's way. None of those deals had been more contentious—although not between Frazee and Ruppert and Huston—than the July sale of renegade pitcher Carl Mays to

New York for two journeymen and forty thousand dollars.

So Frazee called Ruppert, who was only too willing to take the emerging star off Frazee's hands. The price: $125,000 plus a $300,000 loan to Frazee. But before formally signing off on the purchase, Ruppert sent manager Miller Huggins to California to personally talk to Ruth and determine whether the star player could be controlled in New York.

"You've been a pretty wild boy in Boston," Huggins is said to have told him. "In New York you'll have to behave."[2] Ruth agreed to do so but demanded in return that his ten-thousand-dollar salary be doubled. The Yanks signed off.

Privately Frazee told Barrow that the money was too good to pass up, but both men knew better. "You think you're getting a lot of money for Ruth, but you're not," Barrow is said to have told his boss.[3] A fifteen-hundred-word justification of the trade published under Frazee's name in the next day's *Boston Post* betrays the Red Sox owner's own recognition of how bad it looked. "He . . . had no regard for the feelings of anyone but himself," Frazee said of the player. "Ruth is taking on weight tremendously. He has floating cartilage in his knee . . . that may make him a cripple at any time."[4]

Ruth's impact on the field is part of the record, but his impact at the box office was equally dramatic. Prior to 1919 the all-time one-team attendance record had been 910,000, a total drawn by the Giants during the sensational 1908 pennant race. The Major League record, 6.66 million, had been set a year later. The Yankees franchise record was 619,000. With Ruth on board the Yanks drew nearly 1.3 million fans, more than doubling their own franchise record and breaking the 1908 Giants' mark by better than 40 percent. Baseball drew 9.12 million fans overall with Ruth in New York in 1920, breaking the record by 37 percent. And that was despite the war-shortened schedule that saw fourteen fewer games per team played in 1920 than in 1909.

It happened because although baseball games had always attracted a solid core base of fans, the Babe's presence appealed to less-committed fans. In some measure it was his manner: the Babe came across as what his nickname implied, a big kid. He was friendly, approachable, easy. Privately he was also gross. Having grown up on the Baltimore streets, Ruth possessed none of the cultural niceties that most people acquired naturally. He ate like a pig, cussed like a longshoreman, chased women like a sailor home on leave, and farted like a cow. "I wouldn't, nor you wouldn't, nor anybody else who really knew Babe like he was would want their kids to follow in his footsteps," Joe Wood later said of America's idol.[5]

Yet across the nation kids dreamed of following in the Babe's footsteps, and they did so because of his way with the baseball. The Babe hit home runs to places that had never before been visited. He hit them off rooftop cornices, across streets, and onto porches.

Ruppert and Huston wanted Ruth for his drawing power, but also because they were committed to constructing a winner. He got them closer to the goal that they had pursued with zeal and frequent wisdom since acquiring the team prior to the 1915 season.

Those 1915 Yanks weren't much. They'd never won a pennant and hadn't finished within ten games of first in a decade. From the start Ruppert and Huston threw cash at the problem. Almost their first move was to purchase the contract of a lightly used first baseman from Detroit for the waiver price. Wally Pipp only hit .246 as a rookie for the Yanks, but just one season later Pipp led the American League with twelve home runs. He repeated that accomplishment in 1917 (with nine), and in 1918 fashioned a .304 batting average around his war-related duties. Eventually Pipp would gain fame for losing his job to Lou Gehrig, but as the 1920 season began he was viewed as a complement to Ruth in the middle of the New York order.

A month later Ruppert and Huston laid out more cash to acquire George Mogridge, a twenty-six-year-old left-hander of some promise but little accomplishment, from Chicago. Over the next five seasons, Mogridge filled various roles, winning forty-three of ninety-one decisions, sixteen of those wins coming in 1918. That July Ruppert and Huston dipped for the first time into the ongoing fire sale being conducted by Connie Mack in Philadelphia. Their target: twenty-five-year-old right-hander Bob Shawkey, a top-of-the-rotation type. The previous season Shawkey had won fifteen games for the league champions. Given Shawkey's status as a potential prime catch for the insurgent Federal League, Mack unloaded the budding star rather than see the league lose him. In New York Shawkey developed quickly, winning twenty-four games in 1916 with a 2.21 ERA, and adding twenty wins in 1919. At the war's outset he enlisted in the navy. For that decision the New York papers thereafter referred to him as "Bob the Gob."

Another open-wallet visit to Mack, this one in 1916, landed third baseman Home Run Baker for $37,500. In August 1917 Huston and Ruppert found a catcher in twenty-one-year-old Herold "Muddy" Ruel, floating freely in the Browns organization. Ruel did not emerge as a reliable figure until after the war, and when he did it was to share duties with two of the least athletic but most colorfully nicknamed figures in the game. James Harrison Hannah stood six feet one and only weighed 190 pounds, but that was big enough to acquire the sobriquet "Truck" from teammates when he arrived in 1918 as a twenty-nine-year-old career Minor Leaguer and war fill-in. Fred Hofmann made only the briefest of debuts prior to reporting to the team's 1920 training camp and traveled with the big team only sporadically. Teammates called him "Bootnose," for reasons that presumably do not require elaboration.

The only veteran Yank who survived the Ruppert and Huston spending spree was shortstop Roger Peckinpaugh, an occasional bat but a recognized fielding ace. Over time he even learned to hit, grinding out a .305 average in 1919. When the Yanks acquired second baseman Del Pratt from the Browns as part of a seven-player deal, it not only completed the middle infield combo but also gave the Yankees an alliterative top of the batting order. As far as the city's newspaper clan was concerned, the top three spots were occupied by Pipp, Peck, and Pratt.

For the city's ethnic Italian population, all the acquisitions—prior to Ruth, at least—paled alongside the 1918 deal that sent George Burns to Philadelphia in exchange for Francesco Stephano Pezzolo. The latter was a thirty-year-old journeyman out of San Francisco who played under the far simpler handle of "Ping Bodie." Bodie was not the first ethnic Italian to reach the Major Leagues; Ed Abbaticchio had beaten him to that distinction before the turn of the century. But he was very much a rarity in a game that counted its non-Irish ethnics sparingly. The son of immigrants, Bodie in a sense had roots in New York. His dad had helped construct the Brooklyn Bridge before moving the family to San Francisco, where Francesco was born. A product of the city's street teams, Bodie found fame with the San Francisco Seals, hitting thirty home runs (in an expanded schedule) as a twenty-two-year-old in 1910. That got the attention of the Chicago White Sox, who signed him for the following season. He lasted parts of four seasons before being released and re-signing with the Seals for one year, then with the Athletics. Bodie drew attention for both his ethnicity and his mannerisms. Known colloquially as "The Wonderful Wop," his running style was compared to "the waddling of a duck."[6] With a lovably boisterous personality, Bodie became one of the first media darlings. "You should have heard me crash the old apple," he loved to remark of his batting exploits.[7] Like other pros Bodie came and went in the war year of 1918, playing 91 games and batting .256. A regular in 1919, he hit a respectable .278. Never a great player, he was, however, valuable for his appeal to the city's ethnic Italian audience.

Aside from the controversial acquisitions of Mays and Jack "Picus" Quinn, one final trade completed the roster that greeted Ruth in January 1920. In December 1918 Ruppert and Huston sent four players and fifteen thousand dollars to Frazee in exchange for outfielder Duffy Lewis and pitchers Dutch Leonard and Ernie Shore. Their best days were behind all three; in fact, Leonard refused to report to the Yankees, who allowed him to remain Boston property. A month later the Red Sox sold him to Detroit. Lewis, one-third of the famed Red Sox outfield that also included Tris Speaker and Harry Hooper, was thirty years old and had sat idle during all of 1918. With the Yankees he became the regular left fielder in 1919, batting .272, about ten points below his career average. Shore was only twenty-seven years old and a vital piece of the Red Sox championship rotations of 1915–16 when he came to New York. But he had little left. He made just thirteen starts in 1919 and appeared in just fourteen games in 1920.

If Ruth's arrival filled a vital gap in the New York lineup as the 1920 season approached, two less-happy developments created new ones. During the off-season Baker's wife, Ottilie, was stricken with scarlet fever and died. His two small daughters also became ill, although they would eventually recover. Distraught, Baker announced his retirement, expressing a need to take care of things at home. That need lasted one season; Baker returned to the Yankees lineup in 1921. But as the Yankees arrived at spring camp in Jacksonville, Florida, Huggins knew his primary task was to find a third baseman.

There were two logical candidates, one mercurial, the other steadier. Aaron Ward was a twenty-three-year-old middle infielder who had played a kick-around role for the Yanks since 1917. He'd never hit for much, but then Huggins hadn't given him much of a chance. Ward had fewer than one hundred at bats to show for his career to that point.

The more popular bet was a six-feet-three, 190-pound, twenty-three-year-old rookie out of California with a legitimate baseball pedigree. Robert William "Long Bob" Meusel was the younger brother of Emil "Irish" Meusel, star outfielder of the Philadelphia Phillies, who had hit .305 just the previous season. From the start of spring camp, younger brother Bob demonstrated that he could hit just as well as Emil, and possibly better. Line drives flew to all parts of the training field. Unfortunately for Huggins's mental state, so did Meusel's throws from third base. "He's a player I have to get into my club somewhere," an exasperated Huggins said, eventually declaring his intention to try the kid in left field.[8] That experiment proved equally a fielding adventure, especially measured against the reliable Lewis, who was benched when Meusel chased fly balls. Through all of the

1920 season, Huggins never did figure out what to do with Meusel, and he benched him in early August despite a batting average that hung in the .350s at the time. Remarked the *New York American*'s Arthur Robinson, "Never before in the history of baseball has a hitter of his ability been sentenced to a term in the acropolis because of his shortcomings as a fielder."[9]

The second setback, one that presaged the season's pivotal moment, occurred during the fifth inning of an exhibition game against the Brooklyn Dodgers. The batter, Charles "Chick" Fewster, was coming off a 1919 season in which he had batted .283 while playing five different positions, none of them regularly. A fastball from Jeff Pfeffer struck Fewster squarely on the temple, knocking him out and fracturing his skull. Fewster lay on the ground ten minutes before he could be revived. His survival was initially in doubt, he lost his speech for a week, and he required surgery to remove a dangerous blood clot. With the athlete confined to a wheelchair for weeks, few thought Fewster would play baseball again in 1920, and some believed the skulling had ended his career.

Although Fewster did not figure centrally in Huggins's plans, his loss sent serious ripples through the camp. Bodie chose that particular day to bolt from the team after Huggins refused him permission to leave. Having tired of Bodie's antics, Huggins suspended him, leaving nobody to play center field. Recognizing the team's awkward circumstance, Ruth volunteered to take on the job, telling Huggins he was afraid of running into the close right- or left-field wall in the bathtub-shaped Polo Grounds anyway.

The Fewster distraction, the uncertainty over who would play third, and the unsettled situation in center all complicated life for the Yanks as the season opener approached. Labor and legal problems further muddled the picture. The Yanks were scheduled to open in Philadelphia. Their mound ace, Mays, was, however, a wanted man in Philadelphia, with an outstanding warrant for his arrest stemming from his run-in with Bryan Hayes, the overly loud fan, the previous summer. That meant Mays could not accompany the club on its Pennsylvania road trip. For a time it looked as though none of the Yankees might show up. Late in spring training the team staged a brief strike over the dispersal of third-place shares for the previous season. Unbeknown to the players, New York management had seen fit to let various nonuniformed personnel in on a piece of the action. Pratt, Shawkey, and Peckinpaugh confronted the Yankees owners, demanding that each player receive the difference, a sum amounting to about seventy dollars. The players received their money, although when word got around, the city's newspapermen took the cash out of their hides. "Piker conduct," remarked Joe Vila in the *Sporting News*.[10]

The troubled team broke badly, losing four of the first five and carrying a 4-7 record out of April. The very first game set the pattern. It was tied 1–1 in the eighth inning when Ruth—given room to roam in center—fumbled an easy fly ball off the bat of Joe Dugan. That allowed the two winning runs to score. They won the next day, but in Boston for a Patriots Day doubleheader on April 19 the Yankees again showed poorly. Waite Hoyt held them to five hits in a 6–0 morning victory. That afternoon twenty-two thousand fans came out to jeer the returning Mays, who to their delight got hammered.

The April 22 home opener, also against the Athletics, was hardly more inspiring. During pregame warmups Ruth injured a muscle while taking one of his customary cuts. He tried to play, looked bad striking out in the first inning, and called it quits. The prognosis: at least a ten-day layoff. Desperate for anybody who could play center, Huggins swallowed hard and lifted Bodie's suspension. In a sense he acted too hastily. Given steady rain as well as Ruth's powers of recovery, the star missed just three starts.

The Babe found his stroke when the calendar turned to May, and with him so did the Yankees. His first home run came on May 1, a sixth-inning blow against Boston's Herb Pennock that cleared the Polo Grounds roof in right. It was a landmark of sorts, his fiftieth career homer. He would more than double that production by season's end. Duffy Lewis followed with a home run of his own, and the Yankees won 6–0 on their way to taking four of the next five.

Ruth's bat may have provided the inspiration, but pitching carried the New Yorkers. During that early May stretch of five games, Shawkey, Mogridge, Herb Thormahlen, Quinn, and Mays allowed a total of just six runs. In midmonth they hit their stride during a two-week home stand against the four western teams, claiming eight of the dozen games. Early in that stretch Ruth ignited the Yankees fan base with two home runs and a triple in a 6–5 victory over the White Sox. The following Sunday an all-time record crowd of thirty-eight thousand jammed into the Polo Grounds to watch the Yanks play the first-place Indians. Police estimated that another ten thousand fans were turned away for lack of room. The following Sunday Ruth delighted another huge throng by driving yet another ball out of the Polo Grounds. It was the difference in Shawkey's 3–2 victory over the Browns.

In Boston the Yankees swept four games, with Ruth contributing two more homers to the 6–1 victory on May 27. One of them cleared the scoreboard, then in left-center field, and landed in a parking garage. That gave him four home runs in three games. In the series' final game, the frustrated Red Sox tried out an increasingly popular strategy against the slugger: they intentionally walked him twice.

The Yankees returned home for a Memorial Day double-header against the Senators that produced two more victories in front of another all-time record throng, this time 38,698. Ruth sent them home happy, his drive off the facade of the upper deck defeating Walter Johnson 10–7 in the second game. The sight touched off a spontaneous demonstration that would soon become familiar to New Yorkers: people raved, slapped one another, and tossed food, hats, and assorted other items onto the field in a show of joy. From 4-7 in April the Yankees had gone to 19-8 in May. From an uninspired sixth place, they had climbed to third, three and one-half games behind the first-place Indians.

There were explanations for the turnaround almost every-where a Yankees fan looked. Begin with Ruth, who hit a dozen home runs during the month, easily the most by any player during that period in the game's history. Then look at Quinn, the cast-off pitcher whom the Yanks had wrangled away from the White Sox a year earlier. He was brilliant, winning eight of his ten decisions and allowing just thirteen runs all month. Peckinpaugh finished the month batting .329, with Ruth and Bodie also in the .320s.

All that performance must have fired Huggins's nerve, because the following day he bypassed Mays (coming off three days of rest), Quinn (four), and Shawkey (six) and named Ruth his starting pitcher. The Babe lasted only four innings, but that fit the category of "so what?" The Yankees produced fourteen runs in another trouncing of the visitors. The team's ninth straight victory was also Ruth's only pitching appearance of the season. The tenth straight win followed in the first game of the next day's doubleheader, before the Senators drilled Mays 7–6. Yankees fans hardly noticed: Ruth homered twice more in the opener and a third time in the nightcap.

However good May had been, June was better. After the A's snapped their ten-game win streak, a stretch of eight wins in nine starts followed. A 12–6 victory behind Mays on June 8 temporarily lifted New York into a tie for first place with the Indians, both at 28-16. Their only loss of that nine-game stretch the following day cost them that co-hold on the top spot, but they remained within two games or fewer the rest of the month.

The season's first western swing demonstrated both the team's power and Ruth's popularity. The Yankees took four straight in Detroit, savaging the Tigers—who were without Ty Cobb—for thirty-six runs and allowing just fourteen. In Cleveland they drew thirty-five thousand for the Sunday centerpiece of the showdown series between the top two teams. Ruth drove a ball onto Lexington Avenue, and Shawkey coasted to a 14–0 victory. The Indians, however, won the other three games. In Chicago for games on Wednesday through Saturday, the Yanks won the first three, powered by Ruth's eighteenth and nineteenth home runs. They might have swept, leading 4–3 with two out in the ninth, when light-hitting reserve catcher Byrd Lynn lifted an innocuous fly ball in the general direction of Sammy Vick in left-center. Bodie raced over from center in an effort to make his own play and collided with Vick as the ball dropped. The Sox scored the tying run and trumped New York's tenth-inning run with two of their own. The trip closed with two more victories in three starts in St. Louis.

Given the Yankees' fourteen-run outburst, Rip Collins's one-hitter was overkill when the Red Sox arrived at the Polo Grounds late in the month. A day later the Yankees demoralized the Red Sox in another fashion, with three ninth-inning runs for a 6–5 come-from-behind victory. On June 30 Philadelphia visited for a doubleheader pounding that featured home runs twenty-three and twenty-four by Ruth. It was not yet July, and he was already within a handful of blasts of the remarkable home run record he had set just a year previous.

That he would break the record was, by then, a given, assuming the Babe lived long enough. Although Ruth was married and had an adopted daughter, his reputation as a less-than-ideal family man was already firmly established. This in turn made him fair fodder for tales, some true, many made up, and all of them appealing to those who enjoyed baseball for the prospect of a quick financial gain.

One of the true ones unfolded in the predawn hours of July 7 on a road outside Philadelphia as the Babe returned from a series in Washington in the company of his wife, Yankees coach Charlie O'Leary, reserves Hofmann and Frank Gleich, and a quantity of bootleg booze, some of it undrunk. With Babe at the wheel, the car missed a curve, skidded, and rolled into a ditch. There were no serious injuries, although O'Leary was temporarily knocked unconscious, and Ruth walked with a limp for a few days.

Given that the incident involved the nation's best-known celebrity, alarm moved faster than the facts. By morning a Philadelphia newspaper was on the streets with a report that the Babe had been killed in the wreck. Naturally New York papers picked up the rumor, and they too printed it as fact. By then quick-money experts had already seized on what they believed to be the inside information to put down big cash at advantageous odds against the Yankees the following afternoon in Detroit. Ironically, although the report was false and Ruth played, the big-money boys profited when New York lost 4–3.

But Ruth was more than home runs, and the Yankees were more than Ruth. With a .372 batting average, he entered July fourth among all American League batters, trailing only George Sisler, Joe Jackson, and Tris Speaker. Ahead of him Peckinpaugh stood at .323. Behind him in the usual order, Bodie set aside his real or perceived grievances with Huggins to sit at .327. On the mound Quinn had barely cooled off from his brilliant start; his 12-3 record ranked third among all league pitchers in victories. Shawkey added ten more. The only real concern was Mays, locked all season long in a win-one, lose-one mode that to that point had yielded just an 8-7 record. That would soon change: Mays would lose only twice more over the next two critical months.

3. Winter of Their Discontent

For its combination of sustained excellence and simultaneously sustained dysfunctionality, baseball history contains no parallel to the late-teens Chicago White Sox. A few other "great" clubs have from time to time been known for their argumentative natures—the early 1970s Oakland Athletics come to mind. Like the White Sox those A's shared a common antipathy to an owner they viewed as cheap beyond all reason. But the A's collective hatred of Charles O. Finley emerged as a bonding force that drove them to excellence almost out of spite. The White Sox's hatred of Charles Comiskey, although as widely felt, never bonded the Sox clubhouse into anything cohesive.

No evidence exists that allows more than speculation about when or how things went wrong within the Sox's inner sanctum. The closest thing to an identifiable precipitant that emerges is Comiskey's purchase of star second baseman Eddie Collins during Connie Mack's first breakup of his Philadelphia A's. That action, which unfolded over the winter of 1914–15 and was driven by Mack's fear of losing his championship roster to the insurgent Federal League, featured the unloading of Collins, Herb Pennock, Bob Shawkey, Jack Lapp, Jack Barry, and Eddie Murphy. The story goes that

Collins managed to get written into the sale agreement a clause ensuring that Comiskey would continue to pay him the annual salary he earned with the A's, which various sources have put at between fifteen thousand and twenty thousand dollars. Either amount would have been far higher than the salary any of his White Sox teammates made or were likely to make at a time when the average ballplayer could expect to earn between five thousand and ten thousand dollars a season.

But Comiskey's penuriousness, and his players' resentment of it, could be documented. Among the White Sox it rankled that while other teams got four or five dollars a day in meal money, they got only three dollars. They also objected to the high style of living that Comiskey often flaunted. He was well known for periodically inviting dozens and sometimes hundreds of executives and reporters up to his Camp Jerome, Wisconsin, estate for hunting excursions. The group came to be known as "The Woodland Bards" for its customs, which included writing light verse.[1] The accommodations were Spartan—cabins and outdoor plumbing—but the lavish food and drink more than made up for them. "That son of a bitch, he had that big beautiful farm up there in Wisconsin . . . stacked with bourbon," Happy Felsch once muttered. The center fielder expressed interest in spending time up there himself, only to be bluntly informed by his boss, "No ballplayers allowed!"[2]

If resentment were the cause, it may have worked on the Sox in tandem with other factors. In February 1917 Comiskey acquired well-traveled first baseman Chick Gandil from Cleveland for $3,500. Gandil and Collins had what would be referred to today as "a history" dating back to an on-field incident in 1912. Gandil, playing for Washington in his first full season, took a tag from Collins square on the nose and sustained a fracture. Those who knew both players swore that Gandil spent the rest of his career trying to get even with Collins for the injury, both as an opponent and as a teammate.

It may only be coincidence, but Gandil's acquisition coincides both with the Sox's rise to dominance and with the first public notice of dissension within the ranks. The dominance is easier to quantify. Between 1916 and 1920 Comiskey's Sox won 430 games, 10 more than any other team and nearly 70 above the league average over that five-year period. The White Sox won the 1917 world championship, the 1919 pennant, and finished second two other times in those five seasons.

Culture may have contributed, but only culture in the broadest sense. The issue was not as neat or simple as geographical prejudice. Joe Jackson may have been from the backwoods of South Carolina, but Gandil was a native Minnesotan by way of California, and Eddie Cicotte had lived most of his life in Michigan. Rather it seems to have been more an affinity for danger. Again Gandil was the centerpiece, a player who as a youth had kicked around the fringes of organized ball in California, Arizona, and Mexico, meeting a roster of shady characters who could use the game—and a willing player—to their own advantage. One of those men was a rising young gambler named "Sport" Sullivan, who would later figure prominently in the Black Sox fix. That sense of living dangerously bound Cicotte, Felsch, Jackson, Buck Weaver, Lefty Williams, Swede Risberg, and Fred McMullin to Gandil. The team's other clique—Collins, catcher Ray Schalk, pitchers Red Faber and Dickie Kerr, outfielder Nemo Leibold, and a handful of reserves—held no great book for Comiskey. But they played it straight because it would not have occurred to them to do otherwise.

The ability of such a team of dissidents to coalesce on the field is nothing less than a testament to their collective talent. It was a talent that Comiskey had steadily assembled over the course of a decade largely by dint of brilliant scouting. Of the thirteen central figures on the 1919–20 White Sox roster, eight established their Major League credentials with Chicago.

The most senior was probably the least known. His name was John Francis Collins, but everybody called him "Shano," the nickname a locker-room corruption of Sean, the Irish equivalent of his first name. Shano Collins came to the Sox as a twenty-four-year-old outfield prospect in 1910, batted .197, yet somehow managed not to be released. For the next nine seasons, Shano Collins was always around but never a star, usually holding down right field, his average liable to finish almost anywhere between .240 and .290.

The Sox purchased Weaver for $750 in 1910, stashed him in San Francisco for a season, then brought him in to training camp in 1912. Initially, Weaver got by on enthusiasm. Installed at shortstop, he hustled so much that *Chicago Tribune* beat writer Irving Sanborn labeled him "The Ginger Kid." He did not, however, hit. Weaver batted just .224 that rookie season, and five years later his career average remained below .250. For a time Weaver survived on his jocular nature. A 1915 poll of Sox fans selected him as the team's most popular player. A move to third base in 1917 invigorated both his bat and his fielding. Weaver hit .284 in the Sox world championship season and followed that with a .333 average in the World Series. He was, at last, a star.

A native of downstate Illinois, Schalk followed Weaver by a few months; he was purchased from Milwaukee in August 1912 for ten thousand dollars and two players. Physically Schalk's acquisition made no sense. At 148 pounds he lacked the build that allowed catchers to take the day-to-day pounding the position administered. But Schalk was tough. Kid Gleason, at the time a Sox coach, worked with Schalk for hours prior to games. "He had me chasing from behind the plate to field bunts, and running under pop flies . . . to give or yield with the catch, to never hold the ball high when making a throw," Schalk later said of Gleason.[3]

Schalk arrived just in time to become the favored catcher of Comiskey's new acquisition, Cicotte, who had been purchased from Boston a month earlier. The Red Sox gave up on the four-year veteran because they were in a pennant race and could no longer afford to indulge his lack of command. Cicotte had plenty to be wild about, for he may have thrown a larger variety of pitches than any other legitimate big leaguer. His repertoire included a fastball, a knuckle ball, a screwball, a slider, a shine ball, a spitter, and an emery ball. In Chicago, though, Cicotte finally brought that assortment of pitches—and particularly the knuckle ball—under control. The result was dramatic. Having won 51 games in 146 starts in Boston, Cicotte won 18 for the White Sox in 1913 and 28 in 1917.

Cicotte's twenty-eight-game-victory performance in 1917 supposedly led to the contretemps with Comiskey made famous in Eliot Asinof's book *Eight Men Out* and the film of the same name. The story has it that Comiskey promised Cicotte a $10,000 bonus in addition to his roughly $5,500 salary—absurdly low for a frontline pitcher even then—if Cicotte won thirty games. When Cicotte threatened to win those thirty games, Comiskey supposedly ordered him benched for the season's final weeks on what Asinof described as "the excuse" that the pitcher needed rest prior to the postseason. However deep Cicotte's salary-driven animus toward Comiskey, and however powerful the book's description or the cinematic scene, that animus must be tempered by the facts, represented in the following table. Factoring in both off days and doubleheaders, the column at left indicates games from mid-August through season's end that a Chicago pitcher—starting every fourth day—could have started. The column at right indicates games actually started by Eddie Cicotte.

Theoretical start dates	Cicotte start dates
August 15	August 15
August 19	August 20
August 23	August 23
August 27	August 27
August 31	August 30
September 4	September 2
September 8	September 8
September 14	September 14
September 18	September 19
September 22	September 25
September 26	September 29
	October 1

From August 15 through the end of that season, Cicotte started eleven games for the White Sox. Chicago's record in those games was 9-2. Given Chicago's actual schedule, the greatest number of starts Cicotte could have expected to make from mid-August through season's end while starting every fourth day was twelve. In other words, if Comiskey limited Cicotte's opportunities at all, it was a single start, not enough to cost him the bonus that he supposedly missed by two games.[4]

Among those sympathetic to Cicotte's complaint, suspicion has tended to fall particularly on his use during the final two weeks of the season. Had he started (in place of Faber) on September 18 rather than being held back a day, he could have made that one additional start on October 1. But like Asinof's "excuse" charge, this line of argument is unfair to Comiskey and also to Sox manager Pants Rowland. By September 18 the White Sox were eight games ahead with just nine to play. They had all but mathematically clinched the American League pennant and were at the point of setting up their rotation for the World Series. It made no sense for Rowland to set up a rotation that gave his best pitcher an additional start on the season's final day at the expense of his availability to open the Series. It made all the sense in the world for Rowland to do precisely what managers have always done in such circumstances: save their ace for the World Series. In fact, Cicotte did open the Series against the Giants and pitched a 2–1 victory that set the stage for Chicago's four-games-to-two victory.

On the Sox pitching staff Urban Clarence "Red" Faber played the role of the fated prodigy to Cicotte's wily veteran. Signed by Comiskey late in the 1913 regular season, Faber actually debuted during the team's 1913 world tour in company with the New York Giants. He only got the gig when New York star hurler Christy Mathewson backed out of the ocean voyage at the last minute; in fact, despite being under contract to Chicago, Faber pitched for New York on that trip. But the twenty-five-year-old did well enough to win a spot in the 1914 rotation. Mixing a big league fastball and a curve with a spitball, by 1915 he had developed into a twenty-four-game winner.

Faber started twenty-nine times and won sixteen games for

the 1917 world champions. But the same caprice that brought him to prominence when Mathewson jumped ship on the world tour worked against him with the onset of World War I. After winning four of his nine starts, Faber left the team to enlist in the navy and missed the rest of the 1918 season. Stricken by the pandemic flu of 1919, he missed much of the Sox's pennant winning season and did not pitch in the tainted World Series. The illness, however, left no permanent mark, and Faber reported for spring training in 1920 in full health. Faber's warm relationship with Weaver constituted a small bridge between the factions. They had been teammates since 1914, and their mutual admiration survived the tense clubhouse atmosphere.

With a few key exceptions, Comiskey completed his cast by 1916. Felsch arrived out of Milwaukee in 1915 and immediately established himself as a phenom. Barely twenty-five in 1916, he batted .300 while leading AL outfielders in fielding percentage. Leibold came over on waivers from Cleveland in midseason, eventually forming a usable if not intimidating platoon with Shano Collins in right. Comiskey signed Williams prior to the 1916 season following a failed tryout with the Tigers and a far more successful season in Salt Lake City. Williams followed a sixteen-victory season as a rookie with seventeen wins in the world championship season, then avoided the draft by taking a shipyard job midway through the 1918 season. Returning in 1919 Williams started forty games, won twenty-three of them, and posted a 2.64 earned run average, the lowest of his career.

In August of that year, Comiskey picked up Jackson on the cheap from Cleveland when Indians owner Charles Somers decided he was about to lose his star player to the Federal League. The price: three journeymen, $31,500 in cash to the

Indians, and a three-year deal for Jackson at $6,000 per season. Between 1911 and 1914 Jackson had averaged .381 for the Indians. He was no longer up to that—not quite—but he still hit .332 for the Sox between 1916 and 1919, serving as the offensive focal point for the two-time pennant winners.

That did not make Jackson's life in Chicago easy. When war came to America in 1918, he was deferred due to his marriage. But a few months later, his local draft board, embarrassed to appear to be going easy on an obviously fit man, reclassified him as eligible. Jackson did what Williams had done and what numerous other players would soon do; he took an "essential" job in a Delaware shipbuilding plant, renewing his deferment—and playing ball for the shipyard team as the opportunity presented itself.

But Jackson was too prominent a figure to slide seamlessly into such a safe fallback, and he was also the first major figure to do so. Consequently, he got raked both by the league and in the press for his reluctance to fight. Johnson, for one, issued a general "warning" to players not to avoid military service by taking shipyard jobs. Jackson returned for 1919, signing another six-thousand-dollar deal. The figure satisfied his easy-to-please nature yet was far below market value for a player of his prominence. That in turn made Jackson susceptible to lures dangled by less team-spirited teammates.

There were two such human lures, and they both arrived in 1917. The first was Gandil, acquired from Cleveland to play first base. The second was Risberg, whose contract was purchased for four thousand dollars as a replacement for veteran Zeb Terry. Although the two men had not previously known each other, Gandil and Risberg shared hardscrabble backgrounds, reputations as roughnecks, resentment of their salaries, connections with questionable characters, and an affinity for "sporting" propositions. They could, however, play ball. Gandil was a consistent .270s hitter with a reputation for his fielding. Risberg never hit much, but in three seasons he acquired—not entirely justifiably—a reputation as a gloveman. The baseball press described him as "a wonder" with one of the game's strongest throwing arms. Reality tells a different tale; Risberg's fielding averages were generally among the lower half of league shortstops.

The final piece of the 1919 club, left-hander Kerr, joined the team just in time to cover for the stricken Faber. Only five feet seven and 155 pounds, Kerr was a runt with an attitude. Given only four starts the entire first half of the season, he lost three of them. But when Faber's weakened condition forced Gleason's hand, Kerr took advantage. He made thirteen starts after July 1 and won eight.

The Sox won in 1919 despite the fractured cast. "None of these guys felt any friendliness toward each other. . . . There was no contact . . . nothing," remarks Asinof, who interviewed many of the principals. He claims that Felsch told him that the club "almost went on strike against that bastard [Comiskey]" over the meal money question during a July 4 road trip to Detroit.[5]

Even so, the evidence suggests that the conspiracy itself developed almost casually. In his sworn 1920 confession, Cicotte said the plot hatched out of a discussion among the players of talk that some Cubs players had been offered ten thousand dollars to lose the 1918 World Series to the Boston Red Sox.[6] "Somebody made a crack about getting money, if we got into the Series, to throw the Series," he said. "The boys in the club got to talking it over about the fellows [presumably Collins] getting too much money and such stuff as that, and said that they would go ahead and go through with it if they got this money."[7]

Four days before the Series was to open, oddsmakers installed the White Sox as 7-to-10 favorites. Just three days later, on the eve of the first game, the line tightened to 5-to-6, virtually even money. The official reason: a report that twenty-nine-game-winner Cicotte was suffering from a sore arm. The real reason: an unusually heavy amount of "smart money" placed on the Reds.

The next day the Reds humiliated Cicotte and the Sox 9–1 in Cincinnati. The odds shifted to even. A day later the Reds defeated Williams and suddenly became 9-to-5 betting favorites.

When the Series shifted to Chicago, Kerr rallied the Sox with a 3–0 shutout victory in the third game. But Cicotte lost a second time 2–0, and two days later Williams also lost. The Sox offense failed to produce a run between the fourth inning of the third game and the fifth inning of the sixth game, a stretch of twenty-six consecutive fruitless innings. The Series went off the betting boards.

When the Series returned to Cincinnati, Kerr again rallied the Sox, this time to a 5–4 victory. A day later Cicotte also won, 4–1. But Williams was touched for four Cincinnati runs in the first inning of the eighth game of the best-of-nine Series, and Cincinnati won the clinching game 10–5.

The details of what happened in that Series are sufficiently available elsewhere that they can be dispensed with relatively quickly here. But the record is clear on certain aspects.

1. Some Sox players conspired with gamblers in advance of the Series to throw games for a price.
2. At least some crooked plays or slack efforts contributed to all five of the team's losses.
3. Five of the Sox actively participated in the throwing of one or more of those tainted games. Those five were:

Cicotte: He confessed to deliberately throwing the first game and also confessed to deliberately committing two fielding errors at a critical point of his 2–0 fourth-game defeat. Cicotte acknowledged receiving ten thousand dollars for his complicity.[8]

Williams: He lost all three of his starts. At a key point in the second game, a 4–2 loss, he walked three batters and then allowed a triple. In the fifth game, a 5–0 loss, Williams allowed just four hits, but three of them—a double, a single, and a triple—produced four sixth-inning runs. Williams supposedly received a death threat prior to the eighth game, although recent research has called that belief into question. In that game he faced just five batters and allowed four hits. Williams acknowledged receiving five thousand dollars—half of what he said he was promised—for his participation in the fix.[9]

Gandil: The ringleader actually had an average Series. He hit .233, batting nine times with runners in scoring position and collecting three hits. Gandil was charged with one error, and it allowed a meaningless run to score. Between the gambling funds he kept and the side bets he is said to have made, Gandil reportedly reaped thirty-five thousand dollars from the fix.[10]

Risberg: He hit safely just twice in twenty-five at bats and made four errors, none of them, however, in critical situations. As one of the ringleaders, Risberg reportedly kept fifteen thousand dollars of the fix money for himself.[11]

Felsch: Happy batted just .192 and was hitless in nine at bats with runners in scoring position. His throwing error in the fifth inning of game 5 set up a four-run Cincinnati inning. He is known to have received five thousand dollars from Gandil.[12]

4. Three other players—Weaver, Jackson, and reserve infielder Fred McMullin—knew of the fix, although the evidence is not conclusive that they took part. Jackson is known to have received five thousand dollars. Neither Weaver nor McMullin was ever paid.[13]

The Series had barely concluded when allegations surfaced. On October 10, the day after the concluding game, newspapers carried reports that the Series had not been played on the level. *Chicago Tribune* sportswriter Hughie Fullerton predicted, "There are seven men on the team who will not be there when the gong sounds next spring, and some of them will not be in either major league." He did not name his source at the time, but in later years it was identified as Comiskey. Added Fullerton cryptically, "There will be a lot of inside stuff that will never be printed."[14]

Formally those closest to baseball provided cover against any intimation of illegitimacy. Famed former pitcher Christy Mathewson, who had attended all the games, declared, "The rumors and mutterings about the honesty of the Series are ridiculous."[15] Reds manager Pat Moran dismissed the rumors, saying, "If any member of the other team was pulling they can have credit for fooling me."[16] Comiskey released a statement the day after the Series ended expressing confidence that "[his] boys fought . . . on the level, as they [had] always done." He offered twenty thousand dollars to anyone producing evidence to the contrary.[17]

That was for public consumption. Privately the picture was different. Even before the Series, Mathewson and Fullerton had agreed to compare suspicions as the games moved along; Mathewson reported several questionable incidents. Comiskey directed his attorney, Alfred Austrian, to hire private investigators to look into the talk. Those investigators eventually produced a lengthy report that raised suspicions but did not name any suspects. The report was lost for many years, although recently it has come into the possession of the Chicago History Museum.[18] Comiskey also held up the World Series checks of the eight suspected ballplayers. When players complained about not being paid, his chief aide, Harry Grabiner, acknowledged the inquiry but declared that it "had found no evidence to support charges of dishonesty."[19]

One man, former player Joe Gedeon, tried to take Comiskey up on his offer. Gedeon, who had played second base for the St. Louis Browns, happened to have been in Risberg's hotel room just prior to one of the meetings at which the idea of a fix was discussed. Hiding in the closet, he overheard enough of the details to become convinced of the plot's legitimacy.[20] Gedeon placed his own bets when the Series opened, won on the first two games, then lost it all when Kerr won game 3. Presented with the prospect of recovering some of his loss, Gedeon went to Comiskey, Grabiner, and Austrian and told them his story. The Sox brain trust dismissed Gedeon without payment and did no more with his information than briefly discuss it with Illinois state's attorney Maclay Hoyne.

Gradually, over the course of the long winter, the story disappeared from the headlines. Johnson, preoccupied by the Carl Mays imbroglio and his weakening grasp over the American League, could not conduct an investigation. Comiskey decided he was better off not doing so. At that stage, he felt, all he could do was wreck his own business. Only Fullerton tried to maintain momentum for an inquiry, and even he couldn't sell the topic to his own editors at the *Tribune*. He finally found a buyer at the *New York World*, which ran his series of broad-brush indictments in December. "The Major

Leagues, both owners and players, are on trial," Fullerton wrote. "Charges that ballplayers are bribed and games are sold out are made without attempts at refutations by men who have made their fortunes in baseball." Fullerton closed with a demand that federal judge Kenesaw M. Landis head a special investigation.[21] His plea was essentially ignored. Garry Herrmann, former chairman of the National Commission, said, "[The matter] rests with Comiskey, who is responsible for the conduct of his players."[22] A small newspaper near Ray Schalk's hometown reported the catcher's personal suspicions, but Schalk later issued a denial.

Comiskey could hardly tie himself up with Fullerton because he was preoccupied with attempting to reassemble his ball club for 1920. It was no simple task. In January Risberg announced his intention to retire, complaining about his low salary. Gandil summarily rejected Comiskey's contract offer and demanded ten thousand dollars, a sum that would have put him second on the team, behind only Collins. When the inevitable rejection arrived, he too announced his retirement. Weaver, Cicotte, Jackson, and Kerr all returned their contracts unsigned.

Because Jackson was the centerpiece of the club's offense, his refusal to sign presented the biggest concern. Grabiner paid a personal call at the player's Savannah, Georgia, home, to offer a three-year deal at $9,000 a year. Jackson signed.[23] Weaver signed a three-year, $7,500 deal as spring training began. But he regretted doing so almost immediately and was out of camp again in a few weeks. Only a blunt expulsion threat delivered by Comiskey in person brought him back. Risberg held out until early April. Cicotte and Kerr also eventually gave in.

That left just Gandil, who never came closer to a big league camp that spring than a drop-by visit to the Cubs camp in California. He was driving a sporty new car.

When the regular season began, Chicago broke quickly, winning its first six games. By early May the Sox were 10-2, and the roster of the league's leading hitters looked very much like the middle of the Chicago order. At .488 Jackson was first, with Collins (.442) third and Weaver (.400) fifth.

Even so, the Sox offense was inconsistent. Leibold, the most frequently used lead-off hitter, was saddled with a .179 average three weeks into the season. Risberg was at .176, Schalk at .160, and Ted Jourdan, Gandil's replacement at first, managed only a .242 start. Felsch too got off slowly, at just .235. Happy picked things up in midmonth. His home run helped the Sox defeat Boston 4–3 on May 18, and another homer helped sink the hapless A's a week later. The blast was Hap's sixth, tying him with Ruth for the league lead.

Then the Sox turned cold. Between May 5 and May 30, they lost fifteen of twenty-four games to sink into fourth place, just two games above .500 and six and one-half behind the leading Indians. Worse, nearly half of those two dozen games were against their chief rivals, the Indians and the Yankees, and the Sox went 2-9 in those games. Cicotte, the team ace, delivered especially frustrating results, at one stretch losing four of his five starts.

Gleason also could not settle on a reliable fourth starter. Despite his performance in the 1919 World Series, Kerr had broken spring camp in a battle for the final spot in the four-man rotation with journeyman Roy Wilkinson. When Kerr got hammered 12–4 in St. Louis, Gleason gave the job to Wilkinson, who promptly lost six of his next seven starts but looked better doing it. In their fifteen losses between May 4 and May 30, Sox pitchers allowed an average of more than six runs per game. Only Williams demonstrated early consistency, winning his first six starts and carrying a 10-2 record to June 1.

A five-game series in Cleveland at the outset of this dismal stretch has for some time been a focal point of debate. In *Eight Men Out*, Asinof asserts that St. Louis gambling elements tried to blackmail the seven dirty players to lose the first game. Asinof identifies McMullin as the contact man. He notes a strange shift in the odds just before that game, favoring Cleveland. Asinof is not perfect in his details. He says that the Sox came in hot, having won six straight. The team actually had won four straight prior to dropping the final game of a series in St. Louis. He claims that Cicotte, Williams, and Kerr had all been hot, a statement that is certainly not true of Kerr (0-2) and just modestly so of Cicotte (2-0 after thirteen games). It is, however, true that Chicago led 2–1 behind Faber in the eighth inning when Jackson misplayed a fly ball in left, then Risberg threw wildly on the relay, allowing the tying run to score. The Indians won in the ninth and took three of the next four games as well.

Several sources—chiefly Asinof and various players—subsequently asserted that the fixes recurred throughout the summer of 1920. No way exists today to substantiate that claim beyond doubt, but the record of the season demonstrates that the play of the Sox was often unusually inconsistent.[24]

If the White Sox seemed to stumble through May, they looked good in June. Cicotte highlighted his personal 6-1 month with a 7–0 shutout of the Athletics at Comiskey Park that completed an 0-15 road trip for Connie Mack's last-place club. Three days later Weaver's three hits helped Chicago defeat Cleveland 12–7. On June 30 Eddie Collins and Risberg combined for seven hits in a 14–0 rout of Detroit behind Faber.

It was the Sox's eighth victory in their last nine games. They were still five games out of first, but at least they finally had some momentum.

Chicago's .290 team average, second best in the league behind only the leading Indians, carried an offense that was outscoring its opponents by a run a game, producing at least seven runs two dozen times. Only the phenomenal first half enjoyed by St. Louis's George Sisler, hitting .427, denied Jackson a clear run at the batting title. But Joe's .397 required no apologies. Nor did Eddie Collins's .327, Weaver's .351, or Felsch's .327. Elsewhere, though, the offense was in trouble. Leibold labored at .181. He was a millstone at the top of the order, and more so after Comiskey benched Jourdan in early June, handing the first-base job over to Shano Collins, Leibold's former platoon partner in right. On the mound Williams was afire, winning fifteen against just four losses. But he was also virtually the club's only effective weapon against the Indians. Through June 30 the White Sox had already met those chief rivals for the pennant fifteen times. Williams started four of those games and had four wins to show for the effort. In the remaining eleven games, the Sox's record against Cleveland was 1-10.

For public consumption virtually all the concern about gambling had withered. The closest the game came to any sort of action was an increase in patrols among the customers, the goal being to identify and arrest fans making side bets. Such signs were prominent, among other places, at Comiskey Park.

Privately, though, the White Sox remained suspicious and at odds with one another. That fall Jackson told a grand jury of conversations he had with Williams revisiting the previous autumn. At one point, he testified, the two men agreed that Gandil's decision not to return for 1920 was based on the former first baseman's desire not to confront fellow conspirators whom he had gypped by keeping more than his stipulated share of the money. "He must have made an awful lot out of it," Jackson said. "We both decided he crossed them [teammates] up."[25]

The subject came up again during the team's mid-July visit to Washington. "I told him what a damned fool I thought I was, and he was of the same opinion," Jackson said, referring to Williams.[26] However self-damned Jackson felt, it did not hurt his performance. The Sox won three of four in the nation's capital, with Jackson collecting seven hits, among them a double, a triple, and a home run.

As the season's second half dawned, the White Sox did not doubt their ability to win the pennant. They did wonder—openly, in many cases—whether they had the nerve to do so. At least some of the Sox had maintained ties with the gambling elements that remained rife in baseball in those days. These connections were not merely with the major money men in New York and Boston to whom they had sold out the previous October but also with smaller yet powerful elements in Detroit, St. Louis, and other cities. These connections worked periodically, if not daily, preferring to manipulate odds on a game-by-game basis on the theory that such an approach was both less risky and more enduring.

It also gave the gamblers an ongoing blackmailer's hold over elements of the Chicago team, a hold that the players had to respect. This hold did not require Chicago to sell out the season. To the contrary, taking the White Sox out of contention would be counterproductive because it would diminish betting interest in the team. Instead gamblers' interests lay in the Sox staying just close enough to the top of the league to maximize betting interest.

Such a strategy was fraught with peril because it required the White Sox to virtually win on command if they fell behind in the race, then lose once the prospect loomed that they might pull too far in front. This is precisely what occurred. During August and September the Sox would play a dozen times when they trailed the league leader by three or more games; their record in those dozen contests was 9-3. When they trailed by any margin at all during that August–September push, the Sox's record was 32-12, a .727 winning percentage. Once in front, however, it was a different story. The White Sox played eight games those final two months as the American League's first-place team. Their record in those eight games was 2-6.

Even players not directly connected to the rigging sensed that something unnatural was up, although they could not be sure whether the driving force was an ongoing fix or the fear of exposure. "They didn't dare win in 1920," Indians outfielder Joe Wood said years later. That wasn't Wood's opinion; it was, he said, drawn from conversations with the White Sox players themselves. "I think they could have beaten us . . . if this thing didn't happen to the White Sox."[27]

4. The Honeymoon

To be a Cleveland Indians fan in the first decades of the twentieth century was to be a Chicago Cubs fan today. Expectation annually gave way to disappointment. In 1902 Napoleon Lajoie, the game's greatest player and a .426 hitter the previous season, fell into the team's lap when a court invalidated the contract he had signed with the Athletics during the American League's war with the National League. Lajoie batted .378 that season and won batting titles in both 1903 and 1904. But the team called the Naps in his honor couldn't make it above third place.

In 1908 one of the great pennant races of all time unfolded, a three-way battle among the Tigers, the Indians, and the White Sox. Addie Joss, Cleveland's right-handed pitching star, won twenty-four games, one of them a 1–0 perfect game against the White Sox in the season's final week. But the Tigers claimed the pennant by a margin of one-half game. The rules in force at the time did not require Detroit to make up a rained-out contest with Washington. Had Detroit played and lost that makeup, a playoff game would have been required.

In June 1910 the Indians acquired Joe Jackson, an illiterate but brilliant prospect, from the Athletics in a straight-up swap for veteran Bris Lord. It was the kind of age-for-promise trade that rebuilding teams make with contenders all the time, one rife with the prospect of benefit for both clubs, and this one panned out. Lord batted .310 to help the Athletics to the 1911 pennant. Jackson, only twenty at the time of the deal, batted .408 for Cleveland in his first full season. But the Naps again finished third, their aspirations dampened in April when Joss suddenly succumbed to tubercular meningitis. He was barely thirty-one.

The pitcher's death, complicated by Lajoie's age-diminished skills, heralded a noncompetitive stretch. In 1914 the team now known as the Indians won just fifty-one games and finished dead last. They gained only six games and one position in the standings in 1915. In August Charles Somers, the revered but cash-strapped club owner since the creation of the American League, traded Jackson to the Chicago White Sox for three journeymen and $31,500.

It was a desperate move, and it was also Somers's last major action on behalf of the team. Early the following year he gave up and sold the Indians to Jim Dunn, a well-heeled local businessman. Dunn not only had money; he was willing to spend it. He sent fifty-five thousand dollars and two players to Boston in exchange for Tris Speaker, regarded as the greatest center fielder of all time. Speaker responded by hitting .386 to claim the only batting title between 1907 and 1919 not won by Ty Cobb, and the Indians made up twenty games in the standings, finishing with a 77-77 record. They were back to third in 1917 and stood second, just two and one-half games behind the Red Sox, when World War I forced an abrupt halt to the 1918 season on Labor Day. Dunn's Indians were second again in 1919, this time losing to the Chicago White Sox by three and one-half games.

Through its first two decades of play, the American League

superficially divided into "have" and "have not" camps. Four teams—the White Sox, the Tigers, the Athletics, and the Red Sox—had won all the pennants. The Indians, the Yankees, the Browns, and the Senators had won none. But that simple statistic did not reflect the true power balance. Since Connie Mack's self-destruction during the Federal League War, the Athletics had been simply horrid, finishing a distant last every season. The Tigers and the Red Sox too were in obvious decline, the former's problems due to personnel decisions and the latter's due to money, complicated by dissension.

Of the perennial also-rans, St. Louis and Washington approached 1920 with few expectations. The Browns had only George Sisler, and the Senators Walter Johnson. But New York's purchase of Babe Ruth made the Yankees—who had been building in step with the Indians since Ruppert and Huston gained control of the team also in 1915—a feared opponent.

Statistically the war's impact on home attendance made fan excitement in the era difficult to precisely quantify. But there is no doubt that the arrival of Dunn and then Speaker refueled interest in the Indians that had lain dormant since the days of Lajoie and Joss. Speaker was actually Dunn's second player acquisition; his first was first baseman Chick Gandil, purchased in February 1916 from Washington for $7,500. But Gandil wore out his welcome within a year and was sold to the White Sox at a discounted $3,500. Before the 1917 season, at Speaker's urging, Dunn bought Speaker's best friend and former teammate, Smoky Joe Wood, from the Red Sox for $15,000. Wood had once been the most feared pitcher in the league, but his right arm had been rendered useless by shoulder problems. In fact, he made only seven appearances on the mound for Cleveland and never recorded a victory.

But Speaker believed that Wood could make the conversion to the outfield, and Wood worked quietly throughout 1917 on that transition. The result, while hardly a revelation, was the emergence of a perfectly competent everyday ballplayer. As a regular in 1918, Wood hit .296 before settling into a platoon role in 1919.

The player Wood platooned with, Elmer Smith, had arrived from Washington in June 1917, costing Dunn a couple thousand. Smith came cheaply in part because his three-season career had produced nothing to recommend it, and in part because as a healthy twenty-five-year-old, he was draft eligible. Indeed, Smith missed all of 1918 because of military service before returning to hit .278 in split time with Wood in 1919.

Dunn swung his best deal early in spring training prior to the 1919 season, shipping outfielder Braggo Roth to the Athletics for Larry Gardner, Charlie Jamieson, and Elmer Myers. Gardner, a veteran of three Red Sox championship teams, was (with Home Run Baker) one of the league's two best third basemen. Jamieson was an obscure kick-around left fielder with experience in Washington as well as Philadelphia. At five feet eight and 165 pounds, he had no power, collecting more than one thousand official at bats before laying into his first home run. But Charlie Jamieson could run. The Indians' most veteran presence was popular outfielder Jack Graney, the team's lead-off man and soon to become its all-time leader in games played. But Graney's familiarity and popularity masked offensive shortcomings. A career .249 hitter, Graney hadn't even managed that since turning thirty in 1916. Jim Dunn saw something in Charlie Jamieson that the rabidly loyal Indians fans were unable to see; he saw Jack Graney's successor.

Later that year Dunn saw in the decline of the Boston franchise a chance to pick up a player he had always coveted. The Red Sox that spring had obtained veteran Ray Caldwell from the Yankees. A thirty-one-year-old right-hander, Caldwell had won seven of his dozen starts for the Red Sox. But with the team in turmoil that summer, club owner Harry Frazee made almost everybody available, and Dunn snapped up Caldwell in a cash deal. He started six times for the Indians and won five of them. By that time Speaker had replaced Leo Fohl as on-field manager. The move was popular among Indians fans, although Fohl's five-year tenure hardly looked like a failure on paper. Taking over early in the desperate 1915 season, he led the team successively to sixth-, third-, and second-place finishes before falling victim to expectations. A preseason pennant prospect in 1919, the Indians stood third in midseason when Fohl was released. Under Speaker they won forty of their final sixty-one and moved up to second.

While Jamieson, Speaker, Caldwell, Wood, and Smith had been valuable pickups, the core of the Indians—the focus of the building excitement in Cleveland—was homegrown. It consisted of seven players, ranging in age from twenty-five to thirty. One was a Cleveland native, and several lived there year-round. In many respects the Indians approached 1920 as a true hometown team.

That could certainly be said of Bill Wambsganss, the twenty-six-year-old second baseman with the funny name. Born in Cleveland in 1894, the man the newspapers called "Wamby" never wanted to play anywhere else, and he never had. Wambsganss arrived at the depths of the building process, in April 1914, a weak-hitting middle infielder with a good glove. Learning to hit took time, but by 1918 Wambsganss had become a plausible big league stick. A career .233 hitter without a home run to that point, Wambsganss batted .295 in war-shortened duty. He still failed to homer, but his .356 slugging average was a career best by forty-three percentage points and thirty-four points above the league average. He returned for a full season in 1919, and his average moderated to .278. But he did hit two home runs.

At first base the Indians had Wheeler "Doc" Johnston, a thirty-year-old left-hander who had held the position between 1913 and 1914, only to be traded away and then reacquired. "Doc" was the lesser-known older brother of Brooklyn's Jimmy Johnston, a key figure on the Dodgers' 1916 pennant-winning team. He was also the most "adopted" of the Cleveland core, having been born and raised in rural Tennessee. Like Wambsganss, Johnston had learned to hit through a process that was so laborious it's no wonder that the Indians unloaded him to Pittsburgh for $7,500 early in 1915. With the war imminent Pittsburgh released Johnston after two unremarkable seasons. He then signed with the Indians and saw brief action in 1918. With peace at hand the more mature Johnston emerged in 1919 as a .300 hitter.

Joe Evans had come to the Indians in 1915 as a twenty-year-old out of Mississippi, but he had rarely emerged from the dugout. There were two reasons: his hitting and his fielding. The Indians thought Evans was a third baseman, but his fielding averages—between .885 and .935 through his first four seasons—shouted otherwise. The Indians also tried him at shortstop and catcher. Evans came to camp in 1920 hoping to hold a job as a right-handed platoon alternative to Graney or Jamieson in left. But to get any work at all, he would have to improve on his career .214 batting average. Twice before, in 1917 and 1918, the Indians had given Evans a chance to show that he could hit the way they thought he could. The results had been .190 and .263 averages.

Two players Speaker knew he could count on were his pitching aces, Jim Bagby and Stan Coveleski, whose name was often presented in the media as "Coveleskie." Their careers and lives traced several parallels, beginning at the family level. Coveleski's older brother, Harry, had been a pitcher (and three times a twenty-game winner) for parts of nine seasons before retiring in 1918. Bagby's son, Jim Jr., would pitch for ten seasons in the 1930s and 1940s, enjoying a pair of seventeen-win seasons. Both Bagby and Coveleski came to the Indians in 1916 following brief and unsuccessful stints with other clubs in 1912. Both had been thrown into the Cleveland rotation as rookies, made a combined fifty-four starts in 1916, and won thirty-one games against thirty losses. Both blossomed quickly. Bagby's best season, 1917, produced twenty-three victories against just thirteen losses, and he entered 1920 with a career record of 75-58. Coveleski won nineteen in 1917 and topped twenty wins in both 1918 and 1919. His career record was even better than Bagby's, 82-53.

The Indians' hopes could have been legislated toward extinction over the winter. In February a joint rules committee of the two Major Leagues agreed to outlaw all pitches that involved tampering with the baseball, attaching a ten-day suspension as the penalty for violators. That prohibition included the so-called shine ball, whose chief practitioner was Chicago's Eddie Cicotte. But Cicotte was well equipped to get along without that particular pitch because his wide repertoire also included a good fastball as well as a knuckle ball. Of greater potential concern to the Indians was that the prohibition also covered the spitball. There were at the time seventeen recognized spitball pitchers in the Majors, none of whom started more games in 1919 than Coveleski's thirty-four. Combined with Caldwell their fifty-two starts also represented a Major League high for spitballers on a single team in 1919. No wonder the Indians were particularly relieved when the committee attached a grandfather clause to its new rule, allowing those seventeen to continue throwing the pitch. In 1920 Caldwell and Bagby would make seventy-one starts, nearly half of all the games that the Indians played.

For their entire professional careers to that point, Coveleski and Bagby had essentially pitched to one man, Steve O'Neill. An Indians backstop since 1911, O'Neill assumed the regular duties in 1915 and had appeared in 85 percent of all Cleveland games since then. Two years younger than Bagby and Coveleski, O'Neill was the model catcher: durable, only so-so with the bat, but possessed of both a strong arm and a strong brain. In the abbreviated 1918 season, he led all American League catchers in fielding average. As with Wambsganss and Johnston, O'Neill found a batting stroke in 1919. A career .235 hitter to that point, he raised his average to .285 while playing in all but fifteen of Cleveland's games. He compensated for a lack of home run power by producing thirty-five doubles that year and a .427 slugging average that was fifty-one percentage points higher than his previous career best.

O'Neill, Coveleski, and Bagby were the on-field core of the returning Indians. But the emotional core was Ray Chapman. Installed as a regular with Johnston and O'Neill in 1912, Chapman started every game at shortstop in 1915 and again in 1917, batting .302 that year and .300 again in 1919.

At only five feet ten, Chapman lacked the classic shortstop's size. But he was a fan favorite. They saw in his pep, his smile, and his jauntiness a zeal both for baseball and for the Indians that they could relate to. His teammates saw it as well; by 1919 Chapman had been named the team captain.

Chapman was part of the small but growing rank of Major Leaguers coming from a part of the country utterly off the big league map: the rural South. Entering the 1920 Major League season, only four Kentuckians held down spots on the sixteen big league teams. Three were popular figures: Chapman (Beaver Dam), Tigers outfielder Bobby Veach (Island), and likably eccentric Cardinals pitcher Ferdie Schupp (Louisville). The fourth was Carl Mays, a product of the village of Liberty in the state's central region and probably the league's least liked figure with the possible exception of Ty Cobb.

Chapman developed a following in Cleveland in part due to his play on the field, but also due to the community roots he increasingly established. Seen with increasing frequency in the company of socialite Kathleen Daly, daughter of a prominent Cleveland gas company executive, Chapman announced in 1918 that the couple would make wedding plans. The declaration raised eyebrows for two reasons. First, the Dalys were one of the city's most prominent families, residing in a mansion along the section of Euclid Avenue known as "Millionaire's Row." Ballplayers, even those as respected as Chapman, were almost unanimously considered to be of a lower social order. Chapman's own parents cautioned him about the pressures of marrying "above his station."

But there was more than social status to it. The Dalys were members of the city's Catholic community, and Chapman had been born and raised a southern Protestant. Although it was not discussed in public, the interfaith marriage split the previously closely knit Indians. The rift widened further when Chapman openly acknowledged his active consideration of converting to his fiancée's faith. That pleased O'Neill and Graney, both Catholic, but it unsettled others. Speaker may have been Chapman's closest friend, but he was also a Texan, a Protestant, and a ranking Mason. He, Wood, and Gardner found the idea of solemnizing their shortstop's wedding in a Catholic church difficult to come to accept. What evolved was a compromise. The wedding was performed in October 1919 by a Catholic priest but in the Daly home, not in a church. Tris Speaker was the best man.

Publicly the question of Chapman's faith got far less attention than the question of his future. At the elder Daly's urging, Chapman agreed to take a winter job with his father-in-law's company and to consider retirement following the conclusion of the 1920 season. Daly would have preferred that Chapman retire immediately from the ballplayer's nomadic life, buy a home, begin raising a family, and become an officer in the Daly business. But Chapman, who had never played on a pennant-winning team, believed that doing so would cost him a share of imminent glory. Like Indians fans around town, he had an unshakable belief in his team. "I'll play next year, for I want to help give Tris Speaker and the Cleveland fans the first pennant Cleveland has ever won," he said. Then he would hang it up.[1]

As weather permitted, the Indians justified their city's faith when the season opened in mid-April. Nearly twenty thousand fans crowded into a chilled Dunn Field to watch Coveleski shut out the Browns 5–0 on five scattered hits. But cold and rain forced cancellation of the series' final two games and six of the seventeen scheduled April starts overall. The frequent postponements did not, at least, ruffle team chemistry. The Indians won sixteen of the first twenty-two games, including Coveleski's 3–2 victory over the White Sox on April 27, Chicago's first defeat of the season. Cleveland won again the next day and took over first place.

Johnston was the surprising fuel to the early fire, carrying a

.462 average into May. His batting work eclipsed even Speaker, who finished the first month at .402. Playing the second of five games in Chicago on May 6, Chapman handed the Indians a 3–2 ten-inning victory with a base hit. Three days later, when Coveleski beat the Sox 4–3, the Indians left town in sole possession of first.

For the next week they traded that position with the surprising Boston Red Sox. Johnston remained the offensive reason, his average up to a league-leading .466. With the exception of Wambsganss, stuck at .190 in mid-May, all the Indians were hitting well, as their team .309 average attested.

But Speaker did not need to look very far to find cause for concern. The starting pitching was thin, with Bagby and Coveleski having claimed thirteen of the club's sixteen victories as they arrived in New York on May 15 for the first of four games. In the Friday New York opener, the Yanks handed Coveleski his first defeat after seven victories. Mays took the mound in front of a record crowd of thirty-eight thousand on Saturday, and the Indians found special delight in posting five quick runs against a pitcher they disliked every bit as much as the rest of the league did. Chapman delivered three of those hits in the 8–2 victory behind Bagby. Following a Sunday off day, the two teams split games on Monday and Tuesday. The Indians left New York just as they had arrived, a first-place team.

The club returned to Cleveland from that first Eastern swing to confront one of those scheduling anomalies that could only be produced by the exigencies of train travel. Between May 28 and June 23, they were to play twenty-seven consecutive games at home; those games were to be followed by thirty-two straight on the road from late June through late July. Plainly this was a time for the home team to make its move. Yet the fates conspired relentlessly against those prospects. In the first series against Chicago, Speaker ran into the wall catching a fly ball hit by Joe Jackson and knocked himself out. He sustained only a concussion. The news was more dire for Coveleski, summoned home that same week due to the sudden death of his wife. O'Neill too left the team to tend to his wife, who was ill after childbirth. Barely a few days later, an attack of tonsillitis shelved Graney. The veteran was off to the best start of his career, batting in the high .290s at the time. But it was a break for the Indians since it forced Speaker to use a Jamieson-Evans platoon. Jamieson took full advantage, and by the time Graney was again ready to play in mid-June his replacement boasted a .380 batting average that was third best in the league. Graney spent the rest of the season as a reserve.

Crippled as they were, the Indians still finished May with a 26-11 record and a three-and-one-half-game lead on the Yanks and the Red Sox. The offense was producing nearly six runs per game, the defense allowing barely more than four. Johnston finally cooled, his average dropping to .374 by June 3. But that allowed Speaker, at .389, to assume the league lead. Chapman, meanwhile, sat at .323. But with Speaker forced to start reserve pitchers in Coveleski's absence, the club dropped three straight in early June, then welcomed Coveleski back with a fourth straight loss, 6–2 to the Browns. It was the Indians' worst stretch of the season's first half.

Ruth and the Yankees paid their first visit to Cleveland in mid-June, with thirty-five thousand overflowing Dunn Field to see him. The Babe hit his seventeenth home run of the young season, but the Indians won three of four. A week later Smith produced a four-hit game as the Indians hammered Boston 13–5. A doubleheader sweep of the Browns on the twenty-ninth helped the Indians conclude June with seventeen wins in twenty-eight games, in a functional tie with New York for first, with the White Sox four and one-half games behind. Johnston's average had fallen back to the mere .350s, but with Jamieson playing regularly the Cleveland lineup featured seven starters batting .300 or better, led by Speaker at .398. Bagby, pitching brilliantly, already had fourteen victories against just three defeats.

In the stands the new (and pregnant) Mrs. Chapman provided a continuous presence. "She was a lovely woman," Jamieson recalled.[2]

5. Reactive Revolutionary

Ban Johnson's approach to life can be summarized in one sentence. He was a successful revolutionary whose zeal for the revolution he promulgated was equaled only by his visceral hatred of those who threatened his control over what he had brought about.

When it was pitted against a vulnerable structure—the late-nineteenth-century National League—this zeal served Johnson superbly. Armed with a coalition of like-minded allies, he formulated the first insurgency to successfully challenge baseball's established order. For fifteen years the coalition followed Johnson unquestioningly, forging a dictatorship that was as tranquil as it was powerful.

By the latter half of the second decade of the twentieth century, however, the inevitable effects of transition and power eroded that coalition. As new owners emerged in major markets such as New York and Boston, they asked a question that those whose bonds of loyalty had been forged in the shared experience of revolution would never have considered: did the established order possess a vision for changing times and circumstances?

Nobody doubted Johnson's vision when, as a successful young sports reporter in Cincinnati, he led the fight that brought down baseball's established order, the eight-team National League. Over two seasons, in 1900 and 1901, Johnson positioned the entity he called the American League to take full advantage of the opportunities presented by the existing order's recent consolidation from a dozen cities to just eight. Johnson sent teams into three of those abandoned cities—Washington, Baltimore, and Cleveland—while simultaneously invading Philadelphia and Boston, both longtime National League bastions. In company with existing franchises in Chicago, Milwaukee, and Detroit, the league's lineup included every major city in the northeast except New York. Johnson occupied that city two years later, relocating the Baltimore franchise.

The league's success had been founded on Johnson's opportunistic reading of the National League's fractured relationship both with its players and among its own constituents. At the highest levels that fracture revolved around the legitimacy of "syndicate baseball," the method by which a couple of men manipulated the interests of several teams in order to maximize both on-field success and profitability. In effect they fixed the season's outcomes. The existing league's eight owners happened at the time to divide four to four over the efficacy of syndication, prompting them to spend more time warring with one another than guarding against insurgencies.

Johnson correctly sensed a second opportunity as well, this one among the players. The National League's enforcement of the reserve clause, the device that effectively bound players to one team for life, angered almost all the game's stars. By agreeing not to enforce a reserve clause in its contracts, American League clubs were able to recruit virtually at will from National league rosters between 1900 and 1901.

Of forty-six prominent names sought by American League teams in March of that year, forty-five—all but Honus Wagner—agreed to sign with the new league.[1]

Johnson's willingness to concede to players the illegitimacy of the reserve clause lasted precisely as long as his war with the National League. When in 1903 the defeated league sued for peace, Johnson's one major concession on terms was his acceptance of the reserve clause in standard player contracts.

The American League's successful insurgency was substantially a product of Johnson's organizing genius, but the core of allies who organized around him also deserved credit. Two of the most important were Charles Comiskey, a former star player, and Charles Somers, a millionaire Cleveland businessman who financed the team in that city while aiding several others. Comiskey's business sense and Somers's money filled precisely the gaps that Johnson's vision and zeal lacked, and for as long as the triangular alliance held together Johnson ruled a dynamic, successful enterprise essentially by fiat. In time, however, that alliance ruptured. The strains that pulled Comiskey from Johnson's orbit have already been alluded to; they fundamentally flowed from the competitive natures of the principals. In time too Somers's financial situation weakened, and by 1916 he was ready to sell his interests to Jim Dunn, another prominent Cleveland businessman. The American League power structure that Dunn entered bore only a slight resemblance to the one Johnson had created, with only Comiskey and Philadelphia's Ben Shibe remaining from the original cast. Several of the new owners, notably Harry Frazee in Boston and Jacob Ruppert and Tillinghast Huston in New York, questioned whether Johnson's leadership and vision—so productive fifteen years earlier—remained as forceful in the changing times. They found an ally in the increasingly disgruntled Comiskey; their dissatisfaction coalesced around the concept that Johnson applied insufficient diligence to the needs of the league's largest cities, which happened to be theirs. As was often the case in baseball, they were careful for public consumption to couch their complaints in terms of a threat to "integrity" rather than to their collective bottom lines, but the implication was plain.

"We have reached the conclusion that Mr. Johnson is endangering not only the value of [our] properties, but the integrity of the great national pastime known as baseball, and we therefore intend to do everything possible to rid organized baseball of the impediment which we believe is now attached to it," they declared.[2]

Johnson's belief in the efficacy of rebellion did not apply to rebellions that were aimed at unseating him. And since by this time he was clearly the game's dominant presence, any proposal directed toward changing the established structure was almost perforce targeted toward Johnson. His problems grew out of both his role as president of the American League and his status as the best-known member of the National Commission, the three-member body that ruled baseball. That body consisted of Johnson, whoever his National League counterpart happened to be, and Garry Herrmann, president of the National League's Cincinnati Reds but viewed as a staunch Johnson ally. Its concerns merely complicated and intensified the challenges arising from within Johnson's own league. In the five years between 1915 and 1920, the commission had essentially fallen apart over a series of incidents.

The first occurred in 1915, when the commission had been

called upon to settle a Pittsburgh claim to the rights to George Sisler, at the time the most coveted college player in the country and a future Hall of Famer. Herrmann sided with Johnson and delivered Sisler to the St. Louis Browns instead of the Pirates, despite Pittsburgh's preexisting claim. Commission member and National League (NL) president John Tener seethed.

Then in 1918 the Boston National League club paid Atlanta a $500 advance toward a stipulated $2,500 eventual purchase price for the rights to a pitcher named Scott Perry. Perry lasted less than three weeks before bolting the club and signing with an independent team. The commission declared Perry ineligible to play organized league ball and awarded the Boston Braves first rights to him, assuming they paid the $2,000 balance due to Atlanta if Perry returned. Instead, Atlanta defiantly resold Perry's rights to Connie Mack's Athletics. Perry reported and won several games—no simple feat on Mack's tail-end club—prompting the Braves to assert their rights to the player. The commission reiterated its previous ruling and declared Perry the property of the Braves. But Mack, facing the loss of a budding twenty-game winner, filed and won a suit in a local court allowing his team to keep the pitcher.

By taking his case to court—something unprecedented in the ranks of owner-owner disputes—Mack was understood to have at least the tacit blessing of Johnson, a fact that led Tener to refuse to sit with his counterpart on future commission decisions. In fact, Tener soon resigned his commission seat.

As the conclusion of the 1918 season approached, the once-stable and respected commission limped along as a widely discredited entity dominated by Johnson. That put him in the position to receive all the blame for the commission's handling of a dispute involving the payments to participants in that fall's World Series. The problem stemmed from a directive pushed by the recently departed Tener that cut other first-division teams in on a share of the profits from postseason games. This concept, long since accepted, generated plenty of concern among the pennant-winning Red Sox and Cubs, who feared the impact on their own shares at a time of declining interest in baseball. There was, after all, a war on.

Under the circumstances it came as no surprise that the World Series games themselves drew poorly. Looking at the prospect of record low payouts, Cubs and Red Sox players jointly staged a brief strike in advance of the Series' fifth game. Instead of taking the field, both teams stayed in their dressing rooms while Johnson, interim NL president John Heydler, and Herrmann met with the Cubs' Les Mann and the Red Sox's Harry Hooper. In time the combatants agreed to play, but the players' concerns proved valid when they got their checks: just $1,108 to each member of the winning Boston team—a record low—and only $671 to each of the losing Cubs, the second smallest payout to a loser in history.

The fact that Frazee, Comiskey, and Ruppert and Huston at the time constituted a majority of the American League's board of directors had been a recurring nightmare for Johnson. Yet through all of it, Johnson had been able to count on the unified backing of the league's other members—the so-called Loyal 5—to retain his hold on power. Those five were Shibe and Mack in Philadelphia, Frank Navin in Detroit, Dunn in Cleveland, Phil Ball in St. Louis, and Clark Griffith in Washington. But the animosity arising from Mays's sudden departure from the Red Sox in July 1919 set in motion a chain of events that would unravel the National Commission and erode Johnson's power base. Particularly unsettling was Johnson's order withholding third-place money from Yankees players following the 1919 season, his contention being that Mays's presence on the roster invalidated the team's finish. In November league owners formally sided with the Yankees in their challenge to Johnson's refusal to release the team's postseason share. As American League club owners met in February 1920, the New York State Supreme Court refused to uphold Johnson's suspension of Mays and ordered him to release the players' winnings.

Perhaps the winter's distractions were to blame; perhaps it was his animosity toward Comiskey. But Johnson never did engage the many rumors of improper influences affecting the 1919 World Series. It was not that he remained unaware. In the predawn hours following Cicotte's embarrassing loss in the first game, Comiskey had gone to Heydler to report the rumors swirling around his team, and Heydler had taken them to Johnson. "That's the whelp of a beaten cur," Johnson is said to have snarled.[3] For the entire winter and right through the beginning of the following season, it was Johnson's only statement about the prospect that his sport's most visible attraction had been corrupted. He had more important things to worry about.

When Herrmann left the commission under pressure that January, some of the owners urged reconstruction of the governing body's setup. What was plainly needed, the *Sporting News* asserted in February, was a whole new governance structure that would represent "all elements in Organized Baseball . . . [with] a chairman selected by some intelligent action and with full knowledge of just what sort of a job he [was] selected to fill."[4] This was a profound statement for two reasons. First, since Johnson was the leadership face of the commission as well as of his own league, any criticism of the governance structure was automatically a criticism of him. Second and of equal weight was the source. For two decades the Spink family, which published the *Sporting News*, had been an unfailing Johnson ally. In retrospect this declaration did not mark the Spinks' break with Johnson. But it was a clear sign that the American League president could no longer assume the unwavering backing of the publisher of the nation's best-selling baseball periodical.

As the 1920 season began, Frazee privately approached former president William Howard Taft about succeeding Herrmann or assuming whatever leadership position eventually developed. Taft, whose own ambitions for a seat on the United States Supreme Court rode with the Republicans' ascendant chances in that fall's presidential election, dismissed the feeler. But word leaked.

Johnson pointedly opposed the plan and threatened to resign. Owners did not push the issue, but they did create the first direct check on the powers of the presidents of the two leagues. It was a two-person "review board" (Griffith and Ruppert) empowered to validate or overturn any penalties or fines in excess of one hundred dollars or ten days. The action was significant because it required the defection of two of Johnson's reliable supporters—presumably Griffith and Phil Ball of St. Louis—to enact. Thus the proposal could be and was interpreted as a strong vote of no confidence in Johnson.

6. The Record

Why is the mad mob howling,
Hurling its curses out?
Why is the wild crowd yelping,
What is it all about?

Who has committed the murder?
Who has slaughtered a child?
What is the crime incarnate
Driving the thousands wild?

Why do they shirk [*sic*] in anguish?
Why do they yell for gore?
Why do they raise a clamor,
Worse than a tidal roar?

Maybe you guessed the answer
Hung to the bitter truth—
Only the rival pitcher
Starting to walk Babe Ruth.

—Grantland Rice, *New York Tribune*, July 22, 1920

July 15–25

Like howling 1920s-era fans, physicists too dig the long ball.

You can find the evidence in publications as diverse as *Popular Mechanics*, the *American Journal of Physics*, the National Aeronautics and Space Administration (NASA) Web site, *How*

Stuff Works, and the *Baseball Research Journal*. Within the past few years alone, each has dealt in detail with the question that has fascinated and perplexed fans since the days of Grantland Rice. How can you hit a baseball farther?

Scientists doubtless derive some of that interest from modern factors, notably the impact of the steroid era. But the notion of increasing power is a longtime draw regardless of whether the inquisitor grasps Newton's laws or merely roots for his favorite team.

In the Newtonian world the issue of how far a batted ball travels is a product of the interrelationship of several dozen independent variables. We need only touch on them to gain a sense of their complexity. Several involve not the hit but the pitch—its velocity, angle of delivery, spin rate, and horizontal and vertical spin angles. In other words, was it a fastball or a curve, and how was it moving when struck? Scientists must also consider the ball. Although regulation baseballs are built to certain size, weight, and seam-height specifications, those specs tolerate levels of variance that can influence the scientific property known as the coefficient of restitution. In lay terms that's the bounce-back factor, and it means that to a certain extent there are "live" baseballs and "dead" baseballs.[1]

The bat is yet another factor. How heavy or light is it, how fast is it moving at contact, and what is its coefficient of resistance? The latter is more scientific jargon for the friction inevitably applied to the ball by the bat, which retards its momentum away from the bat on contact. When you've factored all those considerations, factor also the bat's vibrational frequency at the point of contact. In 2007 *Popular Mechanics* determined that energy transfer—from bat to ball—depends on the point-of-contact vibrational frequency. You could think of vibrational frequency as "bees in the bat handle." What's important for our purposes is that energy transfer reduces as vibrational frequency increases. In what we characterize as the bat's "sweet spot"—an area about one inch on either side of a point about five and one-half inches from the tip—ball contact creates approximately zero vibrational frequency.[2]

Carry is further influenced by factors related to the flight of the ball from the bat. The most obvious are speed and angle of departure. But external factors also come into play, as anybody who has seen a game at Coors Field in Denver already appreciates. Those externals include altitude, air pressure, temperature, humidity, and wind. When Rockies executives initiated use of a humidor, they were offsetting the impact of altitude by "deadening" the ball.

In December 2003 the *American Journal of Physics* published an article jointly written by Gregory S. Sawicki and Mont Hubbard, both of the University of California at Davis, and William J. Stronge, of Cambridge University in England, trying to express "an optimum strategy for hitting a baseball." Compressed into a paragraph, these were their findings:

The most influential factor is bat speed. If batters could work on only one thing, that would be it. The ideal swing arc is a slight undercut—about 2.65 centimeters below center with a fifteen-degree upward swing angle. Try to get a curve ball to hit. Because of beneficial topspin imparted by the pitcher that is enhanced during impact with the bat, a curve will travel farther than a fastball or a changeup. There is also a relationship between the speed of any type of pitch and the distance that the ball carries. In other words a well-struck ninety-five-mile-per-hour fastball will fly farther than an equally well-struck ninety-mile-per-hour one.[3]

To quantify the variables NASA—which knows something about flight—developed what it calls the "hit modeler." This program allows tinkerers to project how far a baseball struck in each interaction of variables would be expected to travel. Consider a ball hit in New York City (zero altitude) on an average-weather day (60 degrees, 29.62 air pressure, 0 humidity, 0 wind), propelled from a bat with a 0.3 drag coefficient leaving the bat at a speed of 100 miles per hour at a 45 degree angle. Such a ball would travel 375 feet, reaching an apogee of 117 feet slightly more than halfway along its journey. Like many other aspects of hitting a ball, the optimal launch angle is actually a window ranging from about 45 to 53 degrees, with optimum distance (379 feet) achieved at about a 49-degree launch angle. Outside that window performance falls off sharply. For example, a ball struck under the same conditions, but at an angle of 41 degrees, can be expected to travel 10 feet less than one struck at 45 degrees.[4]

As Sawicki, Hubbard, and Stronge determined, however, the big issue is the speed of the ball departing the bat. Although almost all the factors mentioned earlier in this chapter influence velocity, the ones most immediately within the batter's control are those we would automatically think of: the mass of the bat and the speed with which it is swung. That 375-foot drive at a 100-mile-per-hour departure speed travels 380 feet at 101 miles per hour, with corresponding distance increases for each 1-mile-per-hour gain in ball speed as follows:

Ball speed after contact	Distance
102	382
103	387
104	392
105	395
106	400
107	405
108	409

Today the effort to increase ball speed off the bat generally begins with increasing bat speed through the hitting zone. In Babe Ruth's time more emphasis was placed on the other part of the equation: bat mass.

In fact, as 1920 dawned bats underwent their first major series of stylistic experimentation in two decades. This experimentation was prompted by the game's shifting focus from pitching dominance to hitting dominance. For years prior to 1918, and with the sole exception of a freak offensive season in 1911, league batting averages had hovered within a few points of .248, while slugging averages floated between .325 and .350. In 1918 batting averages rose to .254, then to around .263 in 1919, then to .277 in 1920. That amounted to nearly a 12 percent gain in just three seasons. Slugging accelerated even more quickly, to about .372 by 1920, a 15 percent increase. Quick to notice the increased fan attention that their exploits provoked—and the financial benefits that increased attention brought—players fiddled with an eye toward picking up even more of an edge. In Cincinnati, Reds cleanup hitter Heinie Groh swung his "bottle" bat, so named because of its two-and-three-quarters-inch barrel that tapered sharply toward the handle. Groh batted cleanup for the world champs.

Of course no bat was more famous than Ruth's, a Louisville Slugger behemoth by today's standards that measured thirty-six inches in length and weighed forty-two ounces. As the Babe leveled that bat toward a home run record that most believed would last for the imaginable future, fans coveted explanations for precisely how somebody could accomplish feats of strength so far beyond those of his cohorts. The *New York American* commissioned Arthur Robinson, one of its veteran sportswriters, to ask Ruth himself about his "secret." "I use a heavier bat than any man in baseball," Ruth told

Robinson. "And I swing with all my might. If I time my swing perfectly, and if I get the full force of my arms and shoulders and back behind the swing, I get a homer."[5]

Robinson also testified that Ruth paid a physical price for his aggression. He wrote of interviewing Ruth bare to the waist. "White lines . . . run from the hollows of his shoulders under the pits of his huge arms and extend over that portion of his flesh which ties itself into a mass of knotty wrinkles when he swings at the ball," Robinson wrote. The lines, he said, represented torn muscles. "I guess I've done that swinging at the ball and I guess it's a normal condition for me," Ruth told Robinson. "Sometimes I feel a bit sore around the chest, back and arms."[6]

In the search for an explanation of Ruth's power was born one of the first occasions for the application of scientific principles to baseball. The person to do so was a physicist named A. L. Hodges, commissioned by the *Chicago Herald and Examiner* in July 1920 to explain Ruth in terms that the typical reader—who probably lacked a high school diploma—could understand. Hodges's explanation is similar in its basic elements to the factors that are commonly understood today. Unless noted in brackets, what follows is from Hodges's July 1920 article:

> The bat which Babe Ruth wields and the ball which he hits are both fairly elastic, then everything else being equal, the ball will be driven farther the heavier the bat and the faster the bat is moving. Also, as the weight of Babe Ruth's body prevents this bat from doing much bouncing back, the faster the ball comes the farther it will go when he hits it. . . .
>
> A home run depends to a very large extent upon

the direction given the batted ball. The importance of this factor may be estimated as nine times that of the speed given the batted ball. By direction, we mean not only the horizontal angle but also the vertical angle at which the ball leaves the bat. . . . [Hodges offered no basis for his "nine times" weighting, and modern physicists who wrestle with the same question do not address that aspect of it.]

It is plain that the direction given the batted ball must depend to a large extent on the manner in which the ball is travelling before it meets the bat. Provided the ball is given a proper rotation on its horizontal axis by the pitcher, the kind of curve best suited to make it difficult to hit at the proper vertical angle is either the down shoot or the upshoot. On account of the many variable factors concerned, science believes that any home run made with either of these curves is a lucky chance pure and simple. . . . [Not true; as noted earlier, all other things being equal, curves tend to be easier than straight pitches to hit for home runs due to their increased rotation, which makes them fly farther.]

After the ball has been set in motion by the bat with a certain speed, the distance it will go depends upon the vertical angle at which it starts. The most desirable angle is one of 42 degrees to the ground. Other factors which determine the distance a batted ball will travel are the speed of the ball, its sphericity, the smoothness of its surface and its axis of rotation. Atmospheric conditions, of course, enter into the problem. . . .

If science were asked to make it difficult or well nigh impossible for Babe Ruth to hit a home run, it would select a day when the barometer was high with the air so heavy with moisture that it would retard the progress of the batted ball. The pitcher selected would be one good on very slow but curvy downshoots. [Not true; see the earlier comment on curves.] His ability to hit a home run could be made more difficult by compelling the Babe to swing a bat either so heavy that he could not swing it with much speed, or so light that it would tend to hit the ball at the wrong horizontal angle. . . .

There is a certain spot on the bat, usually a few inches from the end, but varying with different bats, which science knows as the center of percussion. If the ball hits the bat precisely on this spot the greatest effect is produced.[7]

Hodges went on at some length, calculating among other things that the power generated by Ruth on the ball would impart an initial velocity of about five hundred feet per second. Using the graphic imagery of his day, he put that at a speed faster than an express train. The Babe himself was estimated to generate forty-four horsepower. Over the course of a fifty home run season, the professor declared, Ruth expended enough energy to lift a fifty-five-ton locomotive six inches off the ground.

As Ruth approached his own home run record of twenty-nine, set the previous season, locomotives were low on his agenda. The schedule graced the Yanks with a twenty-one-game home stand, their longest of the season, involving five of the seven other league teams. During three victories in four games against the Tigers, the Babe had run his total to twenty-eight, leaving him at the absolute precipice of the accomplishment as the fifth-place St. Louis Browns followed Detroit into the Polo Grounds. In an era when weekday afternoon games did well to attract five thousand, crowds approaching fifteen thousand filed into the stadium for three midweek games in the hope of witnessing the record blow. Their hopes were dashed; the Yankees lost two of the three, and Ruth went homerless. Another fifteen thousand fans gathered on Thursday would have gone home disappointed as well when the Yanks scored six times in the fourth inning and carried a 9–8 advantage into the ninth inning on a rain-soaked field. But Rip Collins allowed the tying run. Ruth—with a chance to make his record homer a game winner—whiffed.

On this day, though, that gaffe merely delayed the dramatics. Aaron Ward kicked off the bottom of the twelfth with a line drive past the third baseman against rookie Bill Burwell, who was in the game only because the Browns had run out of pitching staff. Miller Huggins ordered Wally Pipp to sacrifice ahead of Ruth, then got lucky when Burwell slipped on the muddy field trying to make the play.

With runners at first and second and none out, the Browns debated walking Ruth intentionally but decided against doing so because it would have moved Ward—the potential winning run—to third base, where a sacrifice fly could score him. Burwell worked the count to 3-2, then Ruth drove the next pitch, which he described the next morning in a newspaper column as a high fastball, against the cornice atop the far end of the second deck. Witnesses said that had the ball been hit about three feet higher or six feet further toward center, it would have left the ballpark entirely.

The prospect of seeing Ruth break the record drew eighteen thousand to the Friday afternoon wrap-up with St. Louis. Instead they saw Bill Bayne, a rookie left-hander, challenge and defeat both the Babe and the Yankees, giving the visitors the series three games to two. To the surprise of many in attendance, Bayne pitched to Ruth with a runner in scoring position in the first inning—and fanned him. The Babe did get one hit, a late single, but the loss kept New York one and one-half games behind the Indians.

As the Yankees enjoyed their longest home stand of the season, Speaker's team was deep into its longest road swing. The mammoth thirty-two-game cross-country journey—involving more than 40 percent of its entire road schedule—would take the team to every other city in the league, with two stops in Chicago. Such trips remained the norm in an era that moved by train. Cleveland would be on those trains for a month between home appearances on June 24 and July 25. Arriving in Philadelphia on July 13 for the fifth of those eight stops, the Indians had handled the demands of travel well, winning twelve of the nineteen games to that point. The Athletics too proved cooperative, losing three of the four, among them a 5–1 decision that was shortened to six innings due to rain. The A's only victory came in the Friday closer when Tris Speaker tried to get by with second-line hurler George Uhle. He should have made it; Uhle carried a 4–3 lead into the bottom of the eighth, only to allow a one-out single and a walk. When Uhle missed with his first two pitches to rookie outfielder Frank Welch, Speaker went to Bagby in relief. But the seventeen-game winner walked Welch to load the bases. The next batter, Joe Dugan, took a close two-strike pitch that Bagby beefed loudly about to umpire Dick Nallin. Dugan drove the next pitch for a hit that sent the winning runs around.

From Philadelphia the Indians made their way to Boston for a five-game, four-day series involving two doubleheaders—both created by earlier rainouts—wrapped around an idle Sunday thanks to the city's blue laws. They won both Saturday games by identical 5–2 scores, and from that point onward Bagby was the story. On Monday a four-run Indians rally in the ninth broke a 6–6 tie. Bagby, who entered in relief of Coveleski in the seventh, picked up his eighteenth victory against just five losses. He started the second game, taking a 4–2 lead into the eighth. He allowed a run in that inning, opened the ninth by allowing two hits, and was pulled in favor of Uhle, against whom the tying run scored. Boston won in ten innings.

The Indians extended their lead over New York to two games on Tuesday, although Guy Morton, called on by Speaker to give his front-liners some rest, didn't help. He left in the sixth, leading 7–4. Dick Niehaus followed but failed to retire anybody in the seventh as the Red Sox narrowed the Indians' lead to 7–6. Uhle came next, but he was knocked out in the eighth when Boston tied the game 7–7. Having exhausted his second-liners, Speaker turned once again to Bagby, who managed a scoreless ninth and tenth innings. In the top of the eleventh, the Indians loaded the bases on hits by Jamieson and Chapman and a Speaker walk.

With his team in need of a quick out, Boston manager Ed Barrow resorted to trickery, directing third baseman Eddie Foster in on the grass to lull Jamieson into a false sense of security, then scooting shortstop Everett Scott behind him for a pick-off. It might have worked, but catcher Roxy Walters's throw flew past Scott into left field, allowing Jamieson to score and the other runners to advance. Wambsganss's sacrifice fly, which would have scored the first run, instead scored the second, and that made all the difference when Bagby yielded what otherwise would have been the tying run in the bottom half. Over a bit more than one twenty-four-hour period, Bagby had pitched nearly fifteen innings across three games, winning two of them.

In preparation for a six-game series in New York, the White Sox stopped off in Philadelphia and Washington and won six of eight. Heavy rain on July 15 in Washington contorted that day's game into a doubleheader the following afternoon. That set the stage for Swede Risberg and Shoeless Joe Jackson. The first game featured Red Faber and Walter Johnson in a 1–1 tie broken in the ninth when Risberg tripled to the wall in deep left-center field, driving two runs across. Washington led the second game 5–4 behind Harry Courtney entering the ninth. But when Nemo Leibold beat out a high bounder, Courtney gave way to Eric Erickson, whose error allowed Eddie Collins to reach first base, and who failed to cover first on Buck Weaver's grounder, filling the bases for Jackson. His drive traced Risberg's earlier path to the base of the flagpole in deep center more than 420 feet away. Jackson legged all three runners around for an inside-the-park grand slam and an 8–5 victory.

The White Sox arrived in New York on Saturday afternoon two and a half games behind the Yankees and another game behind Cleveland. The situation could hardly have been more profitable for Ruppert and Huston, who had their most attractive draw for a long weekend with Ruth poised to break the home run record. The fans arrived early for the Saturday opener, with thirty-seven thousand of them pouring into the Polo Grounds. They saw Yankees batters maul Eddie Cicotte and two relievers for twenty runs and twenty-one hits, three of them homers. They saw White Sox fielders assist with seven errors, five in the first two innings alone, when New York built a 6–0 lead. But they did not see Ruth deliver anything more dramatic than a mere double. Cracked the *Chicago Tribune*'s Jimmy Cruisenberry, "Just how Babe Ruth could live through a ball game in which the Yankees got twenty-one base hits and not make a home run that would break the world's record is one of the comical things about the alleged game. The chances are that one might have picked a fan at random from anywhere in the grandstand or bleachers, and he could have gone out and knocked out a four-base hit."[8]

Perhaps the only Yankee more frustrated than Ruth was Ping Bodie, who managed to go hitless on a day in which every other Yankees starter got at least two. But Bodie made up for it on Sunday, stealing the spotlight from Ruth before thirty-four thousand fans, their number held down by persistent showers. Bodie's first-inning grand slam quickly put Lefty Williams in a 4–0 hole, his third-inning double drove home Ruth, and his fifth-inning single plated Meusel. It was Bodie's third hit and sixth RBI of the afternoon. Ruth delivered two more hits, one of them a double, but again failed to homer, sending the thirty-four thousand away less than fully satisfied despite New York's 8–4 victory.

Ruth's failure over three days to produce a home run on demand only ratcheted up the excitement so that the next day's doubleheader against the Sox drew twenty-eight thousand fans, an incredible audience for a Monday afternoon. This time the Babe did not disappoint. Facing Dickie Kerr in the fourth inning of the second game, Ruth sent a 2–2 curve ball ripping into the right-field seats, where its arrival touched off a wild battle for the souvenir. With Pipp, who had singled, ahead of him, the Babe cruised the bases to a thunderous ovation from the spectators. He added his thirty-first home run in the ninth inning, although by then the visitors had safely put the game away, 8–5. The Yankees had won the first game 8–2, with Ruth walked twice, legging out a double and hitting into a force play.

In the next afternoon's *New York Post,* William Chipman described the scene in the Yankees clubhouse when "a timid little negro . . . eluded the doorman and presented to Babe Ruth the thing the slugger thought was hopelessly lost": the thirtieth home run ball.[9]

"Ah didn't aim to try to keep de ball, Mistah Babe, but ah jest hadter come an' give it to yo' mah own self," Chipman quoted the young man as telling the star. "An' ah hoped maybe yo' all might let me shake yo' han." As Chipman told the story, the lucky fan got that and more: a season pass "and a bank note of larger denomination than the youngster dreamed existed."[10]

The six-game series concluded on Tuesday, drawing 32,000 for a wrap-up doubleheader that turned into another split. There was at least financial solace for the visitors in the fact that the four days of games had drawn an unprecedented 125,000 fans. Remarked the *New York World*'s pseudonymous Monitor, "The Sox left for Boston with only two victories . . . but with the biggest bundle of greenbacks any visiting baseball team has ever corralled."[11]

The Babe's thirty-second home run came against Faber during the fifth inning of the first game, a 7–5 Chicago victory. The blow was typically Ruthian, clearing the grandstand roof by five feet and landing in a field outside the ballpark. It was the only pitch that Faber had given Ruth to hit the entire game; he walked him the other three times.

The home run notwithstanding, Ruth for once was forced to share top billing because the day's guests included Archbishop Daniel Mannix of Australia, then engaged in a world tour. Ruppert introduced them, which led the *New York Sun*'s William Hanna to imagine Ruth telling the prelate how Sox pitcher Eddie Cicotte had stifled him in the second game:

"Yu [*sic*] see, I've socked these Sox pitchers for three homers the last two games, so no man can keep busting the apple at that rate."[12]

The four defeats in six games sent the White Sox off to Boston a full six games out of first place in what was threatening to become a two-team race. They found no solace in the Wednesday opener there, a 2–1 duel in which Sam Jones out pitched Lefty Williams. Jackson's second-inning home run represented 100 percent of the White Sox's productivity. Kerr turned the tables Thursday, beating Boston 2–1. The Red Sox raced to a 5–0 lead against Faber after four innings on Friday, but Chicago's offense rode to the rescue. With one out in the sixth, Nemo Leibold tripled; then Eddie Collins, Weaver, Jackson, Felsch, and John Collins all singled, producing four runs. Jackson's home run keyed a second four-run splurge in the eighth that completed the comeback, handing reliever Roy Wilkinson a victory. The rain-interrupted Saturday game also went to Chicago when Felsch drove in four of his team's seven runs with a double and a homer, then dashed into deep center for a catch that choked off a Red Sox rally against Cicotte.

The White Sox labored largely in anonymity, though, because attention focused on the Polo Grounds, where the Indians had followed Chicago for four games of their own. By the conclusion of play Saturday evening, it would become the best-attended regular-season series in baseball history. With Cleveland possessing a two-game lead in the standings, the series threatened the tenuous hold on first place that the Indians had maintained for two weeks. Against that concern fans of the visitors took solace from the schedule, noting that the Yankees had just finished consecutive Monday–Tuesday doubleheaders with the White Sox. Yankees management had plugged the extra games that way in order to shore up its gate for what were usually the two lightest-drawing days of the week. Cleveland had also played a pair of doubleheaders in Boston, but they were booked on Saturday and Monday (around a Sunday off day), affording the Indians a fresher staff. "It looks to me as if manager Miller Huggins . . . pulled a boner" in the rescheduling of earlier rainouts, suggested the *Cleveland Press*'s Ross Tenney. By contrast, Tenney said, the Red Sox "treated the Indians kindly."[13]

Tenney's theory made perfect sense on paper, but on the field, not so much. In front of twenty-five thousand, Bob Meusel gave Carl Mays a fast lead in the first game with a long second-inning home run of Ray Caldwell. Pipp opened the third by driving another ball off the facade of the upper deck, and Ward sent two more runs home with a triple off the right-field wall. The score was 4–0 after just three innings, and the way Mays was pitching that appeared to be enough. It was, barely.

Through eight innings Mays allowed just one Cleveland runner to reach third base and just two to get past first. Today such a situation would inevitably bring a call to the bullpen—probably for the "closer"—to start the ninth. But there was no such thing as a closer in 1920, when pitchers working on a shutout were assumed to be okay. So Mays stayed in, only the first of several managerial decisions in the next half inning that illustrate the difference between the game then and now.

Speaker opened the Cleveland ninth with a double, scoring on Larry Gardner's drive to left, which Meusel gloved, then lost off the wall, then caught again for another double. A more sure-handed fielder probably would have snared the ball cleanly for an out, and Huggins had such a fielder on his bench in veteran Duffy Lewis. Like closers, however, defensive replacements were not often used at that time.

With one out Wambsganss followed with a ground ball to short that should have been the second out. But Peckinpaugh threw the ball over Pipp's head, giving Wambsganss second and scoring Gardner. Now it was 4–2. Johnston's single scored Wambsganss and put the tying run on first. When O'Neill followed with a single of his own, Huggins had finally seen enough of Mays. He called on Rip Collins to face Caldwell.

With the tying run in scoring position, Speaker might have been expected to pinch-hit for his pitcher. He had a long list of availables, among them Joe Evans, Joe Wood—both hitting above .300 at the time—and George Burns. But Speaker stayed with Caldwell, apparently more fearful of his own bullpen in the event his team did tie the game than of his pitcher's performance at the plate. Caldwell, a veteran who had played forty-six games in the outfield during a ten-season career, was hardly incompetent at bat; he would retire two seasons later with a career .248 average. But hits had been rare for him in 1920, his average hanging around .200. Indeed, Collins quickly slipped two strikes past his pitching opponent, before missing with a fast ball in a place where Caldwell could reach it. He drove it on a line toward Bodie in center; the outfielder rifled a throw to Muddy Ruel that barely threw out Johnston, preventing the tying run.

That was the second out, but Collins walked Cuckoo Jamieson, putting the issue up to him and Chapman. Collins and the Yankees survived when Chapman swung and missed on a 3-2 fastball. New York had moved within a single game of the lead.

Save for a few percentage points, the race leveled on Thursday when Collins started and beat Coveleski 11–3 before another twenty-five-thousand-fan weekday gathering in a game shortened to seven innings by rain. Coveleski started for Speaker, and the Yankees delivered early notice that they would treat the fifteen-game winner rudely. New York's first batter, Peckinpaugh, homered into the left-field seats. A walk and two more hits produced a second run. Ruel opened the home half of the second with a single, and Collins bunted to Gardner, who threw to second. But neither Wambsganss nor Chapman had covered the base, so the ball traveled unobstructed out to Speaker. That brought Peckinpaugh back to the plate, and his second home run in two innings—again into the left-field seats—made it 5–0. Coveleski left in favor of the lightly used Elmer Myers.

With rain halting play in the second, the only remaining questions were whether Ruth would homer and whether the Yankees would get the requisite four and one-half innings in before conditions interrupted them. When play resumed, the New York offense hardly slowed up, adding a sixth run in the post-shower second. Two more followed in the third and a ninth run in the fourth. The Babe's portion of that sixteen-hit carnage was limited to a walk and a double. That double, which came amid a steady rain in the fourth inning with the Yankees leading 9–3, touched off what amounted to a baseball burlesque as both teams endeavored to work the elements to their advantage. Ruth started it, rounding second and loping toward third base, daring the Indians to retire him, which Speaker did with a throw to Gardner. Meusel followed with his own double, and he too deliberately ran into an out at third. One out and a half inning from the game becoming official, the Indians chose not to cooperate with the Yankees' efforts to speed the process. Bodie lifted a routine single to center and casually drifted toward second. But this time Speaker refused to throw him out. Bodie broke for third on the first pitch, hopeful of being thrown out. But pitcher Tony Faeth—called on in relief of Myers in the third—upset that "strategy" by firing the pitch over the head of catcher Steve O'Neill. On the next pitch Bodie took off for home on what amounted to a suicide steal attempt. O'Neill thwarted Bodie's attempt to be retired by refusing to make a play on the slow-moving runner, allowing a tenth run to cross the plate.

Caught up in the farce aspects, what remained of the twenty-five thousand fans now jeered the Indians for their failure to cooperate in their own demise. Their jeering did not stop the farce. The next batter, Aaron Ward, was deliberately walked, continuing to second and then to third without a play being made on him. That brought up Ruel. He too saw a succession of offerings far outside the strike zone. But Ruel swung at them and after three pitches officially became a strikeout victim, the inning's final out.

The outcome left the two teams in a virtual tie for first place entering the series' third game before another twenty-five thousand on Friday and left Speaker with only Morton, his shaky "fourth" starter, to put up against eleven-game winner Bob Shawkey. Morton made a game of it for three innings, holding the Yankees offense to a lone two-out hit and taking a brief lead when Speaker's fly ball scored Chapman, who had tripled to right center field in the first.

That changed when Pipp opened the fourth with a double, and Johnston threw poorly to Gardner attempting to retire him at third on Pratt's grounder. With Ruth up next Morton exercised discretion and purposely passed him, filling the bases with none out. Meusel gave the Indians a reprieve with a ground ball that Gardner turned into a force at home. But singles by Bodie and Ruel sent three runs across. By the time the Indians touched Shawkey again, with a pair of eighth-inning runs, the Yankees led 6–1. Those runs included Ruth's thirty-third home run of the season in the sixth inning, as well as Peckinpaugh's third of the series with one out in the seventh.

The weather improved for Saturday, eliminating the final impediment between the series wrap-up and the largest audience ever to attend a regular-season big league game to that point. The other elements—a weekend clash of contenders in the largest stadium in the largest city and with Babe Ruth as the star—had long been in place. Fans responded. By early afternoon the Polo Grounds itself was full, as were Coogan's Bluff and nearby roadways from which a partial view of the stadium below could be obtained. Trainload after trainload arrived at the 155th Street subway station, but with little standing room remaining outside—much less inside—authorities soon ordered the trains not to open their doors. Police set up a "dead line" at 155th Street beyond which non-ticket holders were prohibited. The police inspector in charge of the area estimated that twenty-five thousand were denied entrance to that area of town.

"We think even our big day of 38,283 [earlier in the season] has been beaten," Ruppert told the newspaper reporters regarding the in-stadium attendance.[14] The turnstile count validated Ruppert's estimate, surpassing thirty-nine thousand. Counting those on the hills and milling outside, a proximate attendance of close to fifty thousand by game time isn't outside the realm of possibility. Interest in the game spurred speculation in the New York papers about the need for a new and larger stadium to accommodate interest in Ruth. In the

Tribune W. O. McGeehan termed the Polo Grounds—already the largest ballpark in the country—"somewhat obsolete and completely inadequate" for a Ruth-led team. "It looks very much as though a baseball park with a capacity of 100,000 seats must be built in the near future, for New York at any rate," McGeehan offered.[15]

The lucky ticket holders who got in saw a pitching match-up worthy of the billing between Bagby, seeking his twentieth victory, and Jack Quinn. Cleveland scored first, taking advantage of Ruel's overaggressiveness. With two out and Speaker at second, Ruel let a pitch get past him, then threw hurriedly trying to retire Speaker at third. Instead he fired the ball into left field, allowing the run to score. His error was magnified when Cleveland's cleanup hitter, Elmer Smith, made the inning's third out on the next pitch.

Bagby provided the pitching dominance that the reeling Indians desperately needed. He shut down the Yankees on just six hits. Two of them, however, left the park. Meusel led off the second with a game-tying home run into the left-field stands. Then in the fourth Ruth drove his thirty-fourth home run off the facade beneath the roof of the right-field stands before it bounded back onto the field. Yankees players described the ball as lopsided when it was returned to their dugout. The Indians retied the game in the top of the fifth when Wambsganss tripled and scored on Johnston's sacrifice fly.

From that point onward neither Bagby nor Quinn provided the opponent much opportunity. The best scoring chance fell to the Indians, who put Wambsganss at third and Johnston at second with two out. Speaker gambled on a double steal, which almost succeeded when Ruel threw high to Peckinpaugh, forcing him to throw high in return to catch

Wambsganss at the plate. Ruel was knocked backward trying to block the Indians second baseman off the plate, but he held onto the ball and got the "out" call.

The pivotal play, as it turned out, had already occurred, although it was not evident at the time. In the eighth inning umpire Ollie Chill ejected Pipp during a dispute over a play at first base. That forced Huggins to move Ruth in to first and to swap Meusel from left field to right. With one out in the eleventh, those moves undermined the Yankees.

Chapman started the trouble with an innocent grounder behind first that Ruth fielded, then threw over the head of pitcher George Mogridge. Mogridge partially reprieved the out-of-position slugger when he pitched out on a Speaker hit-and-run attempt. In an effort to protect the base runner, the best Speaker could manage was an off-balance swing for an innocent pop-up that Ruel caught for the second out. The next hitter was Wood, a replacement for the left-handed Smith when Mogridge had entered the game a couple of innings earlier. Mogridge hit him. With runners at first and second, Gardner sent a deep fly ball to right. Meusel started in, then tried to back up rather than turn for the ball, and his one-handed stab came up just short. By the time Meusel regained his balance and threw the ball in, both Chapman and Wood had crossed the plate.

Trailing 4–2 in the bottom of the eleventh, the Yankees had one more chance, and it began with Ruth. Leading off against Bagby, he smashed a drive to the deepest part of right-center field, only to see Speaker chase it down for the first out. Meusel followed with a blow nearly as deep to the same general area, where this time Wood grabbed it. The third hitter, Ping Bodie, did manage a single, but Bagby retired Aaron Ward on an easy grounder to end the game.

The clubs left the field in a virtual tie for the top spot, both four games ahead of the White Sox. At the conclusion of the western teams' long eastern swing, Cleveland's eight-percentage-point hold on first was constructed on the fact that the Indians had played four fewer games than the Yankees, having both won and lost two fewer. Before New York's second tour of the West began the following Wednesday, however, the schedule required two more meetings in New York with the Red Sox. With Mays picking up his fifteenth win on a four-hitter, the Sunday game was a snap. New York led 2–1 in the fifth when Ruel, Peckinpaugh, and Pipp bunched singles, then Pratt doubled. That brought up Ruth, whose thirty-fifth home run was soon deposited in the lower right-field seats. The sum of the damage was five runs. The closest the Red Sox came to a highlight worth talking about occurred in the third after Peckinpaugh walked and Pipp reached on second baseman Mike McNally's error. McNally would quickly atone, snaring Pratt's line drive, touching second to double Peckinpaugh, then throwing back to Stuffy McInnis at first to triple Pipp.

Monday's game was as one-sided for the Red Sox as Sunday's had been for the Yankees. Sam Jones shut out New York 9–0 on just three hits, one fewer than the number of walks he accorded Ruth alone. That last did not sit well with the fifteen thousand home fans. "Babe's walk in the eighth with the score 9–0 and the bases empty was the last word in caution," the *New York Times* reporter observed sardonically.[16]

After pitching his club past the Red Sox Sunday afternoon, Mays left the park in too big a hurry and spun his roadster on St. Nicholas Avenue, a short distance away. A nearby officer, seeing the incident, ticketed the pitcher, who answered the summons the next morning and pleaded for time. The Yankees, he noted, had a long western road trip coming up and would not be back in town until August 16. A cooperative magistrate granted Mays the delay he requested and set the case for a hearing during the third week of August.[17]

7. The Last Three Weeks of Innocence and Purity in the History of Baseball

July 26–August 15

Not many years earlier the signing of Amos Strunk by a contender would have been cause for celebration. In his prime Strunk was a good hitter. In the prime of his prime, that was a modest characterization. In 1916 he batted .316 for Connie Mack's Athletics, ranking fourth (behind Tris Speaker, Ty Cobb, and Joe Jackson) in the entire American League. In the summer of 1920, Strunk was a career .281 batter whose biggest weakness had been his absence of power. Across thirteen seasons he had never hit more than three home runs a year. Strunk did place three times in the top ten in the American League in slugging, but that was more a function of his foot speed than anything involving muscles. "The Mercury of the American League," *Baseball Magazine*'s J. C. Kofoed called Strunk for his ability to go from home to second or first to third.[1] He stole twenty bases or more four different times, a notable performance in the years between 1911 and 1920, when the prevailing baseball philosophy transitioned from one run at a time to hit away.

Amos Strunk may not have been a slugger, but he was reliable. A starter on three of Connie Mack's pennant winners (1911, 1913, and 1914), he made it four after being traded to

Boston in 1918. Four times Amos Strunk had led American League outfielders in fielding average, prompting Mack to call him "the most under-rated outfielder in baseball."[2]

Strunk looked like a ballplayer, with a moon face that fairly shouted his inability to get by in any field requiring classic features. He came to the Athletics as a local boy off the sandlots of Shamokin, Pennsylvania, and got periodic brief opportunities until establishing himself with the pennant-bound Athletics in 1910.

But there was also a fragile aspect to Strunk that periodically diminished what might otherwise today be recognized as his talent, if not his greatness. No sooner did he establish himself as a twenty-one-year-old regular with the A's in 1910 than a knee injury sidelined him for most of the season. (He did return for the World Series and produced five hits as the A's beat the Cubs in 5 games.) Even in his prime he played more than 125 games just three times.

Added to that was a disheartening tendency to be the biggest fish in a small pond. When Mack broke up his Athletics after the 1914 season—selling or losing such stars as Eddie Collins, Home Run Baker, Jack Barry, Chief Bender, Jack Coombs, Herb Pennock, Bob Shawkey, and Eddie Plank—the team fell fifty-six games in the standings in 1915. Strunk was one of the few remaining recognizable faces, bringing him to the apex of his personal game precisely at the moment of least relevance. In 1916 Strunk supplemented his .316 average with 30 doubles, 172 hits, and a .393 on-base percentage. But the Athletics lost 117 games.

Eventually even Mack realized that Strunk was of more value to his team as a commodity than as a player. Before the 1918 season Mack shipped him with Joe Bush and Wally Schang to the Red Sox in exchange for three players and—more importantly—sixty thousand dollars.

Given that Strunk had just turned twenty-nine and could be considered in his prime, the deal might have been a godsend. But Strunk batted just .257 for the 1918 pennant winners, his worst performance in seven seasons, and followed that with just four hits in twenty-three World Series at bats. Even that disappointing effort did not prevent the Red Sox from defeating the Cubs in six games, but it did coincide with the thought entering Boston manager Ed Barrow's mind that left-handed pitcher Babe Ruth was too good a hitter to play only every fourth day. So in 1919 Barrow shifted Ruth to the outfield and packaged the now-surplus Strunk and Barry back to the Athletics in a deal rife with ramifications from the Mays controversy.

Strunk found himself back with a tail-end club but now carried the baggage of being an aging veteran. He hit just .211 in Philadelphia the rest of 1919 but seemed to find his stroke again in 1920, threatening .300 while playing more or less full time through the season's first three months. To Mack that made the 1920 version of Strunk look a lot like the 1918 version: a player with more market value than on-field value. That was especially so if Strunk could be marketed to a contender. As July meandered toward August, it was no secret which team needed a calming clubhouse presence and a veteran bat, especially one who could play some outfield. The defending champion Chicago White Sox had replaced first baseman Chick Gandil with Shano Collins, a career platoon outfielder. That was well and good as far as it went, but the fractured platoon's other half, Nemo Leibold, basically proved to be a disaster as a full-timer in right. By mid-July Leibold was well on his way to delivering a .220 batting average with no discernible power. Playing a position whose contemporaries included Ruth, Elmer Smith, and Sam

Rice, Leibold simply wasn't good enough. On July 23 Mack graciously accepted a check from Charles Comiskey for the going waiver price, and Strunk purchased a train ticket for Cleveland, where two days later the White Sox, four games behind the Indians and the Yanks, were to pick up their pursuit of the front-runners.

A Sunday game between two contenders in Cleveland figured to draw well, and that one did. Dunn Field held only twenty-five thousand, so the Indians had strung ropes deep in the outfield behind which the overflow could be accommodated. This had been a common practice in some cities for decades, but there had been little call for ropes in Cleveland until 1920 because the team rarely drew sellout numbers. The ropes shrank the field and thus distorted the playing conditions by frequently turning easy fly balls into ground-rule doubles if they fell beyond the reach of fielders and into the masses. But to the league and its teams, that was an acceptable trade-off for the additional gate. On this Sunday, given the fervor of the Cleveland fan base, an estimated five thousand packed in behind the ropes, bringing the total attendance on scene to thirty thousand, more if you counted the dozen or so brave souls who scaled school buildings and warehouses across Lexington Avenue to watch for free from the right-field rooftops. Many arrived early, saluting every move of their heroes, even during the usually relaxed batting practice.

Despite the absence to that point of any formal investigation, rumors regarding the 1919 World Series—and for that matter of play during the 1920 season—swirled freely in July. That in turn encouraged Indians fans to threaten open warfare on the suspects. Williams, who started on the mound, and Jackson were particular targets. In the fresh aftermath of the world war, Jackson's war "experience" was viewed as fair game anywhere outside Chicago. He had been twenty-seven and obviously fit, and his shipyard duty, however legal, was widely held as a less-than-courageous approach to fulfilling one's obligation. On the road Jackson was routinely greeted with taunts of "Shipyard!" and "Slacker!" by the unforgiving fans, many of them combat veterans.[3]

Williams was subject to the same criticism. Beyond that, because he had lost all three of his 1919 World Series starts, suspicion swirled around his complicity in the "fix" talk. So it brought the thirty thousand no small measure of joy when Speaker's two-out first-inning home run over the screen in right put Lefty Williams in a quick hole.

To Indians fans one run was generally viewed as sufficient for Stan Coveleski, but he would get two more in the third and an additional three in the seventh for an easy victory. From his place on the bench, Strunk watched a team chemistry that was oddly cold by the standards of his impressive experience. Even with the 1919 Red Sox, the problem had been Mays alone. Here the animosity was more widespread. Battery mates Williams and Ray Schalk did not talk except to bark at each other. The team congregated on the bench in cliques. The seven suspects occupied one area; Ray Schalk, Eddie Collins, Shano Collins, Dickie Kerr, Red Faber along with a handful of reserves took the other. The banter that had been so much a part of Strunk's professional life that he barely heard it now passed unheard for a different reason: there was so little of it. Strunk had joined a "team" that fit the definition of the word solely due to its uniform.

His place on that team was obvious: with the Schalk-Collins faction. However else one assessed Strunk's career, he had never been suspected of crookedness, and he saw no value in it now in the waning days of his professional life. A big leaguer for more than a decade, he had shared lockers with players on both sides of the team divide, coming up to the A's with Joe Jackson when they were both sandlotters in 1908 and 1909. But Mack had traded Jackson to Cleveland in the summer of 1910 because he needed a veteran outfield presence. In 1920 the two thirty-one-year-olds barely knew each other.

Of all the Sox Strunk was most familiar with Eddie Collins from their championship days with the Athletics between 1910 and 1914. But if Collins was more in line with Strunk's preferences ethically, that did not mean they gravitated toward each other. Few players gravitated naturally to Collins, a standoffish, often churlish Columbia College graduate playing a game dominated by sandlotters such as Strunk. Not for nothing was he known throughout the league by the nickname "Cocky."

From Cleveland the Sox hopped the overnight Lake Erie ferry and a train for two victories in Detroit before opening an eighteen-game home stand against the East that would continue into mid-August. The end of July represented an especially opportunistic period for the Sox, since they faced seven games against the league's tailenders, the Tigers and the Athletics. They went 5-2 in those seven games, a result that lost them one game in the standings to the first-place Indians.

The brief stay in Detroit proved uneventful, although it might have been otherwise. Tigers pitcher Hooks Dauss hit the game's first batter, Leibold, then beaned Eddie Collins, briefly knocking him out. Given five minutes, Collins recovered, wobbled to first, then fully regained his senses on the run when Jackson followed with a triple. Fred McMullin replaced Collins in the field for the top of the second. Collins also sat out the next day's game.

The five-game Philadelphia series encapsulated every difficulty with trying to determine whether the Sox were playing on the level that summer. Eddie Cicotte's three-hit shutout easily papered over a Swede Risberg error as well as a mental base-running blunder by Happy Felsch in the Wednesday opener. But Risberg also made a brilliant defensive play, and Felsch drove home a run, the sum being no clear evidence of any untoward behavior.

There certainly was untoward behavior during the second game of the next day's doubleheader, but the wrong suspects fouled things up. After Williams beat Eddie Rommel 4–2 in the first game, the Athletics set upon Dickie Kerr for fourteen hits and led 6–4 entering the bottom of the ninth. Hits by Leibold and Collins put the tying runs at second and third with none out, and when Buck Weaver bounced to short, the A's allowed Leibold to score, focusing all their attention on retiring the batter. But Leibold did not score; instead he held at third, surprising the A's, the home fans, and especially Collins, who attempted to advance on the assumption that the base would be his for the taking. It was an easy matter for Philadelphia's first baseman to trot across the field and retire Leibold in a rundown.

Jackson was next, and he homered, a shot that ought to have won the game but instead only tied it due to Leibold's inaction. Kerr was even worse in the tenth than he had been in the first nine innings, allowing six more runs and taking a loss that should have been a win. The two clubs split the Friday and Saturday games, with Dave Keefe, an unregarded rookie used mostly in relief, holding the defending champions to a single run.

Normally a contender winning only three of five from a tailender would at most reinforce the idea that the unlikely can happen in baseball. Perhaps that was all it did mean, but with the Sox one could never easily dismiss alternative theories. *Chicago Tribune* sportswriter I. E. Sanborn publicly questioned the legitimacy of some aspects of the performance. "In the eighth Felsch led off with a double, and before anything more of that kind could happen he was picked off second by a yard," Sanborn wrote. "Risberg dumped a Texas Leaguer safely into right and tried to make two bases on it without one chance in a thousand."[4] Some players, notably Schalk, openly wondered whether Chicago remained under the control of gamblers seeking to manipulate that summer's race for their own ongoing gain. On a given day that might mean losing or winning; the only imperative would be staying close enough to the top to keep the pennant odds contentious and the betting interest high. Any team can lose on command, but it takes a very good team to win *or* lose on command. Nobody disputed that the 1920 White Sox were a very good team.

Seen in that context, and given Chicago's position between four and five games behind the Indians, it was equally possible to read the Cicotte and Williams victories, the Jackson home run, and the Felsch RBI as evidence of their collective commitment to the team—or to the gamblers.

There were no such doubts about the Yankees, a team that frolic followed. New York warmed up for a four-game early-August series in Chicago with five games against the midpack Browns, and even the loss of three of those five did little to dampen enthusiasm. "One thing in favor of the New York club is that it has no nerves," Arthur Robinson suggested in what was intended to be a complimentary remark. "It is not the temperamental, fragile creation of Speaker, whetted to the fine edge of a razor and ready to be dulled almost as easily."[5] The principal reason was, of course, Ruth, approaching forty home runs and setting a new standard with each one.

To a degree the Yankees hurt themselves with wasted opportunities. "The Yankees squandered bright chances like sailors used to squander money before Prohibition," the *New York Times* reporter cynically observed following a 1–0 loss to Urban Shocker.[6] But more so the Browns won by employing the new and widely popular avoidance strategy. Jimmy Sheckard had set the record for bases on balls in 1911 with 147, one fewer than Ruth would finish the 1920 season with. But until that summer it was unheard of for big league pitchers to deliberately and as a matter of policy avoid challenging a particular hitter. In 1919 Ty Cobb had led the Majors with a .384 batting average, yet he drew a pedestrian 38 bases on balls. During his twenty-nine-homer season of 1919, Ruth witnessed intimations of this strategy, drawing 101 bases on balls, the most in the Majors since Cobb had gotten 118 four years earlier.

In St. Louis, however, the Browns made walking Ruth something of a policy. Urban Shocker pitched around him three times in the opener. The New York papers quoted Ruth complaining about the ultradeferential treatment, although given the loose journalistic practices of the day it is hard to know whether Ruth was actually as witty as the writers made him out to be. "If they won't let me use base hits as a means of transportation, they ought to at least issue me a bicycle," he is alleged to have remarked.[7]

New York evened the series by splitting a Thursday doubleheader and then scoring nineteen runs on Friday. Dixie Davis walked Ruth twice in the Thursday opener, then retired him on a fly ball in the eighth inning with the lead runs on base. The Babe managed a triple in the day's second-game victory. The Yanks beat up on Carl Weilman on Friday afternoon, scoring nineteen times for Mays. Perhaps Weilman was too wild to miss the strike zone for Ruth—whose thirty-sixth home run was among three hits and a walk—or he simply may have quit trying. On Saturday Shocker allowed three early runs, but the Browns scored six times in the third and quickly put the game out of reach. Having already walked Ruth once and emboldened by his margin, Shocker took his chances in the eighth, and Ruth put one onto Grand Avenue, his thirty-seventh home run. The blow mattered only to the fans who could say they saw it; St. Louis won 13–8. Ruth did not let his frustration over the persistent walks dampen his spirits. Legend has it that following a visit to a local brothel, he purchased a large quantity of spare ribs and beer for the train ride to Chicago and sold the food to teammates for a half buck a share. Despite their 4-4 record at Sportsman's Park to that point, there's little doubt that the Yanks viewed St. Louis as their collective hoodoo city. "If the Yankees can ever get out of St. Louis they may win the pennant," observed William Chipman in the next afternoon's *New York Post*. "If they had to stay here all season, Connie Mack would stand in grave danger of being dispossessed of his dismal home in the depths, and the Browns would win the rag in a walk."[8]

The Sox-Yanks series opened on a Sunday to unanimous predictions that Ruth's presence would help the home team best its all-time single-game attendance record of thirty-six thousand (set during a 1911 exhibition against the Cubs). Seen purely through the prism of the standings, such a forecast made no sense, since the Yanks came in three games and the Sox five and a half behind the Indians. Yet of course Ruth, not the standings, was the driving force. Newspapers stoked the fanaticism. "If you should happen to see Joe Jackson out on Thirty-fourth Street, Felsch at Thirty-fourth and Wentworth and Nemo Leibold out on Wentworth Avenue as you fight your way to the Sox ballpark, you will know that Babe Ruth is at bat and that the outfielders are 'playing for him,'" remarked Mark Kelly in that morning's *Chicago Herald and Examiner.*[9]

Fans lined up outside the Yankees hotel and a nearby church in the morning to catch a glimpse of the slugger. At Comiskey police ordered the gates opened three hours early so they would have some way to try to control the crowd. The strategy didn't work. Fans filled the stands by noon and were five to six deep on the promenades and on the field. Some who couldn't get in by legal means scaled the outfield wall, climbing ten feet of brick and falling onto the field. The first pitch wasn't scheduled until three o'clock, but at the urging of police Comiskey advanced it fifteen minutes in the hope that some action would help maintain order. By then the official estimate was that forty thousand were on hand, although given the number of on-premises freeloaders nobody actually knew.

The game itself was all Chicago thanks to Cicotte, who limited New York to five hits, none of them by Ruth. He walked once. That was the official story anyway. Unofficially the Yankees believed umpire Tommy Connolly had robbed Ruth of a fairly earned double, and the debate threatened to touch off actual violence in the powder keg that was a fully loaded Comiskey Park.

The problem involved the cohort of fans penned behind ropes in left field, an increasing and particular distraction to the Yankees in their travels around the league. The fuss happened in the fifth, with the Sox leading a bare 1–0. Ruth backed Jackson up in left, toward and eventually into the crowd. At that point all accounts vary; the last point of agreement was that Jackson put up his hands and was reaching for the ball when he tumbled back on his haunches into the crowd. When he finally emerged, it was without the ball.

Under the ground rules a ball hit into the crowd that was not caught on the fly was a ground-rule double. Aware of that Ruth trotted to second base and stood there. Jackson meanwhile loudly pleaded that he had actually caught the ball. Connolly, whose call it was, sauntered to the scene of the action, his senses assaulted by conflicting opinions on all sides and his face displaying the look of a high school sophomore asked to explain Sophocles. Finally Connolly declared Ruth out and motioned him to come in, stating that he believed Jackson had held the ball "momentarily." "Grotesque," the *New York Sun*'s William Hanna said of the ruling.[10]

Huggins and Ruth both argued violently. Huggins declared his intention to formally protest the game's outcome on the basis that Connolly had substituted his own rule for the ground rule (although the Yanks never did file the protest). When action resumed, the decision immediately became consequential. Meusel singled to center, a hit that would have scored Ruth. Ping Bodie singled to center, and Meusel, who tried for third on it, was thrown out. Bodie took second on the throw in, and Ward was thrown out by Weaver. Rewriting history is always a dangerous proposition, but it's reasonable to speculate that if Connolly had called Ruth safe at second, Meusel would have reached second on the throw to the plate to catch Ruth and thus never would have been thrown out at third. In what turned out to be a 3–0 game, the argument can't be made that the call turned the outcome, but things would have been more interesting down the stretch.

The crowd cut back on Monday, but only to twenty-five thousand. And it may have been a Sox crowd, but it was also a Ruthian one. Williams walked the slugger in the first and again in the third, each time to a reaction simmering between unease and outright frustration. The frustration mounted when Aaron Ward homered two outs later. Williams challenged Ruth in the fourth, another mistake, for it resulted in the Babe's thirty-eighth home run, a small contribution toward what would become a 7–0 New York decision. Ruth also popped out to Risberg, but by then even his pop-ups had become the subject of comment. "A perpendicular home run," Sanborn called it.

Ruth moved Harvey Woodruff, the *Chicago Tribune* columnist who wrote In the Wake of the News, to a doggerel form of musing.

> I'd like to have Babe's muscle.
> I'd like to have his swing.
> I'd like to have his hustle.
> And almost everything
> That he rejoices in for which
> The public pines; but if
> I had his chance for real dough
> I'd be a lucky stiff.[11]

Chastened by Ruth's bat, Red Faber dished out three more walks before an estimated thirty thousand fans on Tuesday, demonstrating poor public relations but good baseball sense. The first came with a runner in scoring position and two out in the first. The second, with one out and the bases empty in the fifth, drew a catcall chorus from his own fans. Faber could retort with the box score: he held the rest of the Yanks to five hits and the Sox won 3–1.

If the fans went away unhappy, they weren't alone. So did Ruth, and he let Faber have it in his ghost-written newspaper column the next day. "Those 30,000 fans didn't come out today to see Red Faber walk me three times," he said. "It isn't fair to them to see a pitcher walk a . . . hitter every time he comes up, whether there are men on base or not."[12] Grantland Rice chimed in with his own suggestion, one that could still be considered today: the optional walk. Succinctly Rice proposed that any batter who was walked should be given the option of declining the base on balls, the alternative being a new count. If the batter drew a second set of four balls, he would have the option of taking two bases or declining again. "How many intentional passes would be given in the face of this penalty?" Rice rhetorically wondered.[13]

The thirty thousand at Comiskey that day may not have seen Ruth hit much, but they did see boxing, in the form of Risberg versus Mays. By baseball standards, though, it was a diffident scrap.

Irate for having surrendered early runs, Mays greeted the Chicago shortstop in the second with a high, tight fastball that sent him sprawling. Risberg responded by charging the mound. Baseball etiquette demanded (and still demands) that in such circumstances, teammates rally behind their favorite. But that dictum did not take into consideration the pariah statuses of both Mays and Risberg on their own teams. So the two teams largely stayed in the dugout while the combatants pounded each other. Eventually, fearing they would be labeled as not having done their duty, umpires Connolly and George Hildebrand broke it up.

The Sox's 10–3 victory in the final came in front of 25,000, running the four-day total to 123,000. That figure not only constituted a record for any series not played in the Polo

Grounds, which at the time had far and away the nation's largest seating capacity; it also amounted to 15 percent of Chicago's season-long home attendance. Dickie Kerr pitched to Ruth and got him four of five times, allowing only a single. Sanborn characterized the meeting between the five-feet-six Kerr and the two-hundred-pound Babe as "David and Goliath Redidivous."[14] That was okay with Ruth, as long as Kerr challenged the plate. "It may be the strategy, but give me the pitcher who goes right after you, like Dickie Kerr," he wrote.[15]

Ruth was the series' overriding theme, getting just three hits—one a home run—in eleven official at bats but also collecting six walks. The Sox gained and the Yanks lost a game on the front-running Indians. New York left for Detroit having lost six of its last nine, those losses essentially coinciding with the league's collective decision to avoid Ruth at all costs. Yankees backers were desolate. "The failure of the Hugmen on this trip has been thorough and complete," Chipman remarked. "Since hitting the trail for the West they have been able to win only through brute strength and occasional breaks."[16]

Having revived whatever winning chemistry they possessed against the Yankees, the Sox welcomed Boston and Washington for nine games and won seven of them. The Sox probably should have won all nine. Against the Red Sox, Jackson, Risberg, and Cicotte all failed at key points.

Cicotte faced Sad Sam Jones and the Red Sox in the Thursday series opener and pitched like the ace he was for eight of the nine innings, scattering three hits in those frames. The exception was the third, when the Red Sox touched Cicotte for four hits and three runs. Jones was sailing along in the sixth, helped by Jackson's lack of alertness on Strunk's sinking liner in the third. He let himself get forced at second. In the sixth Jackson sent one to the wall in left-center. It should have been an easy triple. But Jackson ran into McInnis rounding first, and umpire George Hildebrand waved off interference, holding Jackson responsible for the collision and giving him only what he had gotten, which was second base. Strunk sent a deep fly to right that would have easily scored Jackson if he had been at third. One batter more and the inning was over with Jackson still at second. Boston won 4–2.

For six innings Friday, Williams was even better than Cicotte had been a day earlier, leading 2–0 and holding the Red Sox hitless. But Oscar Vitt's double to start the seventh led to the tying runs, and Williams was gone by the time Kerr won the game 4–3 with a tenth-inning hit.

Two Risberg errors sabotaged Faber's generally good pitching on Saturday, although Faber could hardly blame his fielders for the go-ahead run. Risberg's wild throw with a runner at third tied the game in the second. It was 2–2 in the eighth when Faber walked light-hitting reserve Gene Bailey, but the edge seemed blunted from that miscue when pitcher Harry Harper forced Bailey at second trying to bunt him into scoring position. Not so fast. Faber wild-pitched Harper to second and then to third. He retired Vitt, but Risberg muffed Eddie Foster's easy grounder, allowing the lead run to score. Felsch's home run helped Kerr square the series on Sunday.

There was nothing suspicious about the Sox's play against Washington, a second-division club bereft of its identity with pitching ace Walter Johnson disabled by a sore arm. The seventh-place Senators only managed twelve runs in the five games.

After leaving Chicago the Yankees split four games in

Detroit, where Ruth shared top billing with his boss, Yankees co-owner Col. Tillinghast L'Hommideau Huston—for entirely different reasons.

Ruth was the predictable headliner. In the second inning of the series' first game, he sent a fastball over the screen in right field, his thirty-ninth home run. But Howard Ehmke limited the visitors to just four more hits; the 7–1 final loomed as New York's third straight loss and fifth in six games. Ehmke faced Ruth three more times and walked him twice. The day's story involved the Yankees' shaky outfield defense, especially Bodie in center and Meusel in left. Detroit tied the game 1–1 in the fourth when Bodie dove fitfully for Harry Heilmann's drive, failed to snare it, and played it into an inside-the-park home run. In the fifth Cobb lifted an easy fly to left. "Any kind of a cow except a muley cow could have caught the ball on its horn," remarked the *New York Sun*'s William Hanna. "But . . . the fiery and agile Meusel lumbered in, stopped while the ball fell to the ground, and then it jumped over him for two bases."[17] The eventual winning run scored.

That gaffe earned Meusel a spot on the bench for the Friday second game, which was tied at four when Ruth came to bat in the third. Hooks Dauss had walked him in the Yankees' three-run first. This time Dauss pitched to him, and Ruth drove his fortieth homer into the right-center-field seats, the blow met by an ovation from the Detroit fans even though it cost their favorites the lead. New York had already added two more in the sixth when the Babe returned with two more on base. His third homer in two days, which cleared the park's back wall and landed on Trumbull Avenue, set tongues wagging.

As it turned out, nobody's tongue wagged faster than his convivial boss's. Huston had joined the team in Chicago, waiting faithfully through a series of setbacks for precisely such a moment. As that Friday afternoon turned to evening, the question became how to celebrate. With Prohibition newly in force in the United States, Huston directed his full retinue across the international bridge and into Windsor, Ontario, where it was legal to both purchase and consume liquor. He and the retinue proceeded to do so in abundance.

It must have been some party because, sufficiently liquored-up, Huston revised his mission. His new goal involved spreading the gospel of the Babe throughout as much of Canada as could be reached that evening. And so, authorities later reported, a steady stream of American automobiles could be seen and heard rolling through the streets of Windsor incessantly proclaiming to the willing and unwilling alike the Ruthian feats of strength that had been witnessed that very afternoon at Navin Field.

In an otherwise tranquil community, it was the kind of thing likely to be viewed as a disturbance. So in retrospect it should come as no surprise that the celebratory party was eventually waylaid by a detachment of the Royal Canadian Mounted Police led by a Sgt. Percy Harold Stringer. "'Alt in the king's name," the sergeant barked.

Colonel Huston was, of course, only too willing to halt. As far as he was concerned the Mounties in general and Sergeant Stringer in particular were merely one more audience for the glorious news. "Babe Ruth made two more home runs today," the inebriated Huston announced to the sergeant.

Sergeant Stringer's reply turned out not to be in keeping with the spirit of the occasion. "Fuck Babe Ruth," he said. "'Alt in the king's name."

Whatever the measure of Huston's tolerance, that response exceeded it. "Fuck the king," he responded. You can probably guess the rest. The Mounties dismounted, rushed the colonel's car, hauled him out, and arrested him on a charge of disorderly conduct. The matter was settled by the colonel's posting fifteen dollars cash bail, which he effectively forfeited by returning across the bridge to Detroit. "An international outlaw," the next morning's *New York Tribune* sarcastically labeled the Yankees co-owner.[18]

Those three homers were Ruth's last in Detroit, as the Yanks split the final two games, a 7–3 victory for Mays and a 1–0 defeat for Rip Collins. The Babe managed just one hit and was walked just once in eight trips during weekend appearances that drew an estimated fifty thousand—"estimated" because per custom with the Yanks an overflow of Sunday fans again had to be let into the outfield.

Entering that Sunday game three and one-half games behind the Indians, the Yankees experienced a shutout loss made all the more frustrating by Detroit's successful use of the hidden-ball trick to escape a potential game-tying run in the fifth. Bodie had singled to lead off. What appeared to be Muddy Ruel's double play grounder to Ralph Young turned instead to an apparent break for the Yankees when umpire Brick Owens ruled that Babe Pinelli had both pulled his foot off the bag and dropped the ball, leaving Bodie safe at second and Ruel on first with none out.

The requisite argument ensued, after which play resumed with Bodie striding easily away from second until Young raced over and tagged him out. The Yanks' one potential rally went nowhere. "Ping fumed and frothed and raved," remarked the *New York American*'s Arthur Robinson, who decided he knew who to blame. "Bob Shawkey was coaching at first, and it is the reader's privilege to convict any one he pleases," Robinson wrote.[19]

The outcome left New York four and one-half games behind Cleveland entering a midweek series with the Indians to conclude the second swing of eastern teams through the West.

Since beating Chicago in the opener of their three-week home stand on July 25, the first-place Indians had managed to carve some space between themselves and the Yanks while not letting Chicago move more than four games closer to the lead. To some degree Cleveland fans had the schedule maker to thank. Between the Sox's departure and New York's scheduled arrival on August 9, the Indians played thirteen games against second-division teams from the East and won nine. The leaders played the way their fans fantasized: thirteen runs and fourteen hits against the Red Sox on July 30; a six-hitter by lightly regarded Guy Morton on July 31; then a five-hit shutout by Coveleski against Washington on August 2 that went into the win column when pinch hitter George Burns doubled the game's only two runs across in the eighth.

Betting was such an assumed part of public interest that writers thought nothing of translating each team's progress in the standings. That included the Indians, even though they were neither tarred by rumors of the 1919 World Series nor caught up in the Ruth hype.

As the Athletics arrived for a four-game early-August series that would presage the Yanks' own arrival, Ross Tenney, the *Cleveland Press*'s beat writer, reported on his conversation with a source described only as "a man who [made] a business of figuring odds." Tenney confided that the line on the Indians had shifted to 4-to-5, with the Yankees and the White Sox each holding at 2-to-1.[20]

But Tenney's source shared the widespread, if unstated,

concerns about whether the Sox were even yet playing on the level. "I'm not hankering for much of the Chicago stuff at that figure," Tenney related that his source had told him, adding, "It won't take much to drop the White Sox to 9-to-5."[21]

The Indians' performance in the series opener against the last-place A's could not have done much to bolster the confidence of either their fans or the bettors. Coveleski pitched two-hit ball through eight innings. But he lost in ten after Ray Chapman's bad throw set up the tying run in the ninth, and Bill Wambsganss failed to get Elmer Smith home from third with one out in the bottom half. Bagby and Caldwell held the Athletics to a single run in two easy wins. As the Yanks arrived, Cleveland's lead stood at four and one-half games over New York, with Chicago another half game back.

Although all reserved seats for the opening game had already been sold, Indians management promoted both Ruth's arrival and their team's first-place status as if there had been no advance sale at all. A crowd of fifteen thousand—remarkable for a Monday blotched by persistent pregame showers—arrived early for what was being described locally as "the little World's Series." Aside from the game ceremonies included recognition of seventy-five former Indians, which Cleveland owner Jim Dunn followed by making a public show of introducing Ruth to a youth named Donald Dixon. As Dunn explained, Ruth was the home run champion of the world and young Dixon was the home run champion of Cincinnati—with thirty-nine such blows in his own league.

To avoid offending Clevelanders, Speaker was called forward to receive a floral Indian head in honor of taking the team into first place. With another flourish a Cleveland fan presented Ruth a huge bat made of red and white carnations with a handle covered with blue silk. "I hope you hit 100 home runs, if none of them are against Cleveland," the fan is alleged to have told the Babe.[22]

The rain stopped with Morton's first pitch, but Morton's form was soggy. He walked three in the first inning alone—including Ruth intentionally. Those walks coupled with Morton's own wild throw, Pipp's double, and Chapman's throwing error gave New York four runs—all they would need—before Shawkey took the mound in the bottom of the first. For the day Cleveland committed five errors.

For the home fans nothing improved. Rain washed out Tuesday's game—which began in front of twenty-five thousand fans—after just two innings. Since Chicago had used the interval to sweep three games from the Senators, the Sox found themselves just three behind Cleveland, with New York only three and one-half behind.

With Kerr and Cicotte in the process of polishing off the Senators twice more in Chicago, the final three games of the New York-Cleveland series presented another opportunity for the Yanks to tighten the race. That prospect looked doubtful Wednesday when Smith's third-inning grand slam gave Bagby a 4–0 lead before twenty-seven thousand fans, a weekday record audience in Cleveland that overflowed onto the playing field. But the Indians did nothing the rest of the day against Mays, and the pitcher's own double in the tenth set up the winning run. The game's most significant moment may have come much earlier. In the first Ruth slapped a single to center. Seeing Speaker fumble it, the Babe lit out for second and twisted his knee on his slide into the base. He was carried from the field but returned on Thursday and took his customary walk after Ward opened with a single and stole second. Evidence that the knee remained tender could be seen in the way Babe jogged around the bases on

Pratt's triple to the right-center-field gap a few seconds later. New York scored four off Coveleski that inning and won 5–1. When the Yanks finished their series sweep by claiming the Friday makeup of Tuesday's rainout, they and Chicago had both closed to within a half game of the Indians.

All three contenders faced Saturday-Sunday games against also-rans before the race resumed in earnest with the start of the second long eastern swing by western teams. The Sox took two of three from Detroit, while New York split with the Senators and the Indians did the same against St. Louis. Prior to the Yanks' 3–2 victory in Washington, Ruth drove to Walter Reed Army Hospital to visit wounded World War I veterans. About one hundred of the soldiers returned the favor that afternoon, traveling in Red Cross trucks to Griffith Stadium for the 3–2 Yankees victory. Ruth acknowledged their presence with a first-inning home run over the right-field wall. "One of the soldiers threw his arms and his crutches in the air with a joyous shout and danced on his only leg," Robinson observed in the next morning's *New York American*.[23]

Seeking to profit from the frenzied interest in Ruth, that same newspaper sought out a "noted psychologist" to explain the phenomenon of the slugger's unheard-of power. It was, assured Dr. Orlando F. Miller, a simple case of the power of positive thinking.

"Babe Ruth's success as a knocker of home runs is not a question of athletic skill, but of his confidence," the *American* quoted the psychologist as determining. "When he goes into a game, he does so with the conviction that he will knock a home run. Anybody can do anything that he is absolutely sure he can do."[24]

The three contenders' rosters were brimming with confident

ballplayers. As the Indians arrived at the Polo Grounds for the final three games of a scheduled stretch of seven against the Yankees in eleven days, those clubs and the White Sox dominated statistical categories. Bagby already had twenty-three victories; Coveleski, Mays, and Williams all had eighteen; and Faber, Shawkey, and Cicotte all were above fifteen. Speaker's .408 average, trailing only George Sisler, was one of seven in the regular Cleveland order above .300. As a team the Indians were hitting .309. Ruth sat at .387, Jackson .384, Collins .352, and Weaver .334. With forty-two home runs Ruth was far enough ahead of both his old record and the rest of the field to render the issue moot for discussion. The top of the standings could hardly have been closer or more muddled:

Team	Wins	Losses	Percentage	Games Behind
Cleveland	70	40	.636	—
Chicago	72	42	.632	—
New York	72	43	.626	1/2

8. Under Pallor

August 16–18

Nobody goes to a baseball game to see a man get killed.

Fans go to savor the thrill of the occasion, the atmosphere, the pennant race, the sights, and the sounds. They go because their team is in the hunt. They go to see the stars. Stars have star-power, and that's been true for generations, whether the stars are the Babe, Mickey Mantle, or Derek Jeter.

Fans go to cheer on the good guys in their battle against the outsiders. They go because by rooting they can, however vicariously and temporarily, join the team. They go to win.

Fans go because baseball is a family event, as much a part of summer as a trip to the beach or the museum. They go because their dads took them, and they want to take their kids. They go in order to extend those bonds intergenerationally.

Nobody goes to a baseball game to see a man get killed.

And even if, for unfathomable personal reasons, somebody wanted to witness a killing, a baseball game would be a poor choice of sites, given the game's record for fatalities. The various Major Leagues have been playing baseball for more than 125 years, and in that time approximately two hundred thousand paid-admission games have been staged involving roughly twenty players each. Only one of those games resulted in an on-field fatality. That makes baseball's survivability rate approximately 99.99975 percent.

Baseball's the kind of game you can take your child to secure in the knowledge that you'll be able to cheer for the home team, and that your kid's enjoyment will not be marred by anything as gruesome as a fatal injury.

Any event involving the appearance of Babe Ruth—who had already hit forty-two home runs, far more than had been imaginable a bare season before—was a sure draw. The arrival of the first-place Cleveland Indians only added to the match-up's pull. The Indians boasted three strong starters in Jim Bagby, Stanley Coveleski, and Ray Caldwell, as well as a lineup flush with .300 hitters. So it was no surprise that more than twenty-one thousand fans seized the occasion of a Monday afternoon to enjoy the Polo Grounds' attractions on August 16, 1920. Monday, the beginning of the workweek for dads and a wash day for moms to boot, was generally the hardest sell in the game. But that was decreasingly the case in New York, where the combination of Ruth and the pennant race drew fans even on what were usually the sparsest dates. A typical Monday home game at other parks might pull only a few thousand paying customers. Yet the Yanks had topped ten thousand in attendance for each of their five Monday home attractions since Ruth began hitting in late May. This gate was the third time they had surpassed twenty thousand on a Monday.

Plainly a good time was to be had by all. All, possibly, except the Yankees themselves. The New Yorkers had returned from a nineteen-game road trip that appeared superficially to have been more satisfying than it actually was. Casual fans took comfort from the fact that their favorites had won five of the last seven games. But loyalists fretted about the mediocre 10-9 record and the twenty-point drop in winning percentage, from .646 when the trip began in St. Louis to .626 that Monday afternoon. The Yanks could thank their lucky stars—along with the previous week's sweep in Cleveland—that they had finished the venture one-half game behind the Indians, precisely where they had begun it. But that sluggish trip had allowed the defending champion White Sox, winners of seventeen of twenty-three during the same stretch, to draw ahead of New York and even with Cleveland, creating a three-team race.

Amid such stakes both teams offered their best available starters, Mays and Coveleski, and adopted strategic approaches one would expect to see in a tightly contested ball game. For the most part those strategies did not work. When Cuckoo Jamieson led off with a clean single to left, Ray Chapman immediately sacrificed him over to second. Tris Speaker's fly ball to center moved Jamieson to third, but Elmer Smith was unable to make use of his teammates' assistance, flying out to Ping Bodie as well. Again in the third Jamieson led off with a hit, this one a drive off Wally Pipp's glove at first. Again Chapman tried to bunt, lining out to Pipp, who turned the mistake into a simple double play. Bodie delivered New York's first hit to open the bottom half of that third inning, and Muddy Ruel followed with a sacrifice of his own. It was, by some standards, odd strategy, given that Mays followed Ruel in the batting order. The pitcher failed to deliver, grounding right back to Coveleski, who caught Bodie between second and third and retired him with a throw to Gardner.

Ironically in such a tightly controlled game, the first break-through came via a home run—and Ruth did not hit it. With one out in the Cleveland second, catcher Steve O'Neill caught a Mays offering flush and sent it hurtling into the stands in left. O'Neill hit only three homers all season, but on this day he would hit safely three times, score twice, and pick up two RBIs.

In the top of the fourth, the Indians showed what could be made of a single hit and generous assistance. With one out Mays walked Gardner, and O'Neill's second hit, a single, sent the leading runner to third. Gardner should have been retired on Johnston's ground ball to Peckinpaugh, but Ruel dropped the throw, allowing the game's second run to score. Wambsganss followed with an easy grounder to Ward at third, but he fumbled that chance and filled the bases for Coveleski. The Indians pitcher managed a mere fly ball to Bodie, but it was enough to push O'Neill across and extend Cleveland's lead to 3–0.

Although its near forty thousand capacity exceeded any other park in the Majors, the Polo Grounds was an intimate facility by modern standards. The foul lines were about sixty-five feet from the first row, a few feet more than was or is common, but any loss of touch was more than offset by the proximity to the field of both upper and lower decks. Because the park's architects used pillars to support the upper deck, it was not necessary to set thousands of seats back from the field of play, as is common practice today. The sense of intimacy was heightened by the absence of artificial noise. Notably there was no loudspeaker system blaring commercials, music, or cheers. The only sounds generated inside the park were the honest ones, those fans who chose to cheer or boo, plus the field announcer, who spoke through a megaphone.

On any other occasion the sense of intimacy was viewed as a positive. But when Chapman stepped to the plate to lead off the fifth inning, that intimacy became a sickening negative. It meant most of the twenty-one thousand fans on hand had a clear view of the pitched ball crashing into the side of his head. They could see the blood gush as his temple gave way. With no group was this more sickeningly familiar than the dozen or so "beat" writers who routinely covered the Yankees for New York's bustling newspaper industry. The press area at the Polo Grounds was at ground level just behind home plate. Many of those men had been in Jacksonville the previous March to witness the near-fatal beaning of Chick Fewster by Brooklyn's Jeff Pfeffer in an exhibition contest. Fewster, a utility infielder, had lain still on the field for ten minutes with a skull fracture. Many doubted he would survive, and he did so only through the skills of surgeons at Johns Hopkins. Fewster had missed the season's first half.

Although the writers had the best view, their coverage the following morning diverged on many salient details, leaving the question of what occurred in the moments following the beaning an issue of whom you believed. In the *New York American* Damon Runyon said he saw Chapman try to talk but added that no words came forth.[1] In the *New York Sun*, William Hanna said Chapman tried to stagger to first before collapsing.[2] William Chipman, reporting for the *New York Post*, said Mays told him that John Henry, a former big league catcher associated with the Yankees and a close friend of Chapman, had gone to the clubhouse to see the stricken player. "I'm all right; tell Mays not to worry," Chapman was supposed to have told Henry.[3] Some reporters described Chapman's eye as hanging loose when he tried to rise. But if they disagreed on the details, they quickly picked up on the somberness of the situation. "Twenty-thousand people saw a man go drifting into the valley of the shadow of death," Runyon wrote.[4]

Since there was no framework to give context to what had occurred, some reacted initially in a strange, almost detached manner. Mays was among those. His first move was toward the ball, not the batter. The collision of ball and bone, he later explained, sounded so much like the collision of ball and bat that instinct told him the ball had been hit; therefore, he rushed to field it. Chapman's reaction, of course, quickly betrayed the truth. The game was halted only long enough to allow Jack Graney and Guy Morton to carry Chapman to the visitors' locker room in center field.

Today the move of a stricken player would be undertaken only on a stretcher by trained medical personnel, and only after the player's condition had been stabilized on the scene to the extent possible. Braces would have been applied to ensure no worsening of the injury during transit. But neither physicians nor emergency crews were readily available on the grounds in those days, and ballplayers had not been trained in first aid. Theirs was a more basic instinct: the instinct to help. So Chapman was moved, as quickly as possible, with whatever accompanying risk of aggravated injury accrued. The only exigency was that play be resumed in the quickest possible fashion.

Whether Mays was at all emotionally disturbed by his role in the incident would over the next few days become a matter of wide dispute. His approach in the immediate aftermath did little to burnish his image among those who did not already view him as heartless. Mays did not leave the game; in fact, he pitched through the eighth inning, finally departing only for a pinch hitter and allowing just two hits in the interim. Those two hits—successively by Gardner and O'Neill—both came in the fifth and produced Cleveland's fourth and final run.

If Mays didn't rattle, neither did Coveleski, who shut out the Yankees on three widely spaced singles. As Ruth came to the plate in the ninth, having to that moment produced nothing more menacing than a ground out, Yankees fans had already begun to file from their seats. They paused in the aisles, of course, to watch the Babe hit and were rewarded when he found a hole between first and second for a clean single. Pratt followed with a walk, but Jamieson temporarily dampened hopes for a comeback by the home club, racing to the left-field wall to grab what looked like a sure extra base hit by Duffy Lewis. Under other circumstances Johnston might have tried to turn Pipp's grounder into something more than a simple put-out at first, but leading by four runs the Indians first baseman took no chances.

That final out proved tough to get. Bodie's drive landed just inside the right-field foul line for a double, scoring both Ruth and Pratt. Ruel put a single past Gardner at third, getting Bodie across and bringing the Yankees within a single run, 4–3. Finally Coveleski coaxed a game-ending ground ball. There was irony to the conclusion. The last out was fielded by Harry Lunte, a little-used middle-infield substitute who had taken Chapman's place in the fifth. The three-run rally meant that the seemingly meaningless fourth run Chapman had fatally put on base was the game winner.

Sensing the somber occasion, the twenty-one thousand fans filed out even more quietly than usual after a defeat. Among them were Cuckoo Jamieson's mother and sisters, who had made the twenty-four-mile trip from the family home in Hawthorne, New Jersey, that morning to see him play. It was the first big league game they had ever seen—and also the last. "Charles," Mrs. Hawthorne admonished him afterward, "I don't want you playing that game. It's too dangerous."[5]

The stricken Chapman was taken to the nearby St. Lawrence Hospital, where doctors tried to cope with a condition that grew progressively worse. Because X-rays showed a serious fracture, the hospital's chief surgeon, Dr. T. M. Merrigan, was brought in.[6] He operated for more than an hour, removing part of Chapman's skull in an effort to relieve the serious swelling, but it didn't help. Kathleen Daly Chapman had already been summoned in Cleveland, but by shortly after midnight the case was plainly hopeless.

Several of Chapman's teammates, among them Speaker, Graney, and O'Neill, maintained a vigil in the dying man's room. But as the predawn hours brought the end near, all three—assured by doctors there was nothing more to be done—left for their hotel rooms. They were tired and despondent. They did not sleep. Speaker was notified a short time later that Chapman had died.

"We did not care if we ever played baseball again," Graney said. "We cannot imagine ourselves playing with Chapman dead."[7] When the team visited the New York mortuary later that day for a viewing, Graney and O'Neill both fainted.

Speaker issued a formal statement to the press later that morning. "Ray Chapman was the best friend I ever had," he said. "I would willingly abandon all hope for the championship not only this season but in all years to come and retire from the game forever if by doing so I could recall my teammate and best friend to life."[8] Speaker acknowledged "some bitterness" on the parts of various Indians but did not believe it was possible to prove that Mays intended to injure Chapman; following this line of reasoning, he stated, "I am going to do all I can to suppress it."[9] He then retreated to the seclusion of his room at the Ansonia, distraught. When Mrs. Chapman arrived that morning, she was hurried to

Speaker's room, where he confirmed that her husband had already died of his injuries.

The Indians and the Yankees had been scheduled to play another game that afternoon, but the contest was postponed for a host of obvious reasons. Most of the players on both sides used the free time to sleep or at least to distance themselves to the extent possible from what they had seen. The exception was Mays. Recognizing his role in the death of a fellow human being, he left his wife, Freddie, and their baby at their apartment atop Coogan's Bluff a short distance from the ballpark and reported to the district attorney's office to answer whatever questions might be posed. They turned out to be few and perfunctory. "It was a straight fastball that I threw," he told Runyon after the legal interview had been completed. "I cannot understand how the thing happened."[10] He denied ever deliberately throwing at a batter and told the *Sun*'s Hanna that his experience in Jacksonville the previous March had made him particularly careful. "Fewster is my close friend, and after seeing him nearly killed I have been concerned and conscious not to hit anybody," he said.[11]

For legal purposes the matter was put down as an accidental death. Although Mays's many enemies in the ranks of players and newspaper writers stopped short of calling Chapman's death a homicide, their tone cast it as an act of malevolence that required some sort of league response. In Boston, where the Red Sox and the Tigers were playing a series, news of the serious injury prompted a joint meeting on Monday evening. Boston outfielder Mike Menosky told reporters that the two teams had agreed to sign a petition asking American League president Ban Johnson to disqualify Mays if Chapman should die and committing players on the two teams not to go to bat against Mays.[12] Although Ty

Cobb later denied their accuracy, newspaper reports quoted the Tigers player-manager as confirming the discussions. Informed of the two-team call, Johnson initially offered an uncharacteristic deferral, suggestive of a man who was unsure of his own position. He said he would make no statement until he received "more complete" reports.

Although mourning Indians players initially said little publicly, that did not stop others in Cleveland from channeling their sadness into outrage directed at Mays. In an editorial the *Cleveland Plain Dealer* encouraged other American League clubs to sign the Boston-Detroit petition. Mays, the paper said, "has worked on the theory that if now and then he threw a swift ball close to the batter, the batsman would be cautious."[13] The *Cleveland Press*'s Ross Tenney urged Mays to "voluntarily resign from baseball" because "his control is so poor that he is a menace to baseball."[14] Outside Cleveland sentiment was also widely against Mays. Harvey Woodruff, sports editor of the *Chicago Tribune*, cited the meetings involving the Boston and Detroit teams—Woodruff also cited a meeting of Cleveland players, although that session was more about grieving than punishing Mays—as evidence that his fellow big leaguers considered the pitcher culpable in some fashion.[15] Published reports out of St. Louis identified Browns star George Sisler as leading that team's effort to oust Mays. "If the news had come over the wire that a ballplayer had been killed by a pitched ball without naming who pitched the ball, the Browns to a man would have guessed," said an unsigned article in the *Sporting News*. "That was the conviction they had regarding Mays' [brushback] style of delivery."[16]

Only in New York was the pitcher resolutely defended; fans and writers there pointed to Speaker's own concession that Mays had not intended to injure Chapman as the necessary proof. Dan Daniel, writing in the next day's *New York Sun*, agreed that if the evidence suggested Mays had intended to hit Chapman, "he would merit trial for murder." But since that evidence did not exist, Daniel said, griping players should shut up.[17] In the *New York Tribune* W. O. McGeehan took note of a "cowardly campaign" to drive Mays from the game due to his "tragic misfortune." Why, McGeehan demanded, shouldn't Mays pitch again? "The player's conscience is clear with regard to the accident," he wrote, blaming Johnson's failure to act forcefully for the spreading ill will. "He should long ago have cleared Mays by a frank and manly determination," McGeehan wrote.[18]

The man closest to Chapman when he was killed, Yankees catcher Muddy Ruel, remained mum about what he had seen for a month. Not until late September did a reporter, John Sheridan for the *Sporting News*, think to corner Ruel, who put the incident down as a terrible accident. Declaring that he had often previously seen Chapman easily avoid such pitches, Ruel said that he "must have somehow got careless or was in some way dazzled or hypnotized by the baseball." The catcher even went so far as to suggest that Chapman's "supreme confidence in his eye and in his muscles made him a trifle over-confident" in standing his ground as the pitch approached. In any event, Ruel asserted, the pitch, while "wider and wickeder than usual" in its movement, "was by no means a freak shoot."[19]

Some wondered whether the entire debate wasn't academic. In the *New York World*, Alex Sullivan portrayed Mays as too damaged by his role in what had transpired to return anyway. "Baseball players are unusually sensitive," Sullivan asserted. "The knowledge that he caused Chapman's death, accidental as it was, is enough to put the twirler entirely out of commission."[20]

Stung by the criticism of him but still indecisive in his reaction, Johnson issued a second statement Wednesday in which he attempted to satisfy all sides and ended up satisfying none. He said he could find no clear case against Mays and therefore would take no action against him. At the same time he all but invited Mays to condemn himself, strongly suggesting that he would personally prefer to see the player retire, at least for the remainder of 1920.[21]

Speaker delegated himself and Wood to accompany Mrs. Chapman and the body back to Cleveland on Tuesday night, meaning that the Indians would take the field without them when the season resumed on Wednesday. From a baseball standpoint it was to be a jumbled week. Mrs. Chapman scheduled the funeral services for the earliest possible day, Friday, which coincided with the opening of a series in Boston. That game, of course, was postponed. The result was that the decimated and aggrieved Indians—minus Chapman, Speaker, and Wood—played in New York on Wednesday, made up Tuesday's canceled game on Thursday, entrained for home and the funeral on Friday, then immediately boarded a train for Boston to play a Saturday doubleheader that included a makeup of the postponed Friday game.

Witnesses described the Wednesday game at the Polo Grounds as eerie. A crowd of sixteen thousand—a strong attendance for a midweek game—showed up, but they displayed little interest in what was taking place. "Won't be any yelling today," one veteran sportswriter told another before the game. "The gloom's thick enough to keep 'em quiet."[22] He was right. There was none of the cheering and chatter that usually marked pregame batting or fielding practice. Not even Babe Ruth could stir the crowd. During batting practice he drove a home run deep into the right-field seats, an event normally guaranteed to prompt a loud demonstration. Instead it was greeted with subdued and truncated applause. "One got the feeling the fans were ashamed for having yielded to impulse," the *Cleveland Plain Dealer*'s William Slavens McNutt suggested. "It seemed a little like laughing at church."[23]

Flags had been lowered to half staff, and players on both sides took the field wearing black armbands. The only real demonstration took place in the third inning when Lunte, batting eighth, was greeted warmly by the New Yorkers as he came to the plate in Chapman's place. The Indians too played unenthusiastically, although tempers rose briefly in the fourth inning after Doc Johnston tried to check his swing on a low two-strike pitch. The plate umpire, Dick Nallin, called the pitch a ball, but Ruel appealed to Tommy Connolly, umpiring the bases, and Connolly overturned Nallin, ruling that Johnston had fanned. The disgusted batter flung his bat in the general direction of his own dugout, barely missing an unsuspecting Jamieson.

For eight innings the game was as dull as the mood. The Indians scored single runs in the fourth, fifth, and sixth and led 3–2 behind Bagby as the bottom of the ninth began. Some sensed an emotion of entitlement in the outcome. "Glad to see them get it," McNutt reported hearing a Yankees fan concede.[24] But with one out Duffy Lewis singled, and interest perked up. The next batter, Pipp, smashed a shot in the direction of deep left-center field. Normally this would have been the province of the speedy Jamieson, but in the cavernous Polo Grounds he was in center for the departed Speaker. In his place the aging veteran Graney loped hopelessly after the ball. When it eluded him and rolled to the wall, Pipp followed Lewis around the bases for what was scored as a game-winning home run. For the only time that afternoon, fans forgot the communal grief. In New York at least, the pennant race was back on. The next afternoon Elmer Smith's sixth-inning home run broke a 2-2 tie and sent the Indians back home with a 3–1 victory, with Ray Caldwell besting Bob Shawkey in front of eighteen thousand. In the fourth inning Babe Ruth delivered his forty-third home run of the season, a smash into the seats in right. The shot occasioned the second fatality of the week at the Polo Grounds, for a thirty-nine-year-old fan named Theodore Sturm was so excited about what he had just witnessed that he collapsed in his box seat and was pronounced dead. The cause was given as heart failure.[25]

In Cleveland funeral arrangements were hastily drawn that balanced the wishes of Chapman's widow with those of his parents. The rites were to include a funeral mass, although they would conclude with burial in the city's public Lake View Cemetery rather than a nearby Catholic cemetery where the Daly family maintained a plot. Since the crowd desiring to attend was expected to far outstrip the capacity of the family's small East Cleveland neighborhood church, St. Philomena's, diocesan officials made St. John's Cathedral downtown available. Much of the city joined in the mourning process. Mayor W. S. Fitzgerald issued a call for the creation of a Ray Chapman memorial using funds donated by private citizens and to be erected at League Park. In nickels and dimes fans of all ages sent money to a hastily created "flower from a fan" funeral fund, although two-thirds of the money was redirected to the memorial. More than two hundred displays and bouquets could be counted at the Daly home the night before the funeral. The mayor ordered flags at city hall and the courthouse flown at half staff. Ohio governor James Cox, the Democratic nominee for president, sent a telegram expressing his condolences.

Those able to get seats at the Friday-morning service witnessed virtually the entire Cleveland team file in as part of the procession. Team secretary Walter McNichol, to whose lot had fallen the primary responsibility for accompanying Mrs. Chapman from New York, fainted on the way home and was not permitted out of bed. Among players only Speaker and Graney were absent. In both instances the official explanation was that they were too overcome to take part. Given their well-known friendship with Chapman, the story was widely accepted. Graney, it was said, became so hysterical outside the church that former Indians star Napoleon Lajoie seized him and drove him out into the countryside to settle him down. Speaker was said to have been ordered to bed by his physician for recuperation from what was described as a nervous breakdown.

The truth only surfaced over time. As related by Mike Sewell in *The Pitch That Killed*, Bill Wambsganss late in life confirmed that Graney and O'Neill had confronted Speaker at the latter's apartment that morning over the latter's objection to the funeral services taking place in a Catholic cathedral. The result was a fistfight after which Speaker was in no condition to appear in public. Nor did he join the club when it boarded its train that afternoon for Boston. O'Neill sustained serious facial and hand injuries, and although they hampered his play on the field for several days, he was able to attend the funeral. It isn't clear how seriously Graney was injured, and it is possible that all elements of the story are true. He and Speaker fought, after which he became hysterical at the church, prompting Lajoie's intervention.[26]

Johnson also attended the funeral, as did Indians owner James Dunn and his wife, along with Robert Quinn, business manager for the St. Louis Browns. Ernie Shore, Duffy Lewis, and Wally Pipp represented the Yankees.

Rev. Dr. William Scullen, a well-known Cleveland clergyman, delivered the homily. Given the reputation of the widely loved player, he had, under the circumstances, an easy task. "There were two great phases in his life . . . and that was our friend as the ballplayer and our friend as the man," he said. "He played the game of life as he played the game which was his profession." Scullen eulogized Chapman's desire to win, but to do so within the boundaries of the rules, an especially poignant characteristic in the context of the widespread suspicion of graft and corruption then encircling baseball. "Our friend was the spirit of the American youth," he said. He called Chapman "the friend, the friend that understands, the friend that sympathizes, the friend that sees only the best in us . . . the idol of a city."[27]

Playing off the notion of a tough but friendly competitor, Scullen cast Chapman as committed to simultaneous goals: winning ball games and winning friends. "When the moment of consciousness came, a smile broke over his countenance," he told the mourners. "Oh yes, he won both games."[28]

9. Under Shadow

August 19–25

Word of the death of Ray Chapman reached the Chicago White Sox on Tuesday evening when their train from Detroit pulled into the station in Philadelphia. The White Sox and the last-place Athletics weren't scheduled to meet until Wednesday afternoon, giving the visitors plenty of time to digest developments, which by that point already included the meeting involving Tigers and Red Sox players in Boston at which an action against Mays was the principal topic.

With the Indians wounded by the loss of Chapman, no team in the American League at that moment stood to benefit more from Mays's removal than the White Sox. The Sox stood just one-half game behind Cleveland, and one game ahead of New York. Within a week their schedule called for six games against the Yankees in New York, and Mays was virtually guaranteed to start at least one of them. His loss from the otherwise wobbly rotation would have been a serious blow to the only healthy team challenging the defending champs.

Given the Boston-Detroit meeting as well as growing anti-Mays sentiment in St. Louis and, obviously, Cleveland, even a measured call for disciplinary action against the pitcher by the White Sox might have tipped the scales against Mays. It certainly would have put American League president Ban Johnson in a difficult spot since he would be going against the expressed wishes of more than half the teams in his league to defend the player whose walkout had precipitated the initial draining of Johnson's power a year earlier. By the afternoon following Chapman's death, the move within baseball to blame Mays had already begun to spread beyond the ranks of players. Well-known American League umpires Billy Evans and Bill Dinneen both issued statements sharply criticizing Mays as a perpetually dirty ballplayer. They did so after Mays issued his own statement in New York labeling the beaning accidental, and suggesting that it may have been caused by a rough spot on the ball that had been carelessly allowed to remain in play by that day's plate umpire, Tommy Connolly. Although prior to 1920 baseballs had been kept in play virtually until they had been knocked out of shape, a new rule adopted prior to the season required umpires to removed discolored or defaced balls from play. The rule had been motivated in part by other rule changes that outlawed various trick pitches and in part out of concern for safety.

"No pitcher in the American League resorted to trickery more than Carl Mays in attempting to rough a ball in order to get a break on it which would make it more difficult to hit," Dinneen and Evans said. Prior to implementation of the new rules, they claimed, Mays "constantly used to drag the ball across the pitching rubber in order to roughen the surface."[1]

H. G. Salsinger, the best-known baseball writer in Detroit, asserted that the Tigers' beef against Mays was both deep and long-standing. He recalled one game when Ty Cobb, incensed that Mays had tried to bean him, fired his bat at the pitcher in retaliation. Mays retaliated for that by decking Cobb with his next pitch. Cobb got up and dragged a bunt down the first base line, hoping to force the pitcher to make a play on the ball so Cobb could spike him. Salsinger noted that Detroit third baseman Babe Pinelli tried to fight Mays following a game earlier that 1920 season. "Pinelli waited for Mays outside the stands after the game, but the pitcher apparently forgot to meet him," Salsinger said.[2]

Johnson had hardly risen to Mays's defense with much gusto in the forty-eight hours since the beaning. True, by Wednesday he had called the fatality an accident and said for that reason he did not believe formal disciplinary action was warranted. At the same time, he had essentially invited Mays to voluntarily retire, at least for the remainder of 1920, all but openly suggesting that the pitcher would be rendered an emotional wreck by what had transpired if he continued to pitch. "I could not conscientiously attempt to make any trouble for Mr. Mays," Johnson said. "But it is my honest belief that Mr. Mays will never pitch again." He joined others in taking note of the fact that Mays had hit more than forty batters in about 1,000 innings of work since 1917. Among his contemporaries on contending teams, that was certainly an imposing number. By comparison Eddie Cicotte had hit just seven in about 1,100 innings.

Almost the only objections to Johnson's statement came, predictably, from New York. Yankees co-owner Col. T. L. Huston reacted with surprise to even the intimation that his legally exonerated pitcher ought to voluntarily leave the game. The Tribune's W. O. McGeehan, assuming the role as Mays's chief defender in the media, found Johnson's vacillation frustrating. "It strikes me that it all would have ended abruptly if the president of the league had made a statement . . . based on the facts and the principles of fair play," McGeehan wrote on Wednesday. "He has lost a great opportunity to put himself on record as a leader in sports and as a leader of men."[3]

Elsewhere rumors filled the void created by the absence of firm information. Mays, who followed his visit to the office of the district attorney with a brief statement and then disappeared behind the walls of his apartment, was the focus. The *Chicago Tribune* published an anonymous report to the effect that Mays was on the verge of a nervous breakdown. The source turned out to be a team representative standing in for the pitcher at his appearance in traffic court to answer and pay a twenty-five-dollar fine on the speeding charge that had been levied against him the previous month. If that was indeed what the team official told the judge in explaining Mays's absence, the best that can be said was that it represented neither the first nor the last time a judge had been lied to in open court. Mays's backers vocally denied the "nervous wreck" assertions, although even they wondered about his effectiveness. "It is only natural to suppose that his work for a time will be affected," contended Joe Vila.[4]

Whether the White Sox could have forced Johnson's hand on Mays will never be known because they made no effort to do so. The Chicago team that detrained in Philadelphia was a deeply riven bunch, its factions so suspicious of and full of loathing for one another that they barely spoke off the field. Informed of the Mays boycott discussions, Kid Gleason tried to present his team's lack of interest in the topic as evidence of unity rather than division. "The ballclub that determines not to play against Mays lacks courage," Gleason was quoted as saying, adding, "My ballclub will face Mays any and every time he plays."[5] Oscar Reichow, a prominent

Chicago sportswriter, chose to view dissension as altruism. "Some of the White Sox players were for driving Mays out of baseball, but after cooling off a bit realized that an act of that nature would be charging him with deliberately trying to cripple a fellow player," Reichow said. "There are not many who are willing to take that stand."[6]

In fact, there is no record that the Sox players even seriously discussed supporting other teams' calls for league action against Mays. To the White Sox their own feud was more important than any benefit that might accrue from a unified stance.

Instead the Sox took the field on Wednesday at Shibe Park a mere half game behind the Indians. The last-place A's offered in opposition only a twenty-three-year-old rookie right-hander with barely a month of Major League experience and just five decisions under his belt. But that rookie, knuckleballer Eddie Rommel, proceeded to shut out the Sox 1–0 on just five hits, getting slightly the better of Lefty Williams.

With the bereaved Indians in the process of losing in New York, the narrow defeat cost Chicago a chance to move into first place. Rain cost them a second opportunity on Thursday. But in 1920 losing was a difficult proposition for visitors to Philadelphia, and the White Sox rebounded the next day and swept a strange doubleheader that included a makeup of the Thursday washout. Joe Jackson homered in both games, while Red Faber and Dickie Kerr delivered the decisions by scores of 7–4 and 5–2. Those should have been the final scores, except that umpire Ollie Chill actually forfeited the evening game to Chicago due to a strange set of circumstances involving both ballpark architecture and a fan base that, after a long day of inept ball by the home team, was more than ready to chuck it all and go home.

The Sox held that 5–2 lead with two retired and none on base in the bottom of the ninth as Kerr faced Lena Styles, a twenty-year-old up from the bushes whom Connie Mack had called on to pinch-hit for pitcher Scott Perry. Styles offered only a meek grounder along the first base line that Kerr raced over to field; he got it just after it had crossed the foul line and gratuitously tagged Styles for what was nothing more than a foul strike. But the fans in the distant outfield seats did not know that; from their vantage point Styles appeared to have made the game's final out.

At the time no fence separated Shibe Park's outfield spectators from the playing field; they were restrained only by decorum from entering the field. Doing so was a common practice of the era at game's end because it made exiting the park easier. So onto the field the cheap-seat fans poured, not realizing at first that there remained a final out to be recorded. By the time they did realize it, they no longer cared, having given up on their heroes. Chill and base umpire Brick Owens made their own appeals, to no avail. The handful of police at the park were too few to restore order. Asked by Chill to help out, Mack merely shrugged his shoulders in a universally recognized gesture of hopelessness. After five minutes Chill declared he had had enough, turning to the press box and yelling, "Game's over."

On that chaotic note the White Sox departed Philadelphia for Washington, where on Saturday they opened a three-game series in superb position to pad their advantage. Cicotte took the mound on Saturday against left-hander Tom Zachary, the closest thing the Senators had to an ace with Walter Johnson sidelined since midseason by a sore arm. Zachary had won eleven of his twenty-two decisions to that point, a representative showing for a club trundling along with a .500

record. The White Sox scored four early runs and—boosted by Buck Weaver's three hits—led 5–0 entering the bottom of the eighth when Cicotte suddenly lost it. A walk, a line single, and an infield hit loaded the bases before Cicotte walked rookie cleanup hitter Frank Brower to force one run home. A second run scored on a fly ball, and only Weaver's grab of a ground ball, which he turned into a double play, baled Cicotte out. Williams had an easier time of it on Sunday, supported by a thirteen-hit attack off Eric Erickson. Following an oddly scheduled Monday off day, the Sox sent Faber out in search of the sweep and his nineteenth victory on Tuesday afternoon.

For the first three innings, Faber and Harry Courtney battled each other on even terms. The White Sox touched Courtney for a go-ahead run in the top of the fourth with Swede Risberg's single pushing across Happy Felsch, who had walked. What may have been the decisive play opened the Washington half of the fourth when Faber followed a base hit by Joe Judge with a fastball that rattled off the knee of Senators center fielder Clyde Milan. The blow sent Milan sprawling and eventually knocked him out of the game in favor of pinch runner Frank Ellerbe. Milan was not seriously injured. Given the grace of a Wednesday off day, he recovered quickly enough to play all twenty-two innings of a Thursday doubleheader against the Tigers. But at the time of the accident, Faber could not know that outcome, and coming so quickly after the Chapman beaning, the sight of the longtime Washington veteran rolling in agony on the field unhinged him. Following a sacrifice and a strikeout, he walked Bucky Harris and allowed consecutive hits to the bottom of the Washington order, Howie Shanks, Jim O'Neill, and Patsy Gharrity. The hits produced four runs.

Faber struggled on through six innings, and in the interim Chicago bats produced enough activity to tie the game 5–5. Eddie Collins provided help. He reached on an infield hit in the fifth inning, stole second, advanced on Weaver's infield hit, and then stole home. Felsch delivered two runs on a seventh-inning double. But when the reprieved Faber opened the inning's bottom half by surrendering hits to the two lead-off batters, Gleason yanked him in favor of Kerr. The left-hander was good but not good enough and allowed the go-ahead runs to score on a sacrifice, a base hit, and a fly ball.

Road victories in four of the six games played that week against second-division clubs boosted Chicago ahead of the staggering Indians, who had returned to Boston following the funeral service with their hearts and minds anywhere but on the ball field. Worse, the necessities of an extra train trip from New York to Cleveland and then back to Boston presented Speaker's club with an impossible schedule at a time when they lacked not only a shortstop but their emotionally stricken center fielder as well. The original schedule had called for single games on Friday, Saturday, Monday, and Tuesday—Sunday baseball was illegal in Boston at the time. But a May rainout had already forced the addition of a second game on Saturday, and the forced cancellation of Friday's game meant that the Indians—with no more trips into Boston on the schedule—would have to play twice on Monday too.

Joe Wood, acting as manager in Speaker's absence, cobbled together a batting order from the dozen Indians nonpitchers who were actually on hand to play those Saturday games. Facing right-hander Waite Hoyt in the first game and lefty Herb Pennock in the second, he moved Cuckoo Jamieson to center field, inserted Jack Graney in the lead-off spot in left, allowed the still-bruised Steve O'Neill to catch both games, and batted Harry Lunte eighth. His bench consisted of reserve catchers Les Nunamaker and Pinch Thomas, as well as outfielders Joe Evans and himself. Perhaps not since the turn of the century had a Major League team taken the field in such a depleted state.

The Indians looked every bit as thin as they actually were. As a practical matter all they accomplished by showing up was to avoid a double forfeit and thus pick up the visitor's share of the gate. While Red Sox hitters tied into part-time starter Guy Morton for a dozen runs and thirteen hits, Waite Hoyt shut them out on just three hits, one each by Graney, Bill Wambsganss, and Doc Johnston. The second game was not much more inspiring. Herb Pennock reprised Hoyt's three-hitter against Stan Coveleski, and Boston won 4–0.

Speaker remained in Cleveland until Sunday, recovering from the toll—both physical and emotional—imposed by the week's events. He had lost fifteen pounds, slept and ate little, and finally boarded a train to rejoin his team only against the expressed orders of his physician. Publicly those on the periphery of the Indians cast his return in the mode of the crusading hero returning to the battle. "When Spoke's heart is full, it's brimful," wrote Ross Tenney in the *Cleveland Press*. "And his heart is now brimful of that determination to win the pennant as a memorial to the ballplayer-pal he now mourns."[7] Tenney described a Monday pregame pep talk in which Speaker rallied the downcast club, which began play two games behind the White Sox and had lost eight of the last eleven. That was purely for public consumption: The facts were that Speaker had not even arrived at Fenway Park until the second inning of Monday's first game, and his condition when he did could hardly have been described as inspiring. The same was true of his team. No sooner had Speaker, still in civilian clothes, taken a seat on the bench than Boston first baseman Stuffy McInnis lifted what should have been an easy fly ball in the direction of Graney in left. There was a time when the thirty-four-year-old Graney, a longtime Indians star reduced by age to part-time service, would have made easy work of such a chance, but that time was not 1920. Now he loped uncertainly toward it. Only quick work by Jamieson, racing over from center to make the catch, prevented the ball from falling for a base hit.

Speaker's relationship with Graney had been shaky since their religion-based dispute following Chapman's death. He knew the veteran was slowing up; in fact, Graney had committed errors in both of the games that Speaker had missed in New York. The manager was not about to let a game slide away in deference to even a fellow grieving player's seniority. He immediately called time and removed Graney from the game in favor of Wood. Then he retreated to the clubhouse and changed into his uniform.

Aided by Jamieson's quick thinking in the second, Ray Caldwell set the Red Sox down on one hit through the first three innings. But three consecutive hits produced a run, and nearly two, in the fourth. Stuffy McInnis followed singles by Mike Menosky and Tim Hendryx with a double past Wood in left. Menosky scored easily, but Wood's throw to Gardner, relayed to O'Neill, cut down Hendryx at the plate. The play would prove something of a game saver because the Indians produced a tying run in the seventh, then took a 2–1 lead in the eighth on a Larry Gardner base hit that followed walks to Elmer Smith and Jamieson.

By this time Speaker had returned to the bench in uniform,

and one of his first actions was to insert himself as a pinch hitter for O'Neill leading off the ninth. The official reason for the substitution was given as a bruised hand that O'Neill had suffered the previous inning.[8] There has also been speculation that Speaker may have removed O'Neill and Graney out of sympathy, aware that they had been as emotionally drained by the week's events as he was. While either theory is plausible, particularly considering the poor state of O'Neill's hands since the brawl with Speaker less than a week earlier, the record simply shows that the manager's first two actions had been to yank from the game the two men with whom he had fought. The Boston crowd of twelve thousand greeted Speaker's appearance with a sustained ovation. Speaker produced only an easy fly ball, but Caldwell stifled Boston in the bottom of the ninth, and the Indians left with a 2–1 victory they badly needed.

The second game was as closely played as the first, except the outcome was reversed and it took longer to decide. Speaker remained on the bench at the outset, putting Wood in center field and returning Jamieson to left. He sent Jim Bagby to the mound in search of his twenty-fourth victory, and three consecutive second-inning hits produced a 1–0 advantage for the visitors. It was 2–0 in the seventh when Boston scored twice, the tying run coming home on Wood's weak throw to the plate in a futile effort to retire fleet Eddie Foster after Oscar Vitt lofted a one-out fly ball to short center.

As the game wound into extra innings, Speaker pinch-hit for Wood and put himself into center field. The move offered an immediate chance for heroics when Jamieson reached scoring position ahead of him in the top of the tenth. Speaker failed to produce, although Smith, batting behind him, singled the go-ahead run home. A doubleheader sweep would have been the best tonic for a downcast team, but Bagby wasn't up to the task and allowed two hits and the tying run in the bottom half. Speaker batted one more time to no effect before pulling himself in favor of Evans as the game wound into the thirteenth. It ended there when Boston shortstop Everett Scott produced a clean single to center that got Hendryx home with the winning run.

It had been an exhausting day of baseball, and one that left the Indians precisely where they had begun in the standings, two games behind Chicago. It also generated more questions. However much fans applauded Speaker's return to the field, the fact was that he had looked weak and gone zero-for-three. How long would it take for him to return to form? Then there was Lunte at short. The three hits he produced Monday only lifted his batting average since the Chapman death to .217, not much better than his season-long performance in the .190s. Speaker also had to deal with a depleted staff. Two doubleheaders in three days left him with few options for Tuesday's wrap-up of the five-game series. Bagby had pitched all thirteen innings and Caldwell had gone all nine on Monday, while Coveleski and Morton had each worked seven on Saturday.

Finally and more overarching was the issue of the team's basic interest in even playing ball. Chapman's death had removed more than a .300 hitter from what had been the league's best offense; it had drained enthusiasm. In the six games played since that Monday, four of them losses including two shutouts, the Indians had generated just eleven runs and thirty-seven hits, and a dozen of the latter had come in Monday's thirteen-inning defeat.

For the moment there was little Speaker could do about the offense beyond hoping that his own bat helped. And he knew he wasn't physically ready for that challenge yet. So instead he sent Graney back into left and moved Jamieson back to center for the Tuesday series wrap-up against Bullet Joe Bush. Bob Clark, who had started just one other game all season and who would not start again, got the pitching call. Mostly because he had no other options, Speaker left Clark in for the full eight innings. The Red Sox picked steadily at the fill-in, scoring twice in the first and adding a third run in the fifth and four more in the seventh, all the latter coming with two out. The two runs produced on hits by Smith and Gardner in the eighth inning only averted another shutout.

In one sense the Indians had been fortunate. Although they left Boston with just one win in five games, thanks to Faber's defeat that day in Washington they remained only two games behind the White Sox in the standings. And if nothing else the schedule now began to work a bit in Cleveland's favor. Their next port of call was Philadelphia for three games against the push-over Athletics. The Sox, meanwhile, faced a three-game Thursday-Friday-Saturday series of their own against the Yankees in New York.

Before they could worry about Chicago, however, the Yankees faced four games with Detroit. Although solidly in seventh place as the series began and destined to remain there, the Tigers had morphed into a distraction far exceeding their lowly station due to their participation with the Red Sox in the initial discussion of a boycott against Mays. As easy as such talk had been from the safety of Boston, it grew more controversial as the Tigers packed up for New York, where the newspapers ladled up columns of speculation about whether Mays would be so incapacitated by guilt that he would even be able to pitch.

In the Sunday *New York Tribune*, on the eve of the pitcher's scheduled return to the mound, Grantland Rice presented that impact as an open question. He recalled a 1911 incident involving Russ Ford, then a Yankee, who beaned a journeyman White Sox player named Russ Corhan, knocking him into a state between life and death for several weeks before Corhan finally recovered. "During this period, Ford was so badly upset that he was of no further use to his club," Rice wrote. "He lost weight, lost effectiveness, and finally had to take a vacation to build up his shattered nervous system. He was never the same effective pitcher."[9] Rice's finding about Ford, by the way, is entirely subject to debate. In 1911 Ford won twenty-two games for New York, making thirty-three starts and recording a 2.27 earned run average. He pitched twenty-two complete games—more than any pitcher in the league except Walter Johnson and Ed Walsh—finishing fourth in innings pitched and fifth in strikeouts. His was not the profile of a broken man. It's true that Ford followed that strong season with losing records in 1912 and 1913, although in both seasons his ERA hovered around the league average.

Beyond that, for every instance Rice could cite of a pitcher reduced in effectiveness by a sudden, traumatic event, fans could think of another where no impact whatsoever was evident. They didn't have to think long either, only back to the spring-training beaning of Chick Fewster by Brooklyn's Jeff Pfeffer in Jacksonville. Any impact on Pfeffer had certainly been difficult to discern. True, Pfeffer's record to that point was a so-so 9-8, but that had more to do with the erratic support he had received from Brooklyn's batters. Pfeffer's 2.71 earned run average attested to his abilities. In five of his eight defeats, he had allowed four or fewer runs. Since July 1 Pfeffer had been even better, winning six straight starts, completing five of them, and allowing just eleven earned runs.

Although Mays had kept a low public profile, he had assured Yankees management that he was okay and prepared to pitch. That was enough for Ruppert and Huston, who issued a public statement declaring their support for the pitcher. The statement also amounted to a direct refutation of Johnson's speculation that Mays's own grief would render him unable to pitch; in fact, they rebuked Johnson by name. "That gentleman is misinformed as to the player's status," they said. "Mays, while bowed with grief, is not a broken reed. . . . He will take his regular turn in the pitcher's box, and we expect him to win games as usual."[10] They also addressed the prospect of trouble brought on by agitators, not likely in New York but a concern in other league cities. "If he requires protection he will receive it from us to the extreme limit, no matter where that may lead," they said.[11]

The Saturday series opener drew thirty-five thousand to the Polo Grounds, most of them fully prepared to let the visitors know their anti-Mays sentiments were not appreciated. Greeted by hoots and catcalls, the Tigers responded by declaring their collective innocence and blaming the media. Cobb led the way, twice during pregame warmup walking near the plate, facing the crowd, bowing as they hissed, and gesturing toward the press row as if to pass along the responsibility to its proper place. Once the game began, the Tigers took out whatever outrage they felt on the home team, thrashing Rip Collins and two successors for ten runs and a dozen hits. Only once did the crowd stir in excitement, during the eighth inning when Babe Ruth lifted a fly ball deep into the seats down the right-field line. Ruth declared it his forty-fourth home run of the season and ran it out, but umpire Dick Nallin had other ideas. He said the ball had been foul when it left the yard.

The call coincided with a string of sub-Ruthian performances that had begun with the Yanks' return home, an occasion that itself roughly coincided with the start of filming on *Headin' Home*, Ruth's cinematic debut. Designed to capitalize on the slugger's star power, the movie was being produced by a new outfit called Kessel and Baumann, which commissioned *New York American* sportswriter Bugs Baer to write the screenplay. It starred the Babe as a hick-town hero who becomes a baseball star, then returns to thwart a villainous banker threatening to foreclose on his sweetheart. Ruth had signed the deal in late July, with filming scheduled to take place during the late August home stand. The star had good reason to make the movie: a fifteen-thousand-dollar advance from the producers, with an additional thirty-five thousand dollars promised. (Ruth himself would publicly value the agreement at one hundred thousand dollars, but that number is today considered hyperbole.) The larger check eventually bounced.

Headin' Home was being filmed on six mornings in a vacant lot in Haverstraw, New Jersey, on a set located next to a swamp, a fact that within the week would have profound consequences for the Yankees and Ruth. But the immediate issue appeared to be the Babe's commitment to double duty. His contract required him to get up early—itself problematic for the high-living Babe—make the forty-five-minute drive to Haverstraw every morning, then drive back to the Polo Grounds in time for the day's game. Actual filming began on Saturday, a day on which the Babe went zero-for-three. A second zero-for-three followed against Howard Ehmke on Sunday, when the rest of the Yankees mustered ten hits and still lost 11–9 because Tigers batters touched four Yankees pitchers for seventeen hits. Cobb got five of them, each one baiting a crowd of thirty-seven thousand that remained incensed over what they viewed as the Tigers' aspersions against Mays. In the sixth inning umpire Nallin called Cobb safe on a close play at third, triggering the throwing of a flurry of pop bottles from the stands toward the player. None struck anybody, but one fan was arrested and removed from the park. In the eighth inning Cobb spiked Yankees second baseman Del Pratt on a steal attempt, producing more jeers.

Public reaction gave Ruth's offensive failures a pass on the Sunday defeat, primarily because the fans had the colorful Ping Bodie to kick around. Bodie had produced one more hit than Ruth, and it was a triple. But it came in the fourth inning with nobody on base and did not result in a score. Batting with the bases full in the first and with two runners aboard in the eighth, Bodie struck out both times. "The triple . . . would have been worth its weight in granulated sugar in the first or eighth," argued the New York World's "Monitor."[12]

Mays's return to the mound on Monday naturally accelerated, if it did not elevate, the debate over the propriety of his doing so. A sports editorial in that morning's New York Times lamented "the one note of bitterness" developing out of the "unfortunate incident," that being the campaign against Mays.[13] Writing in the New York Tribune, W. O. McGeehan condemned "a disposition in a small part of the baseball world to be cruelly unfair to Carl Mays." In a comment obviously aimed at the Tigers but not naming them, McGeehan declared such efforts "petty," suggesting they stemmed from Mays's reputation among his fellow players, particularly compared to Chapman. "It is unfortunate for Mays that he has not been as popular as the dead player, but he must not be sacrificed because of his unpopularity," McGeehan argued.[14]

A strong Monday showing of twenty thousand fans poured

through the Polo Grounds turnstiles to witness Mays's return on August 23, as well as whatever theater would ensue from it. They cheered Mays when he emerged to warm up and gave him a full ovation when he took the mound. By the time Ralph Young stepped into the batter's box, any real enthusiasm among the Detroiters for a showdown over the pitcher had evaporated. Nor did Mays himself provide any suspense, going about his business as if nothing at all had taken place exactly one week before. The only real drama occurred in that first inning, and Ruth doused it. After Young had been retired, Mays walked Donie Bush, and Cobb drove a hit against the right-field wall that should have sent Bush around to third. But the Babe played the carom expertly, and his throw cut down Bush at third. It was as close as the Tigers would come to a scoring opportunity all afternoon.

The pitcher's performance drew plaudits in New York. "Outwardly, Mays seemed as cool as you please, but his heart probably was thumping violently in his bosom," Runyon concluded.[15] Said Rice, "It was an extraordinary exhibition of courage, but all the time Mays probably was going through mental hell fire."[16] In the *New York Post*, William J. Chipman found the Yankees' mood markedly enhanced "now that it [was] known that poor Mays [had] come unharmed through the brimstone that [had] been his lot for the past week."[17]

Elsewhere public reaction was far less laudatory. "Well, Carl Mays has done what he said he would do," lamented Ross Tenney in the *Cleveland Press*.[18] A week earlier the *Sporting News* had editorially echoed Johnson's effort to voluntarily nudge Mays aside. "Mays knows what the world is saying," the *News* said at the time. "It remains to be seen if . . . [he] realizes the state of mind that exists in his case."[19] Having been ignored by the pitcher, the paper a week later castigated his return, noting that it came just three days after Chapman's funeral, in a stadium where the flags flew at half mast, and where players wore mourning bands. Those tokens of respect "were mocked when Mays was sent into the game . . . an insult to the memory of the dead . . . and to every lover of baseball."[20]

Those sorts of observations, however, amounted more to subjective speculation than inside knowledge. In fact, Mays had never during the week shown any doubt about his own ability to return to the mound. And any sense of an incipient New York tide crashed on Tuesday when Yancey "Doc" Ayres, a winner only five times in sixteen decisions, handed the Yankees their sixth defeat in eight games, beating fourteen-game winner Bob Shawkey 5–3.

Perhaps it is more accurate to say that Shawkey beat the Yankees. Two first-inning walks led to a Detroit run, and two more in the third inning combined with Bobby Veach's triple provided the basis for a three-run inning. The Tigers only got four hits all day, but between them Shawkey and Rip Collins walked five batters, four of whom scored. The Yankees collected ten hits, but all ten were singles. Beyond that Ayres had a magical touch when he needed it. Bodie came to bat with two runners on base in the second, and Ayres fanned him. In the fifth Del Pratt came up with the tying run in scoring position and struck out. An inning later Muddy Ruel whiffed with the tying and lead runs at second and third. Finally in the eighth Ayres struck out Bob Meusel, pinch-hitting with two runners on base.

Aside from Mays's auspicious return, the Detroit series had been a disaster for the Yanks. Starting just a game and a half behind the Indians, they had lost three of four and fallen three games behind the White Sox. They had not won consecutive games in nearly two weeks. Their star had come off the movie set to produce just two hits in eleven at bats. Aside from Mays New York pitchers had allowed the seventh-place Tigers twenty-six runs on thirty-three hits in three games. And the league's hottest team, at the moment anyway, was due in town next.

10. A Chigger in Conspiracy with Gamblers

August 26–September 1

George Hildebrand was a failed ballplayer who took to umpiring because baseball was the only life he knew. The revelation that Hildebrand's future did not lie in the playing end of the game was not long in showing through. A five-feet-eight, 170 pound, twenty-three-year-old outfielder, Hildebrand signed with the Brooklyn Dodgers in the spring of 1902, batted .220 in eleven games, and was invited by manager Ned Hanlon not to return. Considering that this took place in the throes of the National League's "war" with the American League—the number of big league jobs having doubled just one year earlier—Hildebrand had very decisively "flunked out."

If Hildebrand is to be believed, his banishment may have actually worked to the benefit of a lot of the game's best-known pitchers over the next couple of decades. Following his release Hildebrand signed on with Providence, where he later told the *Sporting News* that he and future big league pitcher Frank Corridon fooled around with moistening their fingers before delivering a pitch. Hildebrand finished 1902 with Sacramento, where he claimed to have shown his "spitball" to an up-and-comer named Elmer Stricklett. How the pitch came to the attention of Jack Chesbro—the

Pittsburgh Pirates star generally recognized as the first great spitballer—is not clear, but within a year or two several big league pitchers, including Chesbro, Corridon, and Stricklett, were throwing it.

Whatever Hildebrand's role in the development of the spitter, it did not provide steady work. The search for that took him to the Pacific Coast League, where he played with Los Angeles and San Francisco through 1908, then caught on as an umpire in 1909. By 1913 he was back in the big leagues on Ban Johnson's American League staff, for which he would labor more than two decades. With the exception of 1918, when umpires as well as players contributed time to the war effort, Hildebrand gained notice for his durability, averaging about 150 games a season and claiming to have umpired 3,510 consecutive games. If he was not ranked among the profession's greats, players viewed him as a competent, placid (by umpiring standards) arbiter.

That was not, however, the case in 1920, when Hildebrand, by then forty-one, found himself the focus of running hostile dialogues with players and managers. Those battles led to six player or manager ejections, more than were issued by any of his fellow AL umpires. Prior to that point Hildebrand had averaged fewer than two ejections per season. He would average about two per season for the remaining fourteen years of that career.[1] In 1920, in other words, George Hildebrand had a bad year, or an especially short fuse, or both. Which makes what occurred in the ninth inning of a game played on August 25, 1920, between the Indians and the Athletics in Philadelphia especially noteworthy.

The A's led 2–1 after the first eight innings, Slim Harriss having to that point bested Stanley Coveleski. Harriss might have been working on a shutout had not two errors by his middle infielders permitted Cleveland's lone run to score in the fourth. The Indians approached the ninth in a desperate mood. Since the Chapman tragedy, they had played seven games, lost five of them, and averaged fewer than two runs per game. From a half game in front, they had fallen two games behind the White Sox. Beyond that they were both physically tired and emotionally drained. Of nobody was that more true than Tris Speaker, whose friends commented that his gray hair looked grayer and his wrinkles deeper the past week than was even usually the case.

Perhaps due to that strain, when Speaker led off the top of the ninth by drawing a walk, he chose to play the "safe" strategy. That meant calling on the next batter, cleanup hitter Elmer Smith, to lay down a sacrifice designed to move the tying run—himself—into scoring position for Larry Gardner or Doc Johnston. Smith did bunt, and the ball teased the third base line. Believing it foul, Smith did not leave the batter's box. Speaker, taking his cue from his hitter, stayed at first. But third baseman Joe Dugan fielded the ball anyway, just in case Hildebrand might call it fair, and threw to second, receiving an "out" call in return for his initiative. It was an easy matter for second baseman Jimmy Dykes to double the still-stationary Smith at first.

Hildebrand's decision triggered the emotional release valve that had been pent up in Speaker since New York. He charged the umpire, set his face directly against Hildebrand's, and unleashed a level of invective guaranteed to get any player ejected from any game in any sport. This went on for minutes before the astonished Philadelphia fans, Speaker cursing the umpire and ranting about the just-made call at point-blank range. He raised his fists and gestured as if prepared to punch Hildebrand. Before long Joe Wood raced alongside his teammate and manager from the Cleveland bench and added his own assessment of Hildebrand's professional capacity to the inquisition. And through it all Hildebrand never said a word or offered a gesture in reply. Although in virtually any other circumstance Speaker would have quickly been ejected, the umpire did not even try to halt the diatribe. It was as if Hildebrand had decided to adopt the role of therapist—"get it off your chest and I'll just listen." His fellow umpire, George Moriarty, moved in to ensure Hildebrand's physical safety, but Moriarty too thought it better or more politic not to confront Speaker. After several minutes of this extended public catharsis, the Indians manager finally gave up and returned to the team dugout, out of simple fatigue as much as anything else. One batter later the game was over, and the Indians had lost again.[2]

Dugan sank the Indians further toward melancholy on Thursday, this time in a more conventional manner. His first-inning single sent the game's first run across. Then after Cleveland had tied the game with a run in the second, Dugan came up and drove Clarence Walker home before scoring a third run. That was enough for promising rookie Dave Keefe, who beat Ray Caldwell 3–2. The Indians did manage to claim the Friday game behind Jim Bagby, who not only held the A's to three runs but contributed four hits to the offense. There was, finally, plenty of that; Cleveland led 7–0 by the third inning and won 15–3. Even Harry Lunte helped out, with three of the team's twenty-one base hits. If ever a team needed the morale boost that the rout provided, it was Cleveland, which had lost six of their last seven, seven of the nine games played since Chapman's death, and twelve of sixteen since August 9. "The last ten days have told their story, and it is a sad one," Cleveland sports reporter Wilbur

Wood wrote of the team that seemed to be falling apart. "There is no longer the interest in the game that there was before the disaster."[3]

Rain forced the Saturday finale to the sidelines; the two teams agreed to make it up on the only other possible date, the A's last trip into Cleveland on September 15. The undesirability of giving the Indians a seventy-eighth home game was commonly understood to be more than offset by the practical impossibility—given the reality of train travel—of bringing the Indians back to Philadelphia on a date when the A's would already be there and neither team was scheduled elsewhere. Only two such dates existed. The first was September 2, impossible because both teams were booked on daylong train trips prior to the start of the final swing of eastern teams through the western cities. The other was September 22, a date on which the Indians were supposed to be returning from Boston for what increasingly loomed as a critical three-game series with the White Sox in Cleveland. Connie Mack was far too much a gentleman to insist that the Indians book a quick stopover to play a makeup game in those circumstances.

The Chicago series would be meaningless anyway if the Indians didn't turn around their slumping offense and at the same time solidify their recurring mound depth problem. At the time of Chapman's beaning, every Indians regular except Bill Wambsganss as well as three subs carried an average above .300. Since then Johnston, Gardner, and Graney had fallen below .300, and Speaker had dropped from a league-leading .411 to .394. Lunte's .226 average hardly replaced Chapman's .303. The .298 team average sounded robust, but it had been .310 two short weeks earlier. Speaker sounded defiant in the face of the facts. "Our slump has come to an end," he declared. "The boys have recovered their spirit."[4]

The other serious problem was pitching depth. Speaker could always count on Bagby, already a winner twenty-four times, and Stan Coveleski. Caldwell had at times been shaky, but as long as the team's bats didn't collapse his 3.85 earned run average, not far off the leaguewide average, was good for close to two wins in every three starts. Speaker's problem was that those three arms were all he had. Over the season he had tested six pitchers a total of thirty-four times in the role of a fourth starter, and the team's record in those games was 16-18. The burden fell inordinately on Speaker's offense. In twenty-one of those thirty-eight games, the Indians had failed to score at least five runs, and their record in those twenty-one games was just 5-16.

What Speaker needed was a reliable fourth starter. That, of course, could be said of almost every team with the exception of the White Sox. Speaker had broken spring training with the intention of using twenty-six-year-old Elmer Myers in the capacity. But Myers lost four of his first six decisions on an ERA near 5.00 and was bundled off to Boston in early June when Harry Frazee offered the standard waiver price. Guy Morton got the next shot. Morton had hung around for seven seasons, losing thirteen of his first fourteen career decisions but occasionally showing promise and generally producing respectable ERAs. Not in 1920. Given fourteen starts, he had managed eight wins, but with an ERA that rose a point and a half above his 1919 numbers. Speaker tried George Uhle, a strapping twenty-one-year-old six-footer whose powerful arm was more than occasionally betrayed by control issues. Since late July Speaker had turned to starters other than Bagby, Coveleski, or Caldwell seven times and gotten a 2-5 return on his investment.

The reality, of course, was that there were no obviously available arms of the quality Speaker needed. So the Indians gambled and purchased the contract of a left-hander named John Walter Mails from Sacramento for thirty-five thousand dollars. By the standards of the day, that was holdup money for an arm of Mails's pedigree, but Speaker needed somebody and Mails at least appeared to have learned how to throw strikes. That had not been the case during his only previous big league experience, brief appearances with the Dodgers in 1915 and 1916. Mails had pitched twenty-two innings spread over thirteen bullpen appearances and let 35 of the 102 batters he faced reach base by hit or walk, often the latter. His inability to locate pitches earned him the disparaging nickname of "Duster," although a Mails pitch was as likely to miss low and away as up and in. His only two big league decisions were both losses. When the Dodgers released Mails, he caught on with the Pirates organization, which stashed him in Portland for possible future use, only to have the war intervene. After the armistice Mails signed with Sacramento, where legendary Cubs manager Frank Chance tipped Speaker that the left-hander had refined both his fastball and his curve. Chance's recommendation and Mails's 20-16 record for a team languishing in last place in its league persuaded Speaker to take a costly chance. On August 18, the day after Chapman died, the Indians plunked down the thirty-five grand, sent lightly used pitchers Tony Faeth and Dick Niehaus west with the cash, and took title to Mails.

That did not, however, mean they actually had Duster Mails available to pitch. There remained the matter of getting from Sacramento to the East Coast, no small issue in 1920. Mails was three days delayed even getting out of Sacramento due to his inability to book accommodations. He did not catch up with the team until the day before the final leg of their eastern swing opened in Washington on August 30. When Mails did arrive, he brought something that the Indians had not counted as part of the purchase: an attitude. Mails declared that rather than Duster, he personally preferred the nickname he had given himself, "The Great Mails." The tag never hung, but Speaker worked the left-hander out soon after his arrival in Washington and declared Mails would pitch the final game of that series. He told his new pitcher not to trouble himself with scouting reports. "Just throw the ball over the plate and you'll never lose a game," he said.[5]

The Indians took three of four in Washington, losing only the opener—when rookie Harry Courtney proved the game's unpredictability by outpitching Bagby 3-2. They even survived Mails's debut on Wednesday, a performance that failed to live up to Speaker's expectations, much less Mails's own. Jittery on his return to the big leagues after more than four years, he walked the first man he faced and allowed three runs. When Mails walked the lead-off man in the second, Speaker pulled him in favor of Morton. Given that the Indians did commensurate damage to Washington's staff, Morton arrived to a 5–3 lead, which he managed to parlay into a 9–5 victory. Notwithstanding Mails's inauspicious debut, Speaker resolved to write off what he had seen that afternoon. In the *Cleveland Press* Ross Tenney applauded the manager's patience. "Give this bird Mails a real chance and he's likely to prove all that his advance notices from the Pacific slope would indicate," Tenney wrote.[6]

The performance in Washington also reinvigorated the club's demoralized fan base. The Indians returned home having nearly split the tragic eastern trip, winning seven of the fifteen games. They were only 11-16 for August, their worst month of the season, but they could look ahead to playing twenty-one of the final twenty-nine games at home. Better, neither the Yankees nor the White Sox had taken full advantage of Cleveland's stumble. In fact, Morton's victory in relief of Mails had improbably lifted the Indians back into first place, although by a mere half game over both of their rivals. Those clubs had their own diverse and very problematic issues.

Such a finding would have surprised patrons at the Polo Grounds as the Sox came to New York for the start of their own three-game series with the Yankees on August 26. Certainly the visitors appeared to be threatened by little. The White Sox had won thirteen of sixteen games since August 8, allowing fewer than three runs per game and moving from five games behind the Indians to two and a half games in front of them. Superficially at least the Yankees were more fortunate, the final threat to Mays's continued availability having finally evaporated.

That threat had all but died with the Tigers' refusal to boycott Mays on August 23. Yet discussion lingered, especially in Cleveland, where it was reported that Indians players had petitioned the other teams to step up. "Every team in the league except the Yankees and White Sox is joining the movement," Tenney reported in the *Cleveland Press*.[7] He assured Clevelanders that the Browns, the Tigers, and the Red Sox remained committed to a boycott, with the Senators and the Athletics pondering the matter. But Tenney was wrong. Although several teams discussed a boycott, none wanted to be the first to act, so the idea essentially died leaderless. Tigers veterans Cobb and Donie Bush and Senators captain George McBride all denied even having been approached by anybody affiliated with the Cleveland club. In Philadelphia Mack acknowledged that his players had been contacted but dismissed the idea. "Cleveland is making a serious mistake and will realize this later," Mack said, asserting that the A's would "take no action" against Mays.[8] In Boston an anonymous member of the Red Sox said threats wouldn't work against Mays anyway because the pitcher could not be rattled by them. "Razz on that nervous stuff," the player said. "That guy hasn't got any nerves."[9] By August 30 Tenney abdicated his self-assigned role as agent provocateur, acknowledging that the league would not challenge the hated pitcher. By then the Tigers, the White Sox, and the Browns all had stood in against Mays, who was 3-0 in those games.

The only remaining prospect of a gesture, and it would by that point have been a symbolic one, remained to be taken by the Indians themselves when the Yankees visited Cleveland for the final time on September 8–11. But even the chance of a Mays boycott by the Indians hinged on the unlikely prospect of the Yankees bringing him along on that leg of the trip. "I do not believe that manager Miller Huggins will have the bad taste to send Mays to the slab while his team is in Cleveland," Tenney wrote. "It will be better for all concerned if he does not."[10]

The Yankees' problem wasn't Mays; it was Babe Ruth, specifically the movie's demands on his time and health. The schedule required him to drive each morning to Haverstraw, New Jersey, for the shooting, and return in time for the day's 3:00 p.m. game. It was a testament to the player's endurance that he was any good at all under the circumstances, but the Yankees were not. They had followed their loss of two of three games to Cleveland by dropping three of four to the Tigers and losing three and a half games in the standings. Ruth managed only three hits in fifteen at bats during games that overlapped with the shooting schedule.

George Mogridge faced Dickie Kerr before a Thursday crowd of twenty-two thousand in the opener of that series—but not for long. The Sox hammered Mogridge for four runs in the top of the first, and not even Ruth's forty-fourth home run, a three-run shot in the inning's bottom half, could perk up the cause. When the Sox added three more scores in the top of the fourth, the twenty-two thousand began to abandon the scene, a wise decision given the 16–4 final score. Among other indignities they missed a rare triple steal by Eddie Collins, Buck Weaver, and Joe Jackson in the eighth.

Those twenty-two thousand fans did not know it, but they had just seen the last of the Babe for a while. Following the game the Yankees star reported to the trainer's office with a strange swelling in his hand. It worsened into a full-blown infection by morning, with the lower arm swollen substantially beyond its normal size. Doctors carved a three-inch incision into the arm to drain the infection and ordered Ruth into a sling. When they diagnosed an insect bite as the culprit, speculation mounted as to where the Babe might have run afoul of such a creature. There was one obvious answer: the cinematic lots of Haverstraw, New Jersey. After two days of lying low on the issue, Ruth confirmed the infection in his own newspaper column and reported that he would be sidelined for ten days. He blamed a chigger but pointedly did not fault either himself for agreeing to make the movie or its producers for their choice of the open field as a shooting locale.

"As a baseball fan, what would you do if you were in my shoes?" he asked. "You're at the top of your career and promoters of all kinds are offering you big money. . . . I might have been bitten by a chigger while sitting on the Yankee bench or playing in the field. . . . You can't blame the movies for an accident like that."[11]

Far from blaming the movies, New York publications celebrated them. Although *Headin' Home* wasn't scheduled to be released for three more weeks, "Mae Tinnae," the *New York Post*'s movie critic, seized the moment to assess *Over the Fence*, a little-known short in which Ruth demonstrated various baseball-related functions. It was, in other words, an early instructional film. "Mae" professed not to be impressed with the film itself, designed to appeal to what she considered "a nutty horde." But she did declare Ruth "quite as charming as many movie stars."[12]

Ruth was decidedly not charmed by what he viewed as cinematic rip-off efforts to capitalize on his baseball and film celebrity. He quickly sought and obtained an injunction in the New York Supreme Court restraining the movie's producers from showing their unauthorized version of him on screen. The legal action prompted the *New York Tribune*'s W. O. McGeehan to observe sarcastically that Ruth "has barely strength enough in his left mitt to sign the papers in a suit for a million dollars."[13]

Curiously, with Ruth sidelined the Yankees' fortunes abruptly improved on Friday. Due to face Mays the Sox did meet briefly that morning, although the outcome of the discussion was foreordained. "If Mays has the nerve to go on pitching . . . and if the American League and the American public wants to see Mays pitch, what's the use of trying to tell them about their business?" summarized the *Chicago Tribune*'s I. E. Sanborn.[14]

In fact, Mays was not even the principal topic of the team meeting, which management had called to clear the air about another startling matter. Back in Chicago police had just arrested three neighborhood punks, who had unburdened themselves of an interesting story. They had intended to rob

White Sox offices immediately after the September New York series in Chicago and steal the take. Gleason informed the players that the ringleader, a small-timer known as James Ryan, had told the cops of their intent to kill Comiskey "and anybody else who stood around close enough to see [them]," explaining, "It's bad stuff to go away and leave a lot of witnesses."[15]

Given that Ryan, Louis Maloney, and Milton Brunski were arrested as they tried to make off with a forty-four-thousand-dollar stockyards payroll, police took the threat seriously. They directed Gleason to ask his players whether any of them knew any of the three. None of the players said he did, and no evidence ever surfaced to undermine those denials.

Mays was not at his best, but he was stubborn. He allowed eight hits in the first three innings alone and trailed 3–1. But that only got the Sox a 4–4 tie through nine innings, in part because two Eddie Cicotte walks produced an equal number of runs. In the top of the tenth, Amos Strunk drove Ray Schalk home, only to see the Yanks tie it in the bottom half on hits by Sammy Vick and Wally Pipp. Finally in the bottom of the twelfth, Roger Peckinpaugh chased Muddy Ruel across with a winning hit. Yankees management got a bracer—albeit a belated and by then meaningless one—when league president Ban Johnson ordered teams not to agitate against Mays. Since the threat of a boycott had already collapsed, the statement's timing merely underscored Johnson's inability by that point to lead.

A record crowd of 39,150 jammed into the Polo Grounds for the Saturday wrap-up, and that total was limited only by the size of the facility. "If the park under Coogan's Bluff had been large enough, there would have been nearly 60,000 fans at the game," one press observer speculated.[16] Ticket sales were halted a full half hour before the scheduled 3:00 p.m. start, leaving thousands on the outside. The lucky fans who got in saw Bob Shawkey out-pitch Red Faber 3–0, a decision that reduced Chicago's lead to just two games. A Swede Risberg error let one run in, but the other two were legit, and the total absence of any Chicago offense is what really determined the outcome. Shawkey held the visitors to just six hits.

The Browns followed the White Sox into New York, and Mays provided the critical support in Ruth's continued absence to win two of three. In the Sunday opener he replaced Jack Quinn during a sixth-inning rally in which the Browns assumed a 3–2 lead before thirty-seven thousand fans. Mays held St. Louis scoreless into the ninth while the Yanks marshaled a tying run, then got help from an unlikely source, Aaron Ward. Already a three-time victim of Browns pitcher Urban Shocker on strikes, Ward only got to bat because a Browns error had let Duffy Lewis reach base. Against a din of calls for a pinch hitter, Ward delivered a game-winning double. Following a scheduled Monday off day, Dixie Davis beat the Yanks 3–2 on Tuesday. But Mays started again on Wednesday and rang up his twenty-first victory, a 2–0 four-hit shutout keyed by Ping Bodie's run-producing triple in the second. "The Browns couldn't hit his truck worth a cent," Runyon observed of Mays.[17]

The White Sox left New York for Boston on Saturday evening still in possession of first place by two games and destined to play what remains today one of the most mysterious, little-known series in baseball history. The raw results are pretty straightforward: the fifth-place Red Sox swept the defending champs. Sam Jones pitched a 4–0 shutout against Lefty Williams on Monday, Joe Bush beat Cicotte

7–3 on Tuesday, and Herb Pennock defeated Dickie Kerr 6–2 on Wednesday.

By the general standards of baseball, there is nothing inherently suspicious about a sub .500 team sweeping a first-place club in a three-game series. The record shows that the Red Sox held their own against the White Sox all season, winning twelve of the twenty-two games that the teams played.

Within the team, though, the outcome quickly raised suspicion. Shortly after the indictment of the seven active and one former player during the season's last week, catcher Ray Schalk specifically pointed to the three games in Boston as having been sold out to gamblers. The substance of Schalk's assertion was that both Cicotte and Williams had crossed him up while delivering fat pitches in key situations. Schalk also accused Chicago batters of "laying down" in key spots. James O'Leary, a prominent Boston newspaper writer, echoed the allegations shortly after the season's end.

The accusation is so general that its truth is difficult to assess. About the best one can say is that the Boston series fits the pattern of games on which gamblers might seek to profit, if for no other reason than to keep the pennant race open. This was especially plausible considering the indefinite sidelining of Ruth and Cleveland's ongoing hole at shortstop. If the games were fixed for that reason, they certainly accomplished their purpose. From one game in front at the start of the series, the Sox slipped into a tie with New York for second a half game behind the Indians as Cleveland won three of four in Washington and the Yanks took two of three from St. Louis.

The "fix" theory would wear more comfortably if obviously indictable mistakes on the part of the White Sox had turned the games. Like many contests of skill, those three contain enough blunders to become suspicious if one chooses to view them with a suspicious attitude, but the case is not clear-cut. For one thing the prospect of a Jones victory over Chicago was hardly unprecedented; he had already beaten the White Sox four times that year in four starts.

Much of the case against the White Sox involves what they did not do as much as what they did do. They certainly did not hit. Eddie Collins banged out three hits against Jones, but the rest of the team managed just two. Schalk's ire particularly rose in the home half of the seventh when—with Boston's lead a precarious 1–0—Williams delivered three consecutive extra base hits to the bottom of the order, producing two more runs. Chicago's only serious chance against Jones died in the next inning when Risberg doubled, then was thrown out trying to steal third. It wouldn't have taken a baseball scholar to judge that trying to steal third down by four runs in the eighth inning represented bad judgment on the Swede's part. But there was then as there remains now a difference between bad judgment and deliberate malfeasance.

After twenty-one consecutive scoreless innings, the White Sox finally scored in the second inning of the 7–2 Tuesday loss to Bush. In a sense Chicago's offense came alive, producing ten hits, with Collins again leading the way with three. But White Sox hitters consistently failed in the clutch. In the bottom of the third, a Jackson error yielded two Boston runs. In the seventh Cicotte collapsed and allowed three more runs.

O'Leary particularly indicted the White Sox for their showing in this game, asserting that gamblers had blackmailed the pitcher, threatening exposure. He cited Cicotte's pitching as suspicious during a three-run third inning that included a base hit to the opposing pitcher as well as two walks, and again during a three-run seventh that featured a misplayed suicide squeeze bunt. "Why, they're playing just like they did in the World Series!" O'Leary recalled remarking to a friend.[18] In *Eight Men Out* Eliot Asinof writes that plate umpire Brick Owens would later contend that he had never seen Cicotte groove so many pitches in so many key situations and had never heard Schalk assault a pitcher as he had torn into Cicotte.

The third game is less suspicious than either of the first two. With his team's lead reduced to a half game, Kid Gleason sent Kerr, a sixteen-game winner, against Pennock, and teammates gave him two second-inning runs to boot. It was the suspected Sox who largely carried the rally, with hits by Jackson and Happy Felsch translating into runs when Risberg drove a smash off the shin of Boston third baseman Ossie Vitt. And when the collapse came, by way of a three-run Boston sixth, Kerr deserved the blame. He walked one batter and delivered a single, a double, and a triple.

There was just enough unusual play in the series to raise questions regarding its legitimacy, especially to Schalk and Collins. Asinof reports that following the club's return to Chicago, Collins went to Comiskey's office to accuse the White Sox of selling out the Boston series. Comiskey told Collins there was nothing he could do.[19]

11. A Phosphate at the Edelweiss

September 2–18

The Indians returned from their eastern swing on Friday, September 3, an occasion that doubled as an opportunity for players to unpack more than their bags. Team train travel was a repetitive, boring process within close quarters, and it tested the ability of any team's members to live as well as play with one another. Often—as with the Yankees—these illustrations involved poker or other card games. The manifestation of the Indians' closeness had been singing, generally featuring an ensemble known as the Quartet, although at various times it might include three, four, five, or more players.

For years Ray Chapman and Jack Graney had been mainstays of the Pullman car Quartet, joined more frequently in 1920 by Doc Johnston, Steve O'Neill, Joe Evans, and an occasional drop-in. Chapman had led the group in "That Old Gang Of Mine" as the Indians rode the elevated train out to the Polo Grounds that fatal Monday morning two and a half weeks before. The last note of that train ride had also been the last note struck on the entire eastern trip, for singing would have been too painful, too reminiscent of the Quartet's leader. But as the team Pullman approached Cleveland, Henry Edwards, the *Plain Dealer*'s team correspondent, reported strangely familiar and heartening sounds.

"For the first time since Chapman died, the Indians yesterday morning found heart enough to sing while on their way home," he wrote. This was taken as more than a mere musical omen. "They have reorganized their quartet and are showing some of the old spirit," said Edwards. "They are fighting to the finish."[1]

Club management declared the opener of an eighteen-game home stand—which would bring every league opponent to Cleveland—Ray Chapman Memorial Day, a chance to give fans and players the opportunity to jointly express their sentiments and then, presumably, push ahead with the pennant race. Brief, somber ceremonies were planned. Before fifteen thousand fans, each of whom received a commemorative booklet, members of both the Indians and the Tigers stood in front of their dugouts as a bugler from Chapman's own naval reserve detachment strode to shortstop and played "Taps." The center-field flag was lowered to half staff, and a combined orchestra-chorus numbering more than one hundred performed "Lead, Kindly Light."

The game itself was intended as a more raucous affair. Members of a newly created fan organization, the Stick to the Finish club, distributed miniature Tris Speaker bats that were actually nothing more than noisemakers, the better to rally the remaining Indians out of any lingering dispiritedness. Fans cheered loudly when the home team took the field and provided Harry Lunte, the former benchwarmer who had inherited Chapman's shortstop position, with an especially loud ovation when he came to bat in the second. Lunte came to the plate with a batting average under .200, but that was, for the moment anyway, of no consequence. "They want to give this infielder every chance," *Cleveland Plain Dealer* sports editor James Lanyon wrote. "They are for him from start to finish."[2]

As it turned out, the Indians' real bats proved of little more use against Tigers pitcher Dutch Leonard than those miniatures would have been. The Indians mustered just seven hits. That made tough going for Stan Coveleski, seeking his twentieth victory, but he was game for the challenge. Through eight innings he allowed the visiting Tigers just three hits in return. So the game remained scoreless into the ninth, when Ralph Young hit a one-out bouncer to Bill Wambsganss at second. It was an easy play, and the second baseman inexcusably threw the ball wildly past Doc Johnston at first for an error that allowed Young to reach second. If he could have retired Donie Bush, Coveleski could have intentionally walked Ty Cobb and faced the less dangerous Bobby Veach. But Coveleski walked Bush—his first control failure of the afternoon—forcing him to pitch to Cobb. The Tigers star belted a clean single beyond Johnston's reach, and Young scored.

The Indians might have recovered from this lone misfortune in the bottom of the ninth but for some absentminded base-running by Johnston, who led off with a single and reached second on Steve O'Neill's sacrifice bunt. George Burns pinch-hit for Lunte and was hit on the foot, which put runners at first and second, still with just one out. Speaker sent reserve catcher Les Nunamaker to bat for Coveleski, but he fanned, and the third strike rolled away from Tigers catcher Oscar Stanage. The rules do not now and did not then require a forced runner to run on a dropped third strike, but that fact temporarily eluded Johnston, who took off for third base and was easily retired on Stanage's throw to Babe Pinelli, ending the game.

The defeat reduced Cleveland's advantage over the Yankees to three percentage points, a circumstance made more emotionally calamitous by its occurrence on the day set aside to honor Chapman. The Indians were not, however, out of fight. Before another healthy crowd on Saturday, they leveled a six-run attack in the second inning against Yancey Ayres, aided by Ayres's bases-filled walk to Lunte. Ray Caldwell sprinkled ten hits in claiming his eighteenth victory 12–3. Jim Bagby followed on Sunday with his twenty-sixth, a tighter affair pitting him against Hooks Dauss. The game was knotted 2–2 in the bottom of the eighth when Dauss walked Speaker, and Elmer Smith dropped a double into the gap between Veach and Cobb. Larry Gardner's fly ball was deep enough to score Speaker, and Johnston pushed Smith home with another double to left. That run, which looked like insurance, proved vital when the Tigers managed one of their own in the ninth.

However tragically undertaken, the seventeen days since Chapman's death turned out to be the high point of Harry Lunte's brief career. Arriving as a light-hitting reserve the previous year, Lunte could have harbored no illusions of doing more than filling in occasionally for Chapman. He lacked the regular's charisma, fielding range, and batting skill. Chapman died enjoying his best season, with a .308 average. Lunte had made the least of his rare opportunities as a rookie, batting just .197 in 1919. The result was to render him nearly invisible in 1920. Prior to August 16, Speaker had allowed him a mere seven at bats, with a yield of one single. Nor had talk of Chapman's retirement at season's end breathed hope into Lunte's prospects. In July Jim Dunn came to terms with Joey Sewell, the recently graduated shortstop from the University of Alabama program. Sewell had been shipped off to New Orleans, presumably to be polished and prepared for 1921.

Necessity forced Lunte into the spotlight, but it did not improve his performance. In the intervening three weeks, he had collected thirteen hits in sixty-four at bats, producing another sub-.200 batting average. Yet Indians fans clung to him because he was the best they had at a vital position in a close pennant race. That all changed in the fifth inning of the morning game of a Labor Day doubleheader against the Browns. With two outs and the home team clinging to a 2–1 lead, Lunte drove a base hit past third baseman Earl Smith but pulled up lame at first base. At the time the injury was diagnosed as a severe charley horse—essentially a quadriceps contusion—although one wonders given the circumstances whether Lunte hadn't actually pulled a muscle. The medical facts were immaterial, since for the second time in a short span an Indians shortstop had to be helped off the field. Unlike his predecessor Harry Lunte would live through the experience. He would never, however, play in another Major League game. Leg injuries will do that to career .197 hitters.

The only available candidate to replace Lunte at shortstop was left fielder Joe Evans, a converted infielder with six games of experience at the position, all of them in 1919. Evans handled two chances in the morning game and eight more that afternoon, all without incident. Cleveland pulled away with four runs in the seventh to win the morning game 7–2, with Duster Mails enjoying his first big league complete game. The only noteworthy moment occurred when Browns lead-off man Johnny Tobin got hold of a Mails pitch and smashed it against the right-field wall with Earl Smith on first. The remarkable aspect of the occurrence was that Tobin did not get credit for a base hit. Indians right fielder Elmer Smith feigned catching the ball well enough to freeze Earl Smith near first base. When the ball caromed off the wall, Elmer Smith retrieved it and forced Earl Smith at second, leaving Tobin with perhaps the longest and hardest hit fielder's choice in baseball history.

The afternoon game was more problematic. Speaker started Guy Morton, but he lasted just two-thirds of an inning, in which time the Browns collected three runs. Bob Clark succeeded Morton and held the Browns as much in check as could be expected through eight innings of what was a 5–5 tie entering the ninth. One out and two hits later, Speaker faced a critical decision. Leaving Clark, a tiring second liner, on the mound was tantamount to giving the game away. But Mails had pitched a complete game just that morning, while Bagby, Caldwell, and Coveleski had all delivered complete games since Friday. Speaker had just one available and rested pitcher, but it was George Uhle, a twenty-one-year-old with a fastball he had not mastered, as his 5.21 earned run average attested. Speaker gambled on Bagby, a choice that would be viewed as reckless today given the more than one hundred pitches he had thrown a day earlier. Indeed, Bagby was not sharp; he walked two and forced the lead run across the plate before retiring the side. But successive hits in the bottom half by Graney, Speaker, and Smith set the tying and winning runs on base for Gardner, who sent them both across with a hit to the gap in right center. The victory, perhaps Bagby's least deserved of the season, was his twenty-seventh.

By this time no team could have thought more longingly of home than the Browns, who had not seen St. Louis since August 14 and would not until September 9. Their present road trip, monumental even by the standards of 1920, encompassed twenty-three games—30 percent of their entire road schedule—and took them successively to Cleveland, then Washington, Philadelphia, Boston, New York, Chicago, back to Cleveland, and finally back to Chicago. They had arrived in Cleveland from the first of their run-ins with the White Sox, a team suspicious of itself, largely due to the events a few days earlier in Boston. But with the Browns in town, other factors soon loomed, odd factors that had nothing to do with the White Sox, the Browns, or, for that matter, any of the other American League teams, but which within a few weeks would transcend and overwhelm the pennant race itself.

The trigger was an innocuous ball game between the Cubs and the Phillies played at Wrigley Field the afternoon of August 31. Only the most dedicated of fans would have paid any attention at all to the game given the Cubs' .500 record and the Phillies' secure hold on last place in the National League. The announced pitching match-up was unremarkable. Phillies starter Lee Meadows, 13-10, was enjoying an exceptional season given the support behind him. The Cubs planned to start Claude Hendrix, a thirty-one-year-old, ten-year veteran with a losing record.

The first public sign that something odd was afoot came just a few minutes prior to the game's start when Chicago manager Fred Mitchell sent Grover Cleveland Alexander, not Hendrix, out to warm up. Cubs president William Veeck had reported receiving wires from bookies in several cities alerting him to odd betting activity in the hours before the game, activity that raised questions concerning whether Hendrix and possibly some other Cubs players had consorted with gamblers to fix the outcome. When dawn broke, the Cubs had been 2-to-1 betting favorites. Suddenly those odds had shifted. At 11:00 a.m. a Cincinnati gambling syndicate wired a bookmaker in Chicago seeking to put down ten thousand dollars on the Phillies, only to find that the Phillies had become 6-to-5 favorites. Even at that price gamblers in Detroit reported receiving up to fifteen thousand on the Phillies in the hours leading up to the first pitch. Additional amounts were reported as having been laid down in Boston, Cincinnati, and Philadelphia. By the first pitch estimates put the total amount bet on the ball game in excess of fifty thousand dollars, an amazing sum for a late-August game between also-rans. The sum was so amazing, in fact, that it was almost certainly inflated; subsequent investigations would suggest that as little as one-fifth that amount may actually have been bet on the game before suspicious bookies took the contest off the board.

But in the context of the previous season's World Series, reports of a sudden flood of illogical money renewed suspicion that crookedness was at work. That's why Hendrix was pulled and Alexander, whose reputation was above reproach, put in his place. Although nothing was ever proved against Hendrix, he never again pitched in a big league game. As it turned out, those sure-thing gamblers who actually got money down had the last laugh. Philadelphia won 3–0, scoring two runs in the second inning, both of them suspicious. Cubs first baseman Turner Barber let an easy ground ball through his legs; then second baseman Buck Herzog fumbled an apparent double play ground ball. Both of those runners scored.

Given the heightened sensitivities in Chicago, the suspicious Cubs-Phillies game commanded attention. On September 4 the *Chicago Herald and Examiner* broke news of the "sure-thing" game in inch-high front-page headline type. "Is baseball in danger?" the next morning's *Chicago Tribune* inquired.[3] The same newspaper made public implications that "among the gambling fraternity . . . four members of the Cubs [later identified as Hendrix, Barber, Herzog, and

Fred Merkle] were involved in the plot to throw the game."[4] The *New York Tribune*'s W. O. McGeehan found "altogether too much pussyfooting" in the Major Leagues' handling of gambling rumors to that point. If dishonest players are found, McGeehan said, "the authorities or their employers should make such an example of them that the coming generations would never forget."[5]

Cubs club president William Veeck took the first step, appealing to the Chicago chapter of the Baseball Writers Association of America (BBWAA) to investigate the charges. Although the BBWAA may seem an odd choice for an inquiry of such magnitude, Veeck had few other options. There was no commissioner, the National Commission existed in a state of shambles since the events of the previous winter, and new National League president John Heydler lacked the stature. Beyond that Veeck recognized that the game's credibility had been so damaged by the suspicions of crookedness that only an outside investigation would help. Finally, the BBWAA was more than willing. In fact, chapter president I. E. Sanborn of the *Chicago Tribune* appointed the membership to sit as a committee of the whole on the matter.

Sanborn need hardly have bothered. The day after Labor Day, Criminal Court chief justice Charles McDonald, a long-time baseball fan whose name a few years earlier had been mentioned as a possible successor to Garry Herrmann as chairman of the National Commission, effectively trumped the BBWAA, ordering a newly impaneled grand jury to take up the topic. Jurors greeted the order with a highly indecorous round of courtroom cheers. Assistant state's attorney Hartley Replogle expressed confidence that "honest" players would provide to the grand jury—operating under its seal of secrecy—any information pertaining to "thrown games."[6]

Although the immediate focus was on the Cubs-Phillies game, neither Replogle nor grand jury foreman Henry Brigham, in civilian life the president of an area car company, promised to confine the investigation to that one game alone.

In short, as the White Sox returned from the east for the final month of a dynamic pennant race—having lost five straight including three destructive games in Boston—neither the players nor their fans could be sure what might lie ahead. Nothing that occurred at Comiskey Park on Friday, September 3, assuaged anyone's uncertainty. Dixie Davis held the home team to a single run, and the Browns handed Chicago a seventh straight loss, 2–1. The problem was the Sox offense. Since the streak began a week earlier with a twelve-inning, 6–5 defeat in New York, the White Sox had been shut out twice and produced just six runs. They got nearly that many in the first game of a Saturday doubleheader, but Eddie Cicotte blew up and allowed fourteen Browns hits. The last of them, Earl Smith's home run into the right-field bleachers, broke a 5–5 tie in the tenth inning and sent the Sox to a seventh straight defeat. Some sense of equilibrium returned during the second game of that Saturday doubleheader, when Lefty Williams won his twenty-third victory of the season, 5–2. On Sunday Dickie Kerr held the Browns to one run and four hits in a 4–1 win. The White Sox may have been back in form, but the losing streak had been costly. When it began on August 27, Chicago stood three and one-half games ahead of the staggering Indians, with the Yankees another half game behind. As the Tigers arrived for a Labor Day doubleheader, the White Sox had given back all that advantage and more, sitting a game behind the Indians and a handful of percentage points in front of the Yankees. They did sweep that Labor Day doubleheader, with Red Faber and rookie Clarence Hodge doing the pitching. But that only kept pace with Cleveland's sweep of St. Louis.

Dutch Leonard shut them out 5–0 on five hits Tuesday afternoon. Although the entire Chicago offense looked sick, no one left the field more embarrassed than Happy Felsch. The irony was that Felsch provided three of the team's five hits. The last of those came in the seventh and followed Joe Jackson's infield single. When Shano Collins worked a walk, the bases were full for Swede Risberg. They did not remain full for long. With Felsch taking an inexplicably long lead considering the game situation, Oscar Stanage picked him off second on the first pitch. "There was no alibi for Hap," Sanborn wrote in the next morning's *Chicago Tribune*. "So far as the situation was concerned, he might better have stood on the base until the ball was hit."[7] Felsch looked even worse when Leonard proceeded to walk Risberg, an act that should have, but did not, force a run across the plate. The defeat dropped the White Sox behind New York into third place, a game and a half out of the lead. Since August 27 they had lost eight of twelve games, six of them to noncontenders.

The Yankees warmed up for their final and pivotal trip west by winning five of seven games from the Red Sox and the Athletics. Babe Ruth returned for the second of those, a 5–3 Friday victory over the Red Sox that also marked Carl Mays's first appearance in a road city since the beaning. That the site happened to be Boston made it that much more significant for Mays, who relieved John Quinn in the eighth inning and claimed his twenty-second victory when Bob Meusel's lucky double fell safely among Red Sox fielders. There were two on and two out when Meusel tried to fall out of the way of a 3-2 fastball, only to have the ball collide with his bat and duck into right-center. A Saturday doubleheader brought a turn-away crowd of thirty-three thousand, including a delegation from the Boston Knights of Columbus, to Fenway Park. The Knights were there to present Ruth with diamond cuff links and, simultaneously, to bask in his reflected glory. They and the other thirty-three thousand received a bonus when some enterprising records maven uncovered the fact that more than two decades earlier a fellow named Perry Werden had hit forty-five home runs for Minneapolis, then a member of the Western League. With Ruth sitting at forty-four home runs when the day began, the discovery made the then-fifty-five-year-old Werden suddenly famous as the "world record holder for home runs in a single season." But not for long. In the third inning of the first game, a 5–3 victory, Ruth's forty-fifth left the park in right field. His forty-sixth came with Sammy Vick on base in the sixth inning of the second game, which the Yankees also led 5–3 entering the bottom of the ninth. But the Red Sox touched Mays for three runs, the last scoring when the pitcher's failure to back up home plate allowed Joe Bush to score on Ping Bodie's overthrow. The last-place Athletics, in New York for a Labor Day doubleheader followed by a Tuesday single game, presented less of a challenge. Hank Thormahlen, Bob Shawkey, and Mays successively dispatched them on a single run and just eleven hits. Mays had been scheduled to open the upcoming western swing, but he was advanced because that swing opened in Cleveland, and Yankees management agreed it would be bad form to even bring the pitcher there, much less start him in one of the games. Col. Tillinghast Huston explained that the decision to hold Mays out was not made "because we think there is any danger of trouble, but out of respect to the feelings of the people there. We don't want to offend them."[8]

The Yankees arrived in Cleveland shorthanded by more than Mays. In advance of the Thursday series opener, the club had stopped off in Pittsburgh for a Wednesday exhibition game against the Pirates. It was the kind of thing ownership might force upon players, if ownership had a gate attraction the likes of Ruth who could bring in an easy extra payday. That it proved to be, with more than twenty-nine thousand attending, the largest crowd to see a ball game in Pittsburgh since the 1909 World Series. And Ruth made it worthwhile, driving a pitch by Jimmy Zinn out of the ballpark in right field in the ninth inning. The Babe circled the bases slowly to an ovation from the National League fans. By then, though, the day's real significance had been painfully realized. In the second Ping Bodie tripled to center field, but fractured his ankle while scoring on a wild pitch. The injury forced manager Miller Huggins to move Ruth to center field, with the unpredictable Meusel back in right and Lewis holding down left. Regular catcher Muddy Ruel, injured in the final game of the Athletics series, was also expected to be side-lined for ten days.

A half game behind the Indians as the series opened, the Yankees were accompanied on their western trip by the Boys Band of the St. Mary's Industrial School of Baltimore. That school's most famous alum, of course, was none other than Babe Ruth. So when a fire destroyed part of the structure, Brother Matthias, the St. Mary's headmaster who had dis-covered Ruth's talents, asked the Babe to ask Ruppert to let the band tag along on a fund-raising trip. The idea was for the fifty-piece band, comprised of youngsters aged six to sixteen, to perform in advance of each game on the road swing, pass the hat, and take in as much cash as possible. Knowing the impossibility of saying anything other than "yes" to his best-paid and most-famous player, Ruppert graciously acceded to the request. In gratitude the kids wrote a new song that they performed at each of their stops. The song was titled "Battering Babe."[9]

If you were to believe the rumor mill, Babe's battering on the eve of the Cleveland series had been all too real. Reports surfaced around New York the morning of Thursday, September 9, of a serious train accident the preceding night on the way to Cleveland in which the Babe and several teammates had, depending on the version, either been severely injured or even killed. The story spread on investment wires in New York, Chicago, Pittsburgh, and several other cities. Since in this instance the rumors were utterly without foundation, it was a simple matter for the Yankees and a vibrant Ruth to dispel them in Cleveland. Huston blamed "sure-thing gamblers" for starting the gossip. "I have no facts on which to base any charge," Huston said. "But one can understand the possibility of gamblers getting unfair odds through just such tricks."[10]

Based purely on the showing in Thursday's opener, nobody needed odds to take the Indians. Speaker sent Coveleski in search of his twentieth victory against Quinn and got it easily. Doc Johnston was the main instigator, his four hits—two of them triples—driving home three runs. The Indians lit up Jack Quinn and three successors for fourteen hits overall, while Coveleski gave up just six. One of those six was Ruth's forty-seventh home run, a spitter that cleared the screen above the right-field wall and bombarded the roof of a frame home along Lexington Avenue, startling two women who lived inside it. "There isn't much I can say about homer No. 47 that I haven't said about all the others," the Babe offered in the next morning's syndicated column.[11]

The victory moved Cleveland a game ahead of Chicago and dropped the Yankees into third place, a game and a half behind. Hopes of the home fans were invigorated both by the result and also by the arrival of Sewell, the kid purchased from New Orleans to take the place of Lunte and Chapman at shortstop. But any sense among the home faithful that a pennant was near was quickly dispatched. Before twenty-six thousand on Friday, Shawkey beat the Indians 6–1 on just six hits. Ruth provided sufficient support when, with one out and Wally Pipp on first, he crashed his forty-eighth home run over the same screen and onto the porch of the same house whose roof he had visited the previous afternoon. With the game out of hand early, Speaker let Sewell take over for Evans at short, but the debut was inauspicious. Shawkey retired him twice, and the youngster fumbled one of his only two chances in the field.

Sewell was back on the bench for Saturday's finale, when Bagby, seeking his twenty-eighth win, opposed Thormahlen, taking Mays's place on the mound. That should have been a mismatch, a sentiment with which gamblers apparently agreed, making the Indians a 3–1 favorite at home. A Cleveland record crowd of more than thirty thousand fans somehow found their way inside Dunn Field to witness it, with an estimated fifteen thousand more turned away. But the mismatch did not favor the Indians. With Pipp at first and one out, Ruth worked a 3-1 count, then unleashed a smash that rattled the right-field wall just foul. The Babe straightened out Bagby's next attempt, scattering the excess fans who had been penned behind ropes in the outfield for a ground-rule double. That left Pipp at third, but he scored on Del Pratt's sacrifice fly. The Yankees added a run in the fifth, then knocked Bagby out with four more in the sixth inning. Thormahlen, meanwhile, gave up only a handful of scattered hits until the home team finally touched him for two consolation runs in the bottom of the ninth, abetted by two Pipp errors.

The outcome left the race back where it had been during much of the past two months: in a state of confusion. Technically Cleveland retained first place, its .617 winning percentage one point better than New York's, with the White Sox three percentage points further behind. But because the Indians had played five fewer games than the Yankees and four fewer than the White Sox, they lingered a half game behind New York with three fewer victories and only two fewer losses. Both clubs came out of the series viewing themselves as front-runners.

The Indians could soothe themselves with the prospect of a week's worth of home games against the last-place Athletics and the sixth-place Senators. There was no better time to break Sewell in, so Speaker assigned him the seventh spot in the batting order for the Sunday opener against Connie Mack's kids. The youngster shared the spotlight with Cleveland's other new star, Mails, getting an infield single and a triple in the 5–2 victory. Mails established himself as a fixture in the rotation by scattering seven hits and allowing just one earned run. On Monday Coveleski won his twenty-first, although not without plenty of help from the A's. With the game tied at 2-all and Speaker on base, Larry Gardner lifted an easy one-out pop-up into foul territory behind first. Either second baseman Jim Dykes or first baseman Ivy Griffin could have made the play, but they ran over each other trying to reach it and the ball fell harmlessly. Reprieved, Gardner lined a three-and-two single to right that sent Speaker around to third base. When the next hitter, George Burns, lifted a fly into short left, Speaker bluffed a break toward the plate in an effort to draw a wild throw from Tilly Walker. He got it; the ball bounded away from catcher Cy Perkins and allowed Speaker to score what would be the winning run.

Eddie Rommel handed the Indians their only defeat of that weeklong stretch on Tuesday, his five-hitter silencing them 8–0. Bagby went Rommel two better on Wednesday, holding the A's to three hits in a 14–0 rout. Indians' bats made merry with Dave Keefe, dispatching him in the second inning of what developed into a twenty-three-hit onslaught. Speaker led the way with four hits, but all thirteen Indians who saw action got at least one.

The Thursday through Saturday games with the Senators were walkovers; at least they were once Sewell scored on a wild pitch in the bottom half of the eighth inning of the opener. To that point Tom Zachary and Mails had matched shutout performances, with Zachary allowing just three hits and Mails just four. Sewell played a key role again on Friday with two hits in Coveleski's twenty-second victory, this one by a far more comfortable 9–3. Caldwell stopped the Senators 7–5 on Saturday when Gardner's three hits, including a triple, produced three runs. Sewell completed his first week as a regular—admittedly against weak competition—with an eye-catching eight hits in twenty-three at bats. "I doubt if any big league baseball team can produce anything that parallels the Indians' feat in going to the bush leagues in the stretch of this hectic season and picking up a pair of rookies to fit in as regulars on a pennant-caliber baseball machine," the *Cleveland Press*'s Ross Tenney wrote, referring to Sewell and Mails.[12]

Having left Cleveland in first place, the Yankees crossed Lake Erie for Detroit, where a three-game sweep produced

Ruth's forty-ninth home run. Greeted by boos and hisses from the Sunday crowd of thirty thousand, Mays allowed hits to the only five batters he faced, four of whom scored. His misfortune turned out to be good news for reliever Rip Collins when the Yankees offense produced thirteen runs and fourteen hits, among them home runs by Pipp and Lewis.

The Sunday outing taxed Mays so little that Huggins threw him right back out on the mound Monday, this time with far different results. He scattered nine hits in a 4–2 victory, his twenty-fourth. Ruth's home run came on a 3-2 pitch from Howard Ehmke in the sixth inning with New York trailing 2–1 and Pipp on first base. The St. Mary's Boys Band greeted the homer with a musical tribute. "I give Ehmke credit for taking a chance," Ruth said in his column the next morning.[13] Shawkey completed the sweep on Tuesday, winning his eighteenth thanks to sixteen Yankees hits, three of which he contributed. Tigers pitchers allowed Ruth little opportunity to join in the massacre, walking him three times, but that only heightened the stakes for Del Pratt, who enjoyed batting behind the Babe to the tune of four hits.

The sweep left New York with a lead of one game over Cleveland as the team train pulled into Chicago for Thursday, Friday, and Saturday games. The White Sox lingered another game and a half behind, giving every appearance of being prepared to collapse into civil war.

The Sox prepared for the arrival of the eastern clubs by beating the Browns 5–3 in a makeup of an earlier rainout. They took the Thursday and Friday games from Boston, both on late rallies. The visitors had taken a 5–0 lead into the bottom of the eighth of the Thursday opener, only to see Chicago score five times in the bottom of the inning against Red Sox starter Joe Bush. Happy Felsch provided the winning run with a sacks-full, two-out hit in the ninth. On Friday Boston's 3–2 lead in the bottom of the eighth was undone by daring Chicago base running. The White Sox had the bases full and one out when pinch hitter Eddie Murphy tapped easily back to pitcher Waite Hoyt, who threw home for a force out of the lead runner. Red Sox catcher Wally Schang had plenty of time to double Murphy at first, but his throw hit the base runner in the back, allowing Joe Jackson to score the tying run. When Felsch tore around third and dashed for the plate as well, first baseman Stuffy McInnis threw wildly back to Schang, sending Murphy around to third. Ray Schalk walked; then he and Murphy pulled off a double steal that produced the inning's third run.

Whatever team harmony those outcomes suggested was publicly betrayed in front of a healthy Saturday crowd when Kerr went in search of his eighteenth win against Sam Jones. The trouble started as Boston batted in the fifth, leading 1–0. With a runner at second, Risberg kicked an easy ground ball. Thanks to this and an Eddie Collins error, the Red Sox had two more runs with runners at second and third. When Jones topped a ground ball back at Kerr, the White Sox pitcher saw Oscar Vitt, the runner at third, well off the base and threw to Buck Weaver to get him. Buck dropped the ball, letting Vitt score. By the time the inning ended, Boston led 6–0.

Kerr, known for his confrontational approach, laid into Weaver and Risberg between innings, suggesting another sellout might be afoot. Tempers were quelled momentarily when Jackson's grand slam brought the Sox back within a run at 6–5 entering the sixth. But with a runner on base in the top of that inning, Jackson and Felsch jointly let Mike Menosky's easy fly fall between them for a run-producing triple. Menosky scored a moment later on a fly ball, and a seething Kerr left the mound trailing 8–5.

Kerr was waiting for Jackson and Felsch on the bench when the inning ended and jumped both of them in a plain-sight dugout brawl that soon spread. The game was delayed several minutes while members of the clean and suspicious factions of the team took out their sentiments on one another, and umpires Ollie Chill and Bill Dinneen wrestled with the question of whether to intervene in such internecine strife.

The mental scars of the battle outlasted the physical ones. On Sunday Washington succeeded the Red Sox into town for three games, a set of contests whose integrity would soon be called into question. In the first of those three, Williams got pounded for a dozen hits and journeyman left-hander Harry Courtney shut out the Sox on just five, 5–0. A seven-run sixth and a Felsch home run helped Faber to his twenty-first victory, 15–6, on Monday. But the Sox went dormant again on Tuesday when rookie pitcher Jose Acosta shut them out 7–0. Errors, this time by Amos Strunk, Weaver, and Eddie Collins, again played a part, resulting in three unearned runs.

Some Senators players privately came to the same conclusions that investigators would soon reach: their opponents were not playing on the level. They did not discuss it openly, but they did discuss it, including with the Indians, their next stop on the road trip after Chicago. "[Senators first baseman] Joe Judge tipped me off that Washington smelled something," Cuckoo Jamieson acknowledged decades later of the White Sox's play in those three games. "I didn't know how to pick it up," he said.[14]

While the sports pages detailed the Sox's seeming collapse, the news pages picked up coverage of the gambling rumors. At the Tuesday loss to Washington, a detective patrolling the right-field bleachers arrested three men on charges of betting around $100 on the outcome of the ball game. The *Chicago Daily News* accorded the subsequent trial extensive coverage but also criticized the police and Sox management for what the newspaper viewed as selective prosecution. "Big gamblers were operating almost behind the home players' bench," the paper reported, telling of wagers between $300 and $350.[15] The problem was enforcement. Since the parties all knew one another and operated on mutual credit, no transfer of cash was involved. That made it impossible for authorities to legally prove that wagering had taken place.

The first-place Yankees arrived in Chicago on the night train from Detroit via Toledo, where they played a Wednesday exhibition game in which Ruth hit two home runs. "In first place by right of might," the *New York American* observed.[16] The teams' comparative fortunes made New York a prohibitive favorite to win and possibly sweep the series. Doing so would have effectively eliminated the White Sox from contention and left New York with both a standings and a schedule edge on the Indians. The latter was so because after Chicago only the Browns, the Senators, and the Athletics remained for New York to deal with; the Indians and the White Sox had three games left with each other. Beyond that the Yanks came in having won five straight and eight of their last nine. The White Sox could claim just a .500 record—and that against mediocre competition—since Labor Day.

Those dour sentiments did not prevent twenty-five thousand from showing up at Comiskey Park for the first game on Thursday. What they witnessed both surprised and delighted them. The home team knocked out Quinn in the second inning and worked over a succession of relievers for fourteen hits on the way to an 8–3 victory, Kerr's eighteenth. Ruth batted five times in the quest for his fiftieth home run and failed every time, taking a called third strike in the sixth inning when he represented the tying run. "I shouldn't have let that last one slip over, but that's all in the game," Ruth said.[17] The Yankees had plenty of chances, leaving eleven on base.

The loss threw the Yankees into what amounted to a deadlock with Cleveland for first, with the White Sox another half game behind. It also renewed hope in Chicago in advance of Friday's game pitting Faber against Thormahlen in front of more than thirty thousand. "The fans here have canceled the order for lilies for the White Sox funeral," the *New York Times* correspondent observed.[18]

Huggins's choice of Thormahlen, a season-long fill-in, said something about the status of Yankees pitching for this critical series. The problem was compounded by the disheveled state of the New York defense since Bodie's injury. With two out in the first, Eddie Collins lashed what should have been a double toward Meusel, continued to third when Meusel took his time fielding the ball, then scored when Meusel threw it wildly back into the infield. Jackson and Felsch followed with triples of their own. Risberg added yet a fourth three-bagger in the second, scoring on Faber's squeeze bunt. It was 3–0.

Huggins called Mays, scheduled to start Saturday, out of the bullpen instead for the third inning. Mays allowed three more runs the rest of the way, although two of them were unearned due to an error by third baseman Aaron Ward.

As had been the case on Thursday, Ruth provided no help to the Yankees' comeback efforts. He went hitless in three official at bats, walking once and coming no closer to anything consequential than a fly ball directed at Felsch in the eighth. That catch prompted an exodus from the seats among fans who reasoned that with the Sox leading by four runs and Ruth unlikely to bat again, the game was no longer of interest. They turned out to be correct, although the visitors did add a pair of runs in the ninth.

The crowd Ruth drew later that evening was smaller but no less enthusiastic. Proprietors of a southside establishment called The Edelweiss, which until Prohibition had been an outdoor beer garden, contracted with the slugger to show up both Friday and Saturday nights. He was to smile, have a drink, and entertain the customers, who enjoyed what the emporium advertised as "phosphates."

Although one might expect the key player on a team that had just dropped two very meaningful games—and that had a third coming up the following afternoon—to think better of such a gig, that was not Ruth's way. The gregarious hero arrived right on time, stayed for an hour each night, glad-handed hordes of Chicagoans, signed autographs, posed for pictures, and generally had a swell evening. Eventually somebody in the crowd demanded a "speech," and the Babe was only too happy to comply. As recorded by witnesses, this was the speech in its entirety: "I haven't much to say and I hardly know how to say it, but I hope you all have a hell of a good time."[19] It was the kind of rhetorical expression the Chicago crowd could relate to.

Another forty-three thousand jammed into Comiskey for the Sunday wrap-up. That game was to have pitted Cicotte against Mays, but Huggins's use of his Saturday starter in relief on Friday meant that Shawkey, who had pitched the final game of the Detroit series, had to be moved ahead. The decision proved disastrous for New York. Shawkey recorded only four outs and surrendered seven runs in six innings before Huggins could replace him with George Mogridge. The Sox tore into all four Yankees pitchers they saw, collecting twenty-two hits, four each by Shano Collins, Weaver, and Felsch. Cicotte allowed eleven hits, but it hardly mattered. The Sox led 8–0 after two innings and 13–2 after four, eventually winning 15–9. Again Ruth accomplished less in the sunlight than at night, producing one hit in four at bats. It was his only hit in a dozen official trips against Sox pitchers.

Instead of sinking the White Sox, the stunning series sweep essentially sank the Yankees. They left Chicago in third place, two games behind the Indians and a half game behind Chicago. Worse, the schedule that a few days before had looked so advantageous—with no games remaining against contenders—now loomed as a millstone, for it provided no catch-up opportunities.

The White Sox, by contrast, came out of the series suddenly emboldened. They still had three games to play with the only team in front of them. The games were to be played in Cleveland to be sure, but a sweep could wash away that one-and-one-half-game deficit.

By mid-September the looming question was whether events outside the Sox's control would allow them to contest that series in Cleveland. Day by day the grand jury had been probing around the edges of the gambling rumors. Many in Chicago were dissatisfied with the progress made by investigators to that point and concerned about the prospect of the corrupted Sox again reaching the World Series. One of them, *Chicago Tribune* sports reporter James Cruisenberry, gave the jurors a nudge that was as effective as it was blunt and contrived. Cruisenberry knew that any appeal appearing under his byline would have the appearance of bias, and for that reason would not be taken seriously. So he drafted a powerful letter, then convinced Fred Loomis, a prominent businessman and well-known baseball fan, to sign it. The letter, which was designed to refocus the jury on the rumors regarding the 1919 World Series, appeared on the *Tribune*'s front page on Sunday, September 19, exactly as the sports pages reported the sweep of the Yankees. The Loomis letter, the *Tribune* asserted in an accompanying unsigned article, "asks questions which are upon the lips of nearly every White Sox fan."[20]

The Cruisenberry-Loomis letter had the desired effect.

12. Eddie Chews, Chicago Stews

September 19–25

Jimmy Cruisenberry's "Fred Loomis" letter may have been bogus, but it was also incendiary and effective. In 1920 America entered an era famous for its self-absorption. But that did not mean Americans had abandoned fundamental notions of ethical behavior. The animated paradigm of right and wrong was baseball. This was true in part because baseball proclaimed it to be so, but also in part because there were no viable alternatives. Baseball was the only professional team sport of consequence. And although individual sports could generate heroes of the stripe of boxer Jack Dempsey or golfer Walter Hagen, their games came across as either too elitist (golf and tennis) or too suspect (boxing and horse racing). Nobody cared whether the former were legitimate; the latter were assumed not to be.

Of all its sporting pastimes, the ticket-buying public only invested faith in the integrity of one. That's why when Cruisenberry-Loomis declared, "Up to this time baseball has been accepted by the public as the one clean sport . . . engaged in by men . . . whose honesty and integrity have been beyond suspicion," the sentence carried mobilizing power.[1]

Cruisenberry and Loomis tapped into a widely held concept

of the time: that baseball was important metaphorically as well as in practice. The concept could only be sold in connection with an institution that had actually presented itself as a metaphor for national virtue—precisely what baseball had done since A. G. Spalding. "The game must be protected," the letter asserted. And if the pursuit of any challenge to that national virtue threatened players involved in the institution, then so be it. "The public is interested in the game more than they are interested in the players," Cruisenberry-Loomis wrote. Note that the interests of owners such as Comiskey, whose investments might also have been threatened, were merely assumed to be neutral to the eventual outcome. They were, after all, "sportsmen."[2]

Nothing in the letter evinced a regard for processes or rights; the issue related fully to the end result. It did not even matter that there was no statutory ban against conspiring to fix the outcome of a baseball game. In September 1920 all that was important involved protecting baseball's virtue. "Those who have in their possession the evidence of gambling last fall in the world series should come forward with it and present it in a manner that may give assurance in the whole country that justice will be done in this case where the confidence of the people seems to have been so flagrantly violated," Cruisenberry-Loomis asserted.[3]

Although Cruisenberry's *Chicago Tribune* published the Loomis letter, it was the rival *Herald and Examiner* that initially pushed the investigative process. With a succession of inch-high front-page headlines, the paper fed readers details of the ongoing closed-door grand jury investigation. One of its reporters cornered Henry Brigham, the head of the grand jury, and got from him several admissions. Suspicion focused on Arnold Rothstein, the best-known underworld figure at the time. A little-known former player named Bill Burns and a former featherweight boxing champion, Abe Attell, were also suspected, working either jointly or independently. *Herald and Examiner* investigators claimed to have connected unnamed New York gamblers—one of whom was presumably Rothstein—to $1 million (about $12 million today) in successful bets against the White Sox during the 1919 World Series.

On the field New York's thorough squandering of its prospects in Chicago left the Yankees needing a revival of Ruthian proportions. Entering the season's final two weeks, they trailed the Indians by two and the White Sox by a half game with no games remaining against either opponent. That meant that, aside from the Sox's scheduled three-game visit to Cleveland on September 23–25, Ruth and his teammates relied on also-rans to help them get back in the race. The first of those also-rans—the final stop on their western swing—were the unhelpful Browns.

The problem was Frank "Dixie" Davis, a twenty-nine-year-old rookie of no particular note against any other American League team. For the season Davis's record was eighteen wins, twelve losses. But Davis had a personal hex against the Yankees. As he took the home mound on Sunday, September 19, for the first game of a series that New York had to sweep, the rookie Browns pitcher had already bested New York five times without a defeat. Facing both their nemesis and thirty thousand St. Louis fans, the visitors never had a chance; they collected just two hits and allocated a mere 104 minutes to the 6–1 defeat. The Yankees had to share the St. Louis headlines, however, with the Boys Band of the St. Mary's Industrial School and with Brother Matthias. As had been its standard previously on the trip, the band performed for donations prior to the game, and the Babe's discoverer gave interviews to the local media. He admitted that he used to spank the young ballplayer when he didn't get a hit. "It looks as if he ought to take him over his knee again," the *New York Times* correspondent opined.[4]

In the *New York American* Damon Runyon offered another, and more sobering, perspective on Ruth. Runyon said that ballplayers he had talked to expressed relief that as hard as Ruth hit the ball, his swing had a predictable pull. If he went up the middle, players told Runyon, there would be more serious injuries and even fatalities. "A ball thrown by Carl Mays had sufficient force to crack Ray Chapman's skull," Runyon noted. "Ruth drives a ball from his bat ten times harder than the strongest man can throw."[5]

The Yankees did rebound to win the final two games, one of them Mays's 4–3, eleven-inning victory before a crowd that greeted him with boos and hisses. But those two wins represented a failure measured against the three games that the Indians took from Boston or the three that the White Sox seized against Philadelphia that weekend. Now the Yanks trailed by three games with only seven remaining. It meant that even if they had won all seven games, either the Sox or the Indians could clinch by playing just slightly better than .500 ball. As a practical matter the September 19 loss to Davis, following as it did the humiliation in Chicago, reduced interest in the Yankees to whether the Babe would hit his fiftieth home run. The American League race was down to two teams.

Ruth settled the home run matter at the earliest possible moment upon his return home. Facing Washington's Jose Acosta, a Cuban and one of the game's first Latin players, he rattled the facing of the upper deck in the first inning of a September 24 doubleheader at the Polo Grounds. His fifty-first followed in the first inning of the second game. "The crowd went mad. . . . Babe Ruth is the greatest showman of these times," Runyon wrote.[6]

To the chagrin of a huge crowd, the Babe's fiftieth proved to be Acosta's only failing; he allowed no runs for the remainder of the game, and the Senators won 3–1. New York won the second game, but when Washington beat the Yanks again on Saturday the mourning began in earnest, for the result left the Yankees three games behind with only four more on the schedule. Ruth worked those four games for three more homers; his final total of fifty-four nearly doubled the previous big league record of twenty-nine, which he had hit the year before. His fans were happy, and so was the Babe, who took special delight in delivering in front of the same St. Mary's delegation that had followed the team on its western swing. "It was like coming back to the old home town a millionaire after making a fortune in the big city," he said of the reception given him by the New York crowd.[7]

The fight between Cleveland and Chicago raged as hot as ever on both the playing field and legal fronts. The on-field action was both easier and more uplifting to follow. Entering the final series before Cleveland's showdown with the White Sox, Indians fans had every reason to believe that if their team won that series they would win the pennant. Although the two teams were tied in victories at eighty-eight, Cleveland had played three fewer games, leaving the Indians with a game and a half to lose in the standings. Unless they stumbled in eleven games against lesser opponents—the Red Sox, the Browns, and the Tigers—Chicago would have to sweep the Cleveland series to erase that lead. Only the fourth-place Browns, from whom the Indians had won eleven of the previous eighteen, appeared to present much of an obstacle. Speaker's team had already beaten the Red Sox and the Tigers a combined twenty-six times in thirty-seven games.

Oddly White Sox fans—at least those not driven to distraction by the court proceedings—could derive hope from the same type of math. Their favorites had eight remaining games against the Browns, the Tigers, and the Athletics, against whom their combined record to that point was 43–15.

Bagby's twenty-ninth victory was a 2–0 shutout of Boston on September 19. Red Sox starter Herb Pennock was almost as good, but in the sixth Speaker and Elmer Smith tapped him for consecutive doubles to right, and Doc Johnston singled Smith home one batter later. Bagby wobbled only in the ninth. The first batter, pinch hitter Eddie Foster, drove a pitch to the edge of the roped-off crowd on the field in left, but Joe Evans caught it. With two out Bagby walked the tying runs on base before striking out Tim Hendryx.

A day later Mails allowed a dozen hits and three second-inning runs. But Larry Gardner drove across six runs with two triples and a single in an 8–3 Indian victory. Stan Coveleski's seven-hit performance in the series' final game amounted to overkill, since the Indians led 9–0 after four and won 12–1. Celebrating his twenty-eighth birthday, Smith delivered three hits including a home run, the whole good for four RBIs.

Like the Indians the White Sox lived dangerously in their Sunday series opener with the Athletics. Kid Gleason started Lefty Williams, around whom locker-room suspicions circulated due to ghastly performances in games against the Red Sox and the Senators during the previous few weeks. "He wasn't right," *Chicago Tribune* beat writer I. E. Sanborn succinctly said of Williams.[8] Gleason obviously concurred, for he lifted the twenty-one-game winner after just three innings, with the White Sox already trailing 3–0. Chicago still trailed Ed Rommel, who passed for an ace among the A's, 4–1 entering the sixth when singles by Eddie Collins, Joe Jackson, Happy Felsch, and Swede Risberg set up a four-run inning capped by Risberg's steal of home with the eventual winning run.

After that brush with an upset, the A's performed at Comiskey like the tailenders they were. On Monday the Sox breezed to a 13–6 win. On Tuesday Chicago bats produced four runs in the first inning, knocking Scott Perry from the mound in favor of Rommel. Felsch stifled the last threat by the visitors in the third. Chicago led 4–2 when he raced to the scoreboard in center for a one-handed flag of a potential Joe Dugan triple with the tying runs on base. Reprieved, Cicotte settled down, and the Sox touched Rommel for four more runs in the sixth. The final score was 9–2.

With a Wednesday off day for both contenders, fans in the two cities and elsewhere made an effort to focus on the big series of games about to begin. That was relatively easy in Cleveland, a city that had never hosted a World Series game. Indians officials announced that the World Series itself was already a sellout. "That surely is confidence," remarked Oscar Reichow in the *Chicago Daily News*.[9] Cleveland insiders did not sense such confidence among the Indians backers. They awoke the morning of the first game to S. M. Bell's declaration in the *Plain Dealer*: "About 5 p.m. today Cleveland's thousands of baseball fans who slept last night with their left toes crossed will know considerably more about their World Series plans than they did when they got up."[10]

But as hard as fans—or players, for that matter—tried, focusing on the games was difficult in an increasingly bipolar baseball culture. Part of the distraction was mere talk. In Chicago the *Tribune* reported without attribution that investigators hired by Comiskey had fruitlessly probed St. Louis for evidence of corruption following the 1919 World Series. Word leaked that Comiskey had personally met with suspected gambling figures—almost certainly Joe Gedeon—as part of the inquiry. Comiskey's effort too had produced nothing.

The same newspaper took a shot at Ban Johnson's diminished stature as measured by the absence of any role for him in the inquiry. "So far as is known, President Comiskey has not talked with President Johnson regarding the scandal," it reported. "Meanwhile, the fans are still wondering."[11]

In the *New York Tribune* W. O. McGeehan repeated a rumor to the effect that the Tigers planned to "lay down" for the Indians in their season-ending series. "It might be well for the league officials to watch those last four games," McGeehan asserted.[12]

League officials already had plenty to watch in the Chicago grand jury room. The day before the first game in Cleveland, four members of the Chicago Cubs were summoned from their team as it traveled from Boston to New York and ordered to return to Chicago to answer grand jury summonses. Published reports suggested that the players—pitchers Nick Carter and Claude Hendrix and infielders Fred Merkle and Buck Herzog—were expected to testify not merely about the supposed fixed game involving the Phillies and the Cubs earlier that summer but also about the 1919 Series. Cruisenberry reported that two of the players—he did not identify them—were prepared to tell the grand jury that they had been told by yet another player that the Reds were sure-thing winners of that Series' first two games.

Assistant state's attorney Hartley Replogle, in charge of

the investigation, fed the street talk. "The last World Series between the Chicago White Sox and the Cincinnati Reds was not on the square," he told reporters. "From five to seven players on the White Sox team are involved." He labeled the four Cubs players as critical to the inquiry.[13]

Among players Herzog was suspected of being a shady, if talented, character. A thirty-five-year-old veteran of thirteen big league seasons, he had been a regular on four Giants pennant winners since 1911. But Herzog had bumped around since the last of those pennant seasons, 1917, and had come to the Cubs from Boston for Les Mann and Charlie Pick in August 1919. With each bump rumors accumulated. One identified him and Hal Chase as having offered pitcher Rube Benton $800 to lose a game in 1919. Others implied crookedness in either or both the 1917 and the 1918 World Series, when Herzog played with the Giants and the Cubs, respectively. Indeed, he arrived in Chicago to find Benton also scheduled to talk to the grand jury. "Benton knows a whole lot," Replogle confided to the city. Replogle said Benton "was offered $750 [implying that the offer came from Herzog] to lose a game that he pitched."[14] But Benton, Herzog, Carter, Merkle, and Hendrix all had to wait their turn. That same day the jury also heard behind closed doors from Comiskey, Johnson, and Cubs president William Veeck.

Veeck delivered reports written by private investigators hired by the Cubs but did not publicly indicate whether those reports dealt with the Series rumors. Johnson admitted to the jury that he had heard reports of a Series fix the previous fall, but whether he discussed his own failure to address those reports is unknown; Johnson did not suggest he had. He also claimed to have visited recently with Rothstein in an effort, he told the jury, to get some sort of inquiry going.

The Rothstein visit proved unproductive; apparently no one had told Johnson that big-time gamblers rarely accept opportunities to discuss their accomplishments.

But Johnson offered reporters another bombshell, this one aimed directly at his enemy's team. He openly repeated the rumors that the Sox remained in the thrall of gamblers, who were in the process of manipulating the ongoing race. "I heard several weeks ago a vague statement that the White Sox would not dare win the pennant this season," Johnson said.[15] He asserted that gamblers had "made heavy bets" on the Indians to win the upcoming critical series, and that the Sox players had been instructed to lay down.

Harvey Woodruff, whose In the Wake of the News column had steadfastly denied the fix talk, modified his position. For the first time he conceded that "so many rumors and circumstantial evidence . . . [led] one to believe reluctantly that some games may have been thrown." He would not yet go all in, however. "The Wake never has believed it possible to secure eight players on one team for a frame. . . . Someone would have refused the money lure and blown the whole scheme." The number of corrupt players, Woodruff asserted, must be smaller.[16]

Outside Chicago, though, the desire for a clean breast of things was in full force. "Baseball belongs to the public," Runyon wrote. "The public is entitled to know what sinister forces threaten the safety of the game. Someone knows something, or someone lies. Let's have the whole story."[17]

Comiskey emerged from his half-hour session with no comment on what information, if any, he had delivered. He had, he told reporters, been instructed not to talk. But apprised of Johnson's accusations, he was livid. "It was a terrible thing to report the blackmail of my players just before they went into a series against Cleveland," he asserted.[18] Comiskey more than suggested a conflict of interest on the part of Johnson, who had once privately financed the Indians and, he insinuated, may have retained a share of the team stock. Johnson's backers leaped to his defense. "Charles A. Comiskey makes a rather sorry figure trying to lay the blame for the White Sox not being cleaned out last fall on the shoulders of Ban Johnson," argued Elbert Sanders in the *Sporting News*. "Everyone can imagine what a howl would have gone up from Commy's associates had Johnson ordered the dismissal of a single White Sox last fall, at a time when he was grappling with Comiskey in the Mays case war."[19]

Amid the mutual backbiting Comiskey remained publicly convinced of his team. "The White Sox," he said, "are going to clean up on those Indians tomorrow afternoon."[20]

Gleason awoke in Cleveland to Johnson's intimation of ongoing crookedness with the same sense of outrage expressed by Comiskey. But since the league president himself was the source of the comment, Gleason had no place to turn for refuge. If he challenged Johnson too directly, he risked being suspended at the worst possible moment. So he issued as strong a denial as he could under the circumstances and hoped his team's performance on the field would speak loudest. "We are trying our best to win the pennant, all reports to the contrary notwithstanding," he told reporters at the park.[21]

Some of his players privately told a different story. Decades later Joe Wood said he had run into Eddie Cicotte at the visitors' hotel during that final series. "Cicotte told me . . . 'we don't dare win,'" Wood said.[22]

Nearly thirty thousand fans forced their way into the twenty-one-thousand-capacity park for that Thursday opener.

The overflow meant that ropes went back up in left and center fields. The fans were not only numerous; they had been roused by the morning headlines to approach the point of violence. It was obviously one thing to envision losing the pennant under circumstances as tragic as those presented by the death of the popular Chapman. But losing to a team of crooks was beyond rational consideration. To the standard retinue of calls of "Shipyard" and "slacker" that greeted Jackson and some of the others, new epithets were added. The most printable: "traitor" and "cheater."

Gleason sent Kerr out to face Bagby, who was seeking his thirtieth victory overall and sixth against Chicago. When Risberg's first-inning error let Evans score, conspiracy theorists could read into that bobble whatever they chose.

The correct read turned out to be nothing more than a routine error. With two out, Risberg on third, Schalk at first, and Kerr at the plate in the top of the fourth, Gleason gambled on a double steal. Given Kerr's minimal credentials with the bat, it wasn't actually much of a gamble once you assumed the Sox were playing to win, and it paid off when O'Neill made the jug-headed decision to try to throw Schalk out at second. Schalk made it, and Risberg trotted home with the tying run.

One of the rewards of studying the records of old-time ball games is the prospect of running into an occurrence that simply would not be allowed to happen today because no manager could tolerate the second-guessing that would follow if things went terribly wrong. Such a moment unfolded in the bottom of the fourth inning. Johnston slapped a one-hopper back into Kerr's glove. To call what any fielder was wearing in 1920 a "glove" is to use the loosest possible descriptive form, because concepts such as webbing were only just then being introduced. Most players, Kerr among them, wore something more nearly resembling an oversized leather dress glove with the fingers laced together at the top to form intimations of a pocket. Since the gloves provided only minimal protection, the best fielders depended on their own finger dexterity to make plays. In this case the ball slammed into the middle finger of Kerr's gloved hand and dislocated it. Kerr may not have been on the mound for his dexterity, but he was there for his toughness. Maintaining his composure, he picked up the ball and threw it to first for the out. Then he called time, ran into the dugout, allowed Gleason to put the finger back into its proper place, ran back onto the field, and resumed retiring the Indians in order.

The game remained tied into the sixth, when Jackson lofted a fly ball toward left leading off. Ordinarily Evans would have made easy work of it. But the ball carried into the on-field crowd for a ground-rule double as Evans stood and watched. It was a small bit of misfortune, but it rattled the Indians. Felsch tried to sacrifice the lead run over to third base and got a bonus when Bagby threw the ball over Bill Wambsganss's head trying to retire the batter at first. Jackson scored on the error. With Felsch now at second, Collins reprised the bunt strategy, and this time Wambsganss dropped Bagby's good throw. Risberg's base hit pushed Felsch across, and Collins followed with Chicago's fourth run a moment later when Kerr's ground out took Johnston too far toward second to permit any play at the plate. Six more runs in the seventh and the eighth—for a 10–3 final score—left the Sox just a half game behind the Indians.

But if the Sox won the game on the field in Cleveland, they got pounded in the public relations contest playing out simultaneously outside the Chicago grand jury room. Reports surfaced that noted Chicago gambler Mont Tennes had lost eighty thousand dollars on the first two World Series games, and that famed Broadway producer George M. Cohan had lost thirty thousand dollars. Both principals initially disputed the assertions, then modified their denials, and it is not possible today to sort out the extent of truth in either claim. But the mere assertion was damning. Grand jury foreman Brigham stepped into the hallways long enough to condemn gambling's influence on baseball, and he ominously did so in the present tense. "Chicago, New York, Cincinnati and St. Louis gamblers are bleeding baseball and corrupting players," he told reporters. Brigham vowed to "go the limit in this inquiry," adding, "I am shocked at the rottenness so far revealed."[23]

Friday was Williams's regular turn for the Sox; he would have been working on a standard four days of rest. But Gleason, still suspicious of his veteran left-hander, bypassed him for Faber. Since Speaker had been forced to use nineteen-game winner Ray Caldwell in relief of Bagby Thursday, his only option was Duster Mails, making the sixth Major League start of his life. Speaker also talked Indians owner Jim Dunn into one other adjustment. Frustrated by Jackson's would-be out that fell for a critical double, he lobbied to keep fans off fair territory. Since every paying customer who got through the gates put cash into Dunn's pocket, this was a large demand indeed, but Dunn agreed to restrict fans to foul territory. The Thursday loss depressed Friday's attendance to about twenty thousand, necessitating the placement of just a few fans in the left-field foul territory.

Mails turned out to be an inspired choice, a fact he apparently never doubted. "Have you ever heard of Shoeless Joe Jackson, Buck Weaver, and Eddie Collins?" umpire Billy Evans was said to have taunted him during warm-ups? "Sure," Mails replied "but have they ever heard of the Great Mails?" He backed up the talk, limiting the Sox to just three hits, all of them singles. The Indians touched Faber for a run in the first, another in the second, and nobody reached home plate for either side the rest of the afternoon. Joey Sewell delivered three hits.

All the afternoon's drama was compacted into the top half of the fifth inning, and it is not much of a stretch to suggest that the outcome of the pennant race hung on the making of those three outs. For more than a few fleeting instants during that inning, Mails looked exactly like the bush-leaguer everybody assumed he was.

Risberg's whiff opened the inning, and fans showed only a touch of concern when Schalk worked Mails for a walk. After all, Faber was next, and Faber had a reputation as an easy out even by the standards of pitchers. But Faber did not need to hit; Mails walked him as well, and on four pitches to boot. If Mails was becoming rattled, the veteran Strunk, next up, could be counted on to wait him out. Strunk took a fastball low and away, then a second one high. Speaker called time and dashed in from center field, hopeful of settling Mails down. Speaker had no good options. Morton and Clark were warming up in the bullpen, but both were for use only in desperate circumstances. Bagby and Caldwell had been burned in the Thursday torching, and Coveleski was needed for the Saturday finale. Worse, the heart of the Sox order—Weaver, Eddie Collins, and Jackson—followed Strunk.

Speaker returned to his position, hopeful that Mails could find himself against Strunk. No such luck. Ball three almost hit the batter. The fourth pitch cut the plate for a strike with Strunk taking all the way. The 3-1 was six inches outside.

The bases were full on walks, as Weaver, batting .330, was at the plate.

The stadium was apoplectic with fear as Buck took the first pitch high. Mails followed with a strike. Weaver sent one foul into the seats, then took the fourth pitch wide. The fifth was down the middle, and Weaver missed with his best hack. Strike three. Now there were two out. But Collins, a .360 hitter, remained.

Suddenly hope vied with despair inside Dunn Field; Mails and the fans regained their lost poise simultaneously. Mails's first pitch tied Collins up, glanced off his bat, and rolled foul. So did the second. A notorious contact hitter, Collins shortened up his grip to maximize his chances for contact. Collins was more than just savvy; he was also superstitious. An inveterate gum chewer, he had developed the habit of removing his gum and placing it atop the bill of his cap when he hit. But superstition dictated that it remain there only until there were two strikes; then he would begin chewing again. So Collins called time, plucked the gum from his cap, and placed it back in his mouth.

Mails tried for the corner, but veteran plate umpire Brick Owens wouldn't give him the call. Mails fired waist-high and just outside, and Collins lashed it high toward left. Had the ball stayed fair it would have tied the game and put runners at second and third for Jackson. But it landed foul among the overflow spectators.

Collins stepped out, got back in, and took another pitch high. Now the count was 2-2. Collins swung again and sent another screamer on a long arc down the left-field line. Again it flew deep into the crowd, barely foul. The next 2-2 was a fastball letter high. Collins cut and missed. The Sox second baseman would make nearly seven hundred plate appearances in 1920 and strike out fewer than twenty times, but that's what he had done in the decisive moment of the pivotal game against a pitcher who had been in the Minors a month earlier.

The din that erupted with Collins's missed contact was so loud that Indians players resorted to shielding their ears with their fingers as they approached the dugout. Having survived that crisis, Mails held the Sox to one hit the rest of the way and retired the final ten Chicagoans he faced in order. Cleveland was again ahead by a game and a half and by three in the loss column. Even if Chicago won on Saturday, the Indians would hold first place entering the season's final week. It was enough to sweep even the staid editorial page of the *Cleveland Plain Dealer* into fandom. "The average Clevelander . . . knows, not merely guesses, that the pennant is ours. And then—and then! Words fail. What will it matter that a presidential campaign is on, that the League of Nations referendum is about to be settled, that bolshevist Russia gnashes its teeth at civilization?"[24]

White Sox players, already frustrated by the unlikely shutout, arrived in their locker room to face something more dreaded. It was a phone call from Charles Dryden, sports editor of the *Chicago Herald and Examiner*. His paper had prepared an article publicly identifying eight players as under investigation for fixing the 1919 World Series. The eight were Weaver, Felsch, Williams, Risberg, Jackson, Cicotte, Fred McMullin, and the retired Chick Gandil. Although there had been open talk much of the summer, it was the first time any publication had actually committed the names and charges to paper. The article implicated Attell, as well as Chase, in what was described as a one-hundred-thousand-dollar gambling ring.

Dryden's particular focus was Cicotte, who vociferously and repeatedly denied the allegation, having no other choice in the presence of his teammates. He told Dryden that he had never bet on a game and dismissed talk of a World Series fix as idle gossip. Cicotte did admit to having his check for the loser's share held up, but saw that as a bookkeeping issue. His tone was defiant. "I'm pitching tomorrow," he told Dryden, "and we're going to beat the hell out of the Indians."[25]

Cicotte got it half right. The Sox did win 5–2 in front of thirty thousand that Saturday, but he never saw the field. Instead Gleason turned back to Williams, playing a hunch founded on the left-hander's four wins in five previous starts against Cleveland.

Given that the suspects' names now freely floated around the park, the Sox knew there would be hell to pay once they took the field. Among the accused eight Gandil was safe in California, while McMullin and Cicotte watched from the bench. But the other five all played key roles in the day's events. "Cincinnati! Cincinnati!" That's all Williams heard when he took the mound. Jackson delivered a fifth-inning home run, then circled the bases to the kinds of hisses a vaudeville villain might expect. Jackson flipped the thirty thousand off rounding third, so they hissed even louder. If not a noble gesture, Jackson's was at least an expressive one.

The Sox had no defense, though, for the public lashing they were now taking. In the *Herald and Examiner* Dryden ridiculed any World Series contested by the White Sox, face-tiously declaring that the paper had "secured the services of the well-known crooked gambler, Mr. Montague Buzzard, to cover the series for [it]." Dryden assured readers that "after reading Mr. Buzzard's inside dope, the timid fish [would] know which side to bet on and make a cleaning."[26] In the same paper columnist George Phair riffed on a baseball classic:

> Oh somewhere in this favored land the sun is shining bright.
> And somewhere fans are singing in their uncontrolled delight.
> But in the town of Mudville there is bitterness and shame.
> For Casey, Mighty Casey, went and threw the game.[27]

13. Losers Laugh, Winners Cry

To the average American who follows baseball more closely than he follows affairs of state, recent revelations may well destroy all faith in the general rightness of the world. From the 10-year-old boy burrowing under the fence of a baseball field to the middle aged and hilarious fan, the shock will be deep and pitiful. It is literally true, perhaps, that nothing could so undermine the average American's confidence in society as the discovery of corruption in organized baseball. —*Chicago Daily News*, September 25, 1920

September 26–October 3

This editorial was published by a serious and respected American daily newspaper to express the commonly held values of contemporary culture. It was neither intended nor interpreted as hyperbole. Can you imagine a way to meaningfully update the final sentence for a contemporary audience? "It is literally true that nothing could so undermine the average American's confidence in society as the discovery of corruption in . . ." Government? Business? Religion? Professional sports? The closest I can come to a serious answer—*American Idol*—illustrates the real difference between American society nearly a century ago and the modern version. Our grandparents were not jaded. They actually, wholeheartedly, and sincerely believed in some things, notably including baseball.

And us? Not a chance. You can't slip anything past us because we're too cynical to believe in higher standards in the first place. We understand we're all basically in it for ourselves, some just more competently than others. In the modern interpretation steroids are more a means to an end than a violation of any morality code. The violation is the classic Spartan one, getting caught without a good explanation.

In 1920 people actually believed ballplayers lived by a code, and that the game was overseen by a benevolent structure. The structure's ongoing collapse—first the undermining of Ban Johnson, then Ray Chapman's death, and finally the exposure of the Black Sox—cumulatively revealed the absence of the code and by extension the fallacy of public faith. It became important to the nation's cultural well-being that the Indians, and not the White Sox, reap the reward of the pennant race. "Hard-boiled as some of these players may be, they must sense the feeling that the public has against their appearance in the World Series at this time," argued the *Sporting News* in a late-September editorial. Unlike the *Chicago Daily News*, its publisher, C. C. Spink, did not go so far as to link a White Sox pennant with the destruction of civilization, but he did see in the outcome the game's future. "It would be a calamity for that team to participate," Spink wrote. "It might be said that the fall of the league is at stake."[1]

Fortunately they could and would turn to Babe Ruth. In the absence of true faith, entertainment value is often a welcome substitute.

The final week of the 1920 schedule featured an odd contrivance which, in retrospect, suggests that whoever made it up saw the scandal's exposure coming and carved out a window for precisely that dramatic purpose. Following the conclusion of their series in Cleveland on Saturday, the Sox closed out the home season with a scheduled Sunday game against the Tigers. Then, while most of the other teams played a next-to-last series of games against each other, the Sox (and the Tigers) were scheduled to sit idle from Monday through Thursday before embarking on season-ending Friday–Sunday assignments. In Chicago's case that season-ending series was to be played against the Browns in St. Louis. (The schedule did require one adjustment, a Monday replay of an earlier rainout with the Tigers.) The idle Tuesday through Thursday happened to be a superb opportunity for, oh, perhaps a few confessions.

The White Sox returned from their series victory in Cleveland to as positive a hometown reception as they could have hoped for Sunday morning, given the circumstances. "Regardless of the recent scandal talk, the South Side is loyal to her White Sox," wrote Larry Woltz in the morning *Herald and Examiner*.[2] Twenty-five thousand fans proved their loyalty by buying tickets for the scheduled game against the Tigers that afternoon.

Even assuming no condemnatory intervention by outside forces—an unlikely assumption at that stage—the Sox's task was daunting, their victories over the Indians notwithstanding. In the standings Chicago trailed Cleveland by only one-half game. But the midweek break left Chicago with just five games remaining, Sunday and Monday against Detroit, then the following Friday through Sunday in St. Louis. Even in the unlikely event that Chicago won all five, Cleveland could claim the pennant outright with seven victories in the Indians' final eight games against the same two opponents.

In other words the White Sox lacked control on the field. More significantly they lacked control in the courtroom, where grand jury indictments could force the sidelining of key figures at the worst possible moment for the team's chances.

Increasingly the accused Sox lashed out against the speculation. Weaver and McMullin acknowledged the truth of an unnamed woman's testimony to the grand jury that McMullin had delivered a package to Weaver's home during the 1919 World Series. But they both denied anything nefarious in the event. "The report that McMullin was delivering money, supposedly my share of the 'graft,' is a lie," Weaver said.[3] McMullin confirmed only the visit. "Why I went there is nobody's business but my own," he said.[4]

At least—and for the first time in months—the court developments had quieted all speculation concerning the legitimacy of Chicago's final games. The press, the public, and the players all understood that the legal heat was so directly on the Sox that even the most involved gambling interests would find them too hot to touch. That being so, Cicotte took the mound against the Tigers at Comiskey Park on Sunday afternoon free of speculation concerning his motives.

In what turned out to be a valedictory performance, Cicotte scattered seven Detroit hits and walked just one. The Tigers' only run came in the top of the first; the Sox responded with three of their own and led 8–1 by the end of the fifth. Every positive development—beginning with the team's appearance on the field to start the game—drew a loud and supportive cheer from the throng. There were plenty more occasions to cheer, among them superb defensive plays by Risberg and Jackson. The victory was Cicotte's 21st of the season, and the 209th of his fourteen-season career. At the conclusion of nine uneventful innings, he walked off to a final, resounding cheer from Sox fans. Within forty-eight hours, he would supply them reason to never welcome him back to that mound again.

The Sox's hopes of making up that elusive half-game difference hinged on Cleveland's play in St. Louis. Ray Caldwell started against the Browns, but he surrendered five runs and did not make it out of the first inning. Essentially in desperation Speaker turned to George Uhle, a lightly used twenty-two-year-old in his second big league season. Ten times a winner as a rookie in 1919, Uhle had not enjoyed nearly as much success this year. Preferring to lean on his veterans for the pennant race, Speaker limited Uhle to just six starts and fewer than one hundred innings. Uhle hadn't helped his own cause most of the summer, allowing a base runner and a half per inning and amassing a 5.21 earned run average with just four victories. But on this afternoon he checked the St. Louis threat in the first, then delivered five more shutout innings, almost certainly his strongest performance of the season. In company with Joey Sewell, Uhle also led the winning rally. Sewell produced the first blow, doubling off the wall in right to send the tying runs home with the bases loaded and one out in the third. O'Neill failed to get the lead run home when the Browns turned his infield grounder into an out at the plate. But Uhle's clean single to center sent Sewell across with the sixth run in an eventual 7–5 victory.

Both the Monday schedule and the results reprised Sunday. In Chicago Kerr shut down the Tigers 2–0 on six singles. The Sox hardly fared better against Hooks Dauss, managing just four hits themselves. But they made two of those hits stretch into the game's only two runs. All the action occurred with two out in the sixth when Dauss fired a pitch squarely into Weaver's back. Eddie Collins followed with a single to right, and Jackson parachuted another hit into left, sending Weaver across and moving Collins to third. He didn't stay there long, scoring on Cobb's short-hop throw that skipped away from Tigers shortstop Donie Bush.

Among the spectators at the game was assistant state's attorney Hartley Replogle, reportedly prepared to look into fresh rumors that gamblers had ordered the Sox to lose to the Indians. Given the microscopic lens under which the Sox were playing, the existence of such talk said more about the neurotic mood of baseball than about the legitimacy of the outcome of that particular game. Replogle had to content himself with brief visits with Comiskey, Schalk, and Gleason. Even so, there was legitimate fodder. Felsch was absent, having failed to make the start for reasons that were formally explained as an infected toe. "The brilliant fly chaser will be back in the game Friday afternoon," reported Woltz in the *Chicago Herald and Examiner*.[5] The reality was that whatever the status of Felsch's toe, he had left both the team and the town for Milwaukee. The other reality was that he—like his companions in suspicion—would never play another game of organized baseball.

Again the Sox failed to gain on the Indians, and as had been the case the previous Friday, the reason was Mails. His seventh victory and sixth complete game in seven starts since joining the rotation earlier that month beat Dixie Davis 8–4. As had happened a day earlier, there was an early stumble, this time George Sisler's bases-loaded single that produced a 2–0 St. Louis lead. But the Indians scored in each inning between the fifth and the eighth to take sure command. Cuckoo Jamieson was the batting star, clicking off four hits including a three-run home run, his first of the season.

From such results did confidence spring, and although their lead continued at a mere half game the Indians drew World Series plans. Dunn formally commissioned the construction of six thousand temporary seats in a pavilion situated in deep right-center. Dunn also formally appealed to the National League champion Brooklyn Dodgers to be allowed to use Sewell at shortstop in the Series. Under the rules established by the National Commission—rules essentially identical to those in force today—Sewell was ineligible to play in the Series since he had not been on Cleveland's roster on September 1. Harry Lunte remained crippled by his early-September injury. Barring an exception agreed to by the Dodgers, Cleveland's only option would have been to try to get by with outfielder Joe Evans—the six-game fill-in between Lunte's injury and Sewell's arrival—at shortstop. "Never has any exception to the September 1 rule been made in any World Series, but never has there been an emergency like the present one," Tenney declared in the *Cleveland Press*.[6] The Dodgers consented to Cleveland's use of Sewell.

In Chicago the White Sox spent Monday's postgame hours in full denial mode. "The talk of the World Series being fixed is all a joke; I know nothing about it," Cicotte told the *New York Post*.[7] Comiskey remained formally resolute. He expressed confidence in his team's pennant prospects and vowed that "every player now with the team [would] enter the series."[8] Comiskey did declare that if the players were proved guilty, he would order their immediate ouster. But he viewed himself and his players as more sinned against than sinning. "This entire matter looks to me now as propaganda designed to disturb the morale of the team, and thereby cause it to lose the championship," Comiskey said.[9]

That was not the prevailing sentiment. The *New York Sun*

speculated that Schalk would soon spin a juicy tale for the grand jury. "He may explain why he punched one of the Chicago pitchers on the jaw during the 1919 World Series. . . . He may be able to confirm a report that one of the White Sox bought four houses immediately after the 1919 World Series. He may tell why the Chicago club has been a house divided all season, and why he and Eddie Collins and others decline to pass even the time of day with certain of their teammates."[10] The *Sun*'s indictment of Sox team chemistry, by the way, is—like much of what passed for informed analysis at the moment—a rich mixture of truths, part truths, and untruths. It is beyond question that the Sox played all of 1920 as two teams rather than one. But while Gandil certainly made elaborate purchases funded by a rumored thirty-five thousand dollars in gambling winnings following the Series—including a large automobile and real estate—there is no evidence he spent as wildly as the published reports suggested. Nor is there any evidence that Schalk actually came to blows with Cicotte or Williams during the Series itself.

But eager fans did not have to wait long for the story to straighten itself out. Gleason paid an early visit to Comiskey, one of the men informing the other that Cicotte was on his way down to make a clean breast of things. "I've got to tell you how I double-crossed you," Cicotte is said to have confided. "I'm a crook."[11]

"Don't tell it to me; tell it to the grand jury," the Sox owner is said to have replied.[12] Cicotte did; he went directly downtown to the courthouse, ironically trumping Schalk, who had gone there first thing that morning in hope of being allowed to spill his guts. The Sox catcher remained stuck all day in the grand jury corridor while Cicotte commanded the attention. One of the jurors reported that the pitcher broke down as he recounted his deeds. He named Gandil, Risberg, and McMullin as the ringleaders, saying, "[They] were at me for a week before the World Series started."[13] At the same time, he confirmed the involvement of all eight players, an aspect that would later play critically against Weaver's particular protestations of noninvolvement. "The eight of us . . . got together in my room three or four days before the game started," Cicotte said. "We talked about throwing the series—decided we could get away with it. We agreed to do it."[14]

Cicotte had recently purchased a new farm outside Detroit and needed the money to meet the four-thousand-dollar mortgage. The *Chicago Tribune* reported his motivation succinctly and memorably: "I did it for the wife and kids," he said. The formal indictment of all eight accused players beat Cicotte out the door.[15]

At 1:00 p.m. Jackson succeeded Cicotte into the chamber, where Replogle drew him out on his own role in the business. The transcript of that testimony reveals a deposition replete with embarrassing factual errors, by both Replogle and Jackson, and in that sense raises questions about the reliability of the entire enterprise. At one point, for example, Replogle elicited from Jackson an admission that "a couple" games played in New York during the most recent eastern swing also "looked bad," although Jackson would not go so far as to indict any of his teammates for throwing them.

"Who pitched?" Replogle asked.

"Williams got one awful beating up there, 25 to something there," Jackson replied.[16] The reality is that Williams did not pitch at all during Chicago's final series in New York. Those games were started by Kerr, Cicotte, and Faber. The record shows that Williams's worst loss of the season did come in

New York, but it was a 14–8 loss on May 12; Williams allowed ten of the runs before being relieved after five innings.

At another point Replogle asked Jackson whether he recalled Washington's final visit to Chicago, a three-game set played two weeks earlier. "You lost three straight games," Replogle remarked.[17] In fact, the Sox, their feud having recently broken out into the open, had lost two of the games, both by shutouts. But they did win the middle contest 15–6.

Jackson denied there was anything fishy about the September 1920 losses to Washington. He did acknowledge to the jury that Williams had delivered five thousand dollars to him following the fourth game of the 1919 Series. But he said that he himself had been gypped out of another fifteen thousand dollars promised him by Gandil. He also noted his .375 batting average and errorless defensive play during the series as evidence that, however much he had been paid, he had not actually thrown games. The assertion, which he repeated for the press following the conclusion of his testimony, had the effect of presenting Jackson simultaneously as a fixer and a double-crosser.

The ballplayer told reporters that he decided to testify after concluding that another teammate had done so. "I called up Judge McDonald and told him I was an honest man," Jackson said. "He said to me, 'I know you are not.'"[18] To hear the player tell it, the judge was heartless. "I got $5,000 and they promised me $20,000," Jackson said. "He said he didn't care what I got, that if I got what he thought I ought to get for crabbing the game of the kids I wouldn't be telling him my story. I don't think the judge likes me."[19]

Despite having just confessed, Jackson left the chamber voicing confidence that he would not be convicted of any crime. "When all this blows over, old Joe Jackson isn't going to fall," he said. He did, however, pledge not to stray far from the bodyguard he had been provided in the interim. It wasn't the gamblers or the wronged fans he feared; it was Risberg. "The Swede's a hard guy," he remarked.[20]

By late afternoon word of the confessions was on the street. Despite having his pennant chances apparently dashed, Gleason expressed relief. "I have felt for some time that some of my players were not going at the speed they should have been going," he said.[21] Alderman Joseph McDonough, who was said to have lost $750 on the previous year's Series, sounded off. "It isn't the change that I lost that bothers me," he said. "It is the thought that a bunch of cheap skates could ruin a great national game."[22] The extent of the sincerity of the alderman's regret might have been open to question, though, given his follow-up observation. "There is nothing left to bet on now," he said, "but lawn tennis."[23]

Two of the eight players—Weaver in Chicago and Felsch in Milwaukee—issued immediate denials. But the remaining players—dubbed the Clean Sox—reacted cathartically. They gathered at a downtown restaurant for dinner, then repaired to Eddie Collins's apartment, where they basically celebrated the termination of their own pennant prospects during a nightlong rendezvous with Prohibition hooch. Schalk drove in from Gary, Indiana, for the occasion.

By the time they sobered up, it was Wednesday morning and the newspapers were full of the story. The players piled into an available car and motored down to the courthouse, arriving just in time for the formal handing down of indictments alleging two counts of conspiracy. Leibold hugged Eddie Collins, who swatted Strunk on the back, who punched Murphy in the ribs. "We don't need to be cheered up; we're still in the game and still fighting," Kerr told reporters.[24] An unidentified player declared, "No one will ever know what we put up with all summer."[25] Never in baseball history had there been a more jubilant cast of losers.

The players might have been in a less celebratory mood if they could have talked to state's attorney Maclay Hoyne. The case dynamic between Hoyne, the elected public official, and Replogle, his appointed assistant, was from start to finish a testy one. Prior to the scandal's surfacing, Hoyne had announced his intention not to run for reelection, and Replogle had declared for the position. That may have contributed to Replogle's far more aggressive approach to pushing the case. In fact, Hoyne had never expressed much enthusiasm for or confidence in the whole business. Literally as word of the indictments was being made public, Hoyne went public with his own indictment—of his office.

"I am uncertain whether any crime has been committed," he told reporters.[26] Although the state's attorney did not spell out his uncertainty in detail, reporters inferred from his statements a view that throwing ball games was not in and of itself against the law. As to any assertion of fraud, the *Chicago Tribune* interpreted Hoyne as follows: The players took money to throw games. They did throw the games. How is that a fraud?

Judge McDonald and Comiskey's attorney, Alfred Austrian, both took immediate exception to Hoyne's downplaying of the charges. McDonald said he was "sure" that Hoyne had been misquoted. Austrian alleged the players were guilty of two crimes. The first involved a fraud against ticket buyers, who, he said, paid to see an honestly contested game and did not. The second alleged a conspiracy to injure Comiskey's "property"—his contracts, his team's drawing power, and its good will. Austrian collectively put that damage at three hundred thousand dollars.

Across baseball, club owners responded to Comiskey's suspension of his star players with declarations and offers of assistance that made themselves look good, while coincidentally being impossible to fulfill. In New York Ruppert telegrammed Comiskey that the suspension of the eight "challenges our admiration . . . excites our sympathy, and demands technical assistance."[27] He offered to place the entire Yankees roster at the Sox owner's disposal to complete the season, "and, if necessary, the world's series." In Boston Frazee declared it the responsibility of every AL team to give the White Sox one player in order to flesh out the team's roster in the event the suspensions were not revoked. Obviously neither proposal was taken seriously.

The Indians took the field in St. Louis knowing of the indictments and suspensions of the eight. Hoping to pad his team's lead to a full game, Speaker selected twenty-nine-game winner Bagby to make the start. The Sarge was hardly at his best and allowed single runs in each of the first three innings. One of them, a Sisler home run, helped the newly crowned batting champion break Ty Cobb's all-time record of 248 base hits. But the Indians scored three times in the second to take a lead they never relinquished. Joe Evans hit safely three times, drove in two runs, and scored two more. The final score was 9–5, and it—combined with the day's events in Chicago—infused confidence across Cleveland. "The unstained and unindicted [White Sox] members remaining never will be able to beat out the Indians," the next morning's *Cleveland Plain Dealer* asserted.[28] On Wednesday afternoon Coveleski picked up his twenty-fourth victory with a 10–2 breeze against the Browns. The decision boosted the Cleveland advantage to a game and a half, although few noticed. Only three hundred were in attendance at Sportsman's Park; all attention was fixed on the events in Chicago.

As had been the case the previous day, some of the discussion never advanced beyond the frivolous. In the *New York World*, columnist George Daley proposed that the Sox forfeit all their 1920 games in which either Jackson or Cicotte—"not eligible under the moral code"—participated.[29] Others proposed cancellation of the 1920 Series, a notion that particularly nettled fans in Cleveland and Brooklyn. "I fail to see where anybody can get any sense of the idea of preventing [the] Indians and [the] Dodgers . . . from meeting," Ross Tenney wrote in the *Cleveland Press*.[30] The *Plain Dealer* rose in editorial defense of its own heroes. "The pennant comes to this city clean," the newspaper asserted.[31]

Comiskey opened his office to all comers, conspicuously displaying piles of letters and telegrams of support. He made it a point to publicly work with Gleason through a "new batting order" for the final St. Louis series, one that would involve the replacement of Felsch, Jackson, Weaver, and Risberg. Gleason said reserve Ted Jourdan would step in at first; Shano Collins would for the first time in his life take third base; Bibb Falk, with three big league at bats, would replace Jackson in left; and Leibold would take over for Felsch in center. Harvey McClellan, as lightly used as Falk, would play shortstop in place of Risberg. "Are you going after the pennant?" a reporter asked him. "As hard as we can," he replied.[32] A reporter, tipped to the prospect of a personal appeal by Weaver, asked a secretary whether Buck had yet shown up. "He hasn't and he better not," the secretary tartly replied.[33] In fact, Weaver did show up and got a brief audience with Comiskey at which he denied involvement in impropriety. Beyond whatever personal satisfaction he derived from the effort, the audience yielded him nothing.

At the courthouse Williams added his confession to those

of Cicotte and Jackson, presumably seeking a more lenient deal in exchange for his cooperation. The deal he outlined involved payments of $5,000 for each loss up to $20,000. Williams insisted he had received only one of those $5,000 payments. From Milwaukee Felsch granted an interview in which he too acknowledged the story's basic truth. "I'm going to hell, I guess," he told the *New York Sun*. "I got my $5,000 and I suppose the others did, too."[34]

Opinion in Chicago turned hard against the players. The *Tribune*, whose columnists had reserved judgment during the worst of the rumors, now went so far as to refuse to editorially acknowledge the suspects' names. Without naming Jackson, it castigated a player "who dodged the firing line in war by seeking refuge in the shipyards [and who now] rail[ed] and ravage[d] because he got only $5,000 in a dirty envelope when he had been promised $20,000."[35]

Rain washed out the scheduled Thursday game in Detroit between the Tigers and the Indians. But it did not fully assuage fan anger regarding cheating in baseball. In Joliet, Illinois, Cubs infielder Buck Herzog took part in an exhibition game with his teammates, in the process catching heck from spectators who had heard of the charges leveled by Rube Benton against him. After the game Herzog entered a waiting automobile and prepared to leave the grounds for the team hotel. A man climbed onto the vehicle's running board, stuck his head inside the car, and yelled at Herzog, "You're one of those crooked Chicago ball players. When are you going to confess?"[36]

An enraged Herzog scrambled out of the car and socked the man, knocking him down, then jumped on top of him. What Herzog failed to consider was that his opponent had friends, one of whom slashed the ballplayer across the hand and the leg with a knife. Herzog escaped with minor injuries.

In soggy Detroit, meanwhile, talk among the players posed another threat to whatever remained of the pennant race's integrity. There were no gamblers involved this time. But in the context of a "fixed outcome," that was a distinction without a difference. Members of the Tigers informally agreed to "lay down" that weekend in order to ensure a Cleveland pennant. Late in his life Joe Wood conceded hearing the damning discussion. "I did know from a couple of fellows with the Detroit club that they weren't going to play their heads off," Wood said. "They would rather see us win . . . that was the idea."[37] The record does not fully condemn the Tigers, by the way, since the hosts did win one of the three games played between the teams while the pennant race remained unresolved—and did so thanks to a five-run late-inning comeback.

While the Indians and the Tigers waited out the rain in Detroit, the remains of the White Sox entrained Thursday morning for St. Louis. They stopped along the way in Schalk's hometown of Litchfield for an impromptu gathering. Several hundred fans turned out at the train station to salute the team, refusing to let the train pass until Schalk agreed to disembark and spend Thursday night with his neighbors.

The Indians' rained-out Thursday game in Detroit was rescheduled as part of a Friday doubleheader. That meant that by the time the revamped White Sox took the field in St. Louis, they already knew the Tigers had beaten the Indians 5–4 in ten dramatic innings. Cleveland could have clinched with a sweep and a White Sox loss, and would have if the Indians hadn't made hash of their own prospects. Mails took a 4–0 lead into the eighth inning of that morning game but gave it up in his worst inning of the season, a four-run burst compounded by errors on the parts of Jamieson and Gardner.

Then Bagby, pitching in relief, allowed the winner to score in the bottom of the tenth.

Back within a single game of the lead, the Sox sent Faber to the mound that afternoon in the hope that their twenty-three-game winner could shut down the Browns and give what remained of Chicago's offense a fighting chance. It helped that the inspired Sox scored three times in the top of the first, the key hit being Shano Collins's bases-loaded single. But Faber broke down in the third inning, which featured a five-run shower capped by outfielder Earl Smith's home run into the right-field bleachers. Faber's exit forced Gleason to resort to lightly used Clarence Hodge, nicknamed "Shovel" because at six feet four inches and 190 pounds it was said that he resembled one. Hodge worked a couple of innings, then gave way to Joe Kiefer, who was making his big league debut. It was hardly the pitching plan Gleason would have hoped to put in play for the most pivotal game of the season, as the results illustrated. The Browns won 8–6. When the Indians hammered ten runs across the plate in their second game in Detroit, a contest halted after eight innings due to darkness, Caldwell had his own twentieth victory of the season and Speaker's team stood two ahead with just two to play.

The official coronation occurred Saturday afternoon in Detroit, when the new champions thoroughly dismantled the Tigers. Bagby, who gained his thirty-first victory, could hardly have been called dominant. He allowed eleven base hits. But the only Detroit score came with two out in the ninth. By then Cleveland had scored three times in the third, twice in the sixth, four more in the seventh, and a final run in the eighth. At game's end the Tigers crowd of ten thousand formed a gauntlet through which the visiting champions were saluted, none more so than Speaker. In St. Louis, where Cleveland's victory rendered the outcome without consequence, the Clean Sox ran up ten runs against Bill Bayne, enough for Kerr even on an off day.

In Chicago, meanwhile, four of the Black Sox issued a public statement declaring their innocence and vowing to fight the charges. Weaver, speaking for himself, Risberg, McMullin, and Felsch, promised to "hire the best legal talent available and vindicate [themselves]."[38] Weaver pointed to his own performance as self-justification. "I fielded 1.000 and batted .333 [in the World Series]," he said. "Does that look as if I were 'fixed.'" He asserted that Jackson, Cicotte, and Williams were "crazy."[39]

By now, though, Hoyne was adopting a more aggressive posture—regarding not 1919 but 1920. He told the *Herald and Examiner* that he believed at least a half dozen games from the current season had been fixed by gamblers. Hoyne did not specify which games, although in addition to the Cubs-Phillies game that had triggered the original inquiry, the three-game late-August visit by the White Sox to Boston was widely assumed to be suspect. "I will venture the assertion that there is more and bigger scandal coming in the baseball world," he said.[40]

That same day Albert Lasker unveiled his proposal for reorganizing the management and oversight of big league baseball. Lasker, a stockholder in the Chicago Cubs and a well-known advertising executive in that city, intended to address what he saw as one of the fundamental management problems that had bedeviled the game to that point, decentralized leadership, at the same time suggesting recognition of two other problems, vision and ethics. His plan had grown out of two related elements: widespread dissatisfaction with the National Commission lingering from its handling of the Sisler and Perry cases, and equally strong dissatisfaction with Johnson stemming from his interference in the Carl Mays case. That context is important to understanding the willingness of the game's leadership to even consider his approaches.

Lasker proposed to substantially distance team managements' influence on the game's direction, a proposal that began with abolishing the National Commission. By October 1920 this initial step was almost a given. Since the more or less forced resignation of commission chairman Garry Herrmann earlier in the year, the three-person governing body had been leaderless anyway, and the fights over player-related decisions left it with few supporters. National League owners had essentially no faith in the commission, and the American League remained rent over the 1919 Mays case.

Seen in that context Lasker's audience for the initial airing of his plan seems less than coincidental. That audience consisted of Cubs owner Bill Veeck, Sox owner Charles Comiskey, National League president John Heydler, Pittsburgh club owner Barney Dreyfuss, and John McGraw, manager and vice president of the Giants. Conspicuous by his presence was Dreyfuss, a frequent and vocal lobbyist for Landis in the position of central authority. Conspicuous by his noninvitation was Johnson.

Lasker proposed to replace the National Commission with a new commission comprised of men "with no interest whatever in any club or league, and which should also represent the minor leagues, the players and the public."[41] He believed that the game should, through an evolution of power, become truly national in deed as well as in word. This commission, Lasker stipulated, should be composed of three men of "unquestionable reputation and standing in fields other than base ball . . . [and] in no way connected with base ball." The presence of such persons in positions of authority, he concluded, would "assure the public that public interests would first be served, and that therefore, as a natural sequence, all existing evils would disappear."[42]

Under Lasker's plan such a commission would be given "sole and unreviewable power over players, managers and magnates, even to the extreme of declaring an offending magnate out of baseball." It would also, Lasker stipulated, "be empowered to establish proper relationship between the major and minor leagues . . . [and] would have the sole unimpeachable right to prescribe the rules of the game. And to regulate the conduct of the players on the field and in public."[43]

In short Lasker proposed a triune dictatorship. He went so far as to propose the dictators, suggesting some combination of Gen. John H. Pershing, former president William Howard Taft, and Landis. The inclusion of Taft, at least, was obviously unworkable. Although one of the nation's best-known baseball fans, with Harding's election to the presidency all but certain, he also was an obvious potential nominee to the position he had always coveted, chief justice of the United States Supreme Court.

Without specifically endorsing Lasker's proposal, new National League president John Heydler issued a statement all but recommending its adoption. Heydler called for replacement of the National Commission by a new supervising body composed of men of "nation-wide prominence with no financial interest in the sport," the Lasker proposal in all but name. Newspapers also rallied behind the idea of placing the national pastime beyond the reach of its owners.

"There will be opposition from certain interests," the *Chicago Herald and Examiner* predicted. "But the feeling that a great wrong can by wiped out only by a great right will be strong enough to carry it. Mr. Lasker has started something. The public will put it over."[44]

Heydler and the *Herald and Examiner* were wrong on that count. However heartfelt the sentiment behind it, the idea that owners would yield control over their own enterprise was not realistic. Given a year's worth of further revelations and testimony, a scaled-back version of Lasker's proposal—with Landis sitting as sole dictator—would be implemented. But even then owners retained the right to hire and fire the commissioner, and in time they would rein in his powers. Ownership's ability to do that, which Lasker opposed, constituted the real difference between what might have been enacted and what eventually was enacted.

With the Indians' formal clinching of the pennant race, though, attention shifted at least momentarily back to the on-field activities. There was at last a pair of contestants for the world's championship, and the reputations of both the Indians and the National League–champion Dodgers were unquestioned. More than that the Indians had become sentimental favorites. Much of the appeal involved the Chapman tragedy, although the Sewell and Mails stories remained compelling in their own ways.

The city of Cincinnati passed a resolution formally backing their Ohio rivals to succeed the Reds as champions. Cleveland residents staged what was widely characterized as a muted celebration of the city's first championship in forty-two years of play. The *Plain Dealer*'s Henry Edwards may have touched on why in a published congratulation that was equal parts paean and obsequy. "When Ray Chapman . . . heard the voice of the greatest Umpire of all . . . Ray's colleagues cared not one iota whether they won the pennant or finished last," he said.[45] The same newspaper editorially asserted that "few teams could have recovered from such a stunning blow" as the Chapman fatality. "The spirit of Chapman," it declared, "helped materially to lead them to their final triumph."[46]

The Indians players themselves reflected that sense of ambivalence: happy to have won but unsure how to react to it. In their own dressing room following the clinching in Detroit, the usual gaiety was punctured to silence when a player whose name is lost to history called above the din for his teammates to vote Chapman's widow a full World Series share. Speaker assented for the team. Then he found a handy bench, covered his eyes with his hands, and sat quietly for several minutes, determined to regain his composure.

14. Aftermath

In the autumn of 1965, Joe Falls, a popular columnist with the *Detroit Free Press*, knocked on the door of a modest brick house in that city. Eddie Cicotte answered. A lifetime earlier Eddie Cicotte had been among the greatest pitchers in baseball. Now he was eighty-one and living out the final years allotted to him farming a strawberry patch. But Eddie Cicotte wanted to talk.

Among the eight players known historically as the Black Sox, that in itself was unusual. None of the others had ever spoken about his complicity in the events of that time. Prior to his death in 1951, Joe Jackson gave numerous interviews, always protesting his innocence, always pointing to his team-leading .375 batting average in that series, always highlighting his errorless fielding record, never disputing the contention that he had received at least five thousand dollars in cash from gamblers. Eliot Asinof, author of *Eight Men Out*, told of meeting both Happy Felsch and Chick Gandil in the mid-1960s. The discussion had been long and involved—until Asinof brought up the fix. Then both men clammed up.

By 1965 the attention generated by Asinof's recently published book had revived distant memories, and eighty-one-year-old Eddie Cicotte was finally ready to talk. "I admit I did wrong," he said. "I've paid for it the past 45 years." What, Falls asked, did he tell kids who asked him about his role? "I tell them I made a mistake and I'm sorry for it," he said. "I try to tell them not to let anyone push them the wrong way."[1]

Occasionally the other disgraced players' self-exoneration took an unusual form, such as in 1922 when journalist Jim Kilgallen interviewed Buck Weaver for the International News Service. Weaver used the article to rationalize his involvement in an "everybody does it" tone. In fact, he accused the Sox of having bribed the Tigers in an effort to help ensure Chicago's 1917 pennant.

"We wanted to win the pennant badly," Weaver told Kilgallen. As the race wound down, the Sox were in a heated battle with the defending world champion Red Sox. "We knew Detroit hated the Red Sox' guts," he said. With that in mind Weaver said Gandil and Risberg propositioned the Tigers on behalf of the whole team: just enough money, Weaver said, "to buy each of them a new suit of clothes." In exchange Detroit was to lay down during the teams' final mid-September two series. The White Sox won six of those seven games labeled by Weaver as suspicious and cruised to the pennant. Yet even as he implicated his teammates, Weaver exonerated himself: at the time the collection was taken up, he said, he had been visiting relatives. He had, he declared, taken no part in that fix either.[2]

Joe Jackson adopted a similar consistency of denial. Despite his own admission that he had accepted five thousand dollars—a detail Jackson rationalized by noting that gamblers had gypped him out of more than he said they owed him—he never accepted his own complicity. Like Weaver in 1956, Jackson in 1951 went to his grave protesting his innocence.

In October 1975, when Swede Risberg became the last of the eight Black Sox to die, the first-person record closed without any of them having elaborated beyond Cicotte's confession.

However ill-fated the Black Sox appeared to be in retirement, they were more favored by fortune than the Chapmans. At the time of her husband's death in August 1920, Kathleen Daly Chapman was pregnant with the couple's first child. A daughter, Rae Marie, was born in February 1921. Mrs. Chapman remarried a year later but never fully recovered from the emotional blow of her first husband's death, and in 1928 she poisoned herself. Depending on whether one believed family members or official records, the fatal dose might have been administered accidentally or deliberately. Rae Marie was seven at the time. The following April the girl contracted measles, and she died as well.[3]

If fate cursed the Chapman family, it showered blessings on Ray Chapman's teammates. With Joe Sewell granted an exception from the rule restricting postseason rosters to players who were with the team on August 1, the Indians defeated the Brooklyn Dodgers five games to three in that season's best-of-nine World Series. The fifth game, played in Cleveland on October 10, became one of the most famous in baseball history when Bill Wambsganss completed an unassisted triple play in the fifth inning. The same contest also featured the first grand slam in Series history—Elmer Smith hit it—and the first home run by a pitcher (Jim Bagby). The final score was 8–1. Stan Coveleski started three games and won them all, including the clinching eighth game, a 3–0 shutout in Cleveland on October 12.

From that baseball highpoint the Indians gradually receded into the game's background, finishing second in 1921, then contending only once again (in 1926) through the 1930s. As individuals, though, the members of that 1920 club prospered. Of the twenty men who wore a Cleveland uniform in that fall's World Series, all but two (Joe Evans and Bagby) lived to see their seventieth birthday, and six—Wambsganss, Sewell, Wood, Elmer Smith, Coveleski, and Graney—were more than ninety years old when they died. The average age at death of the 1920 Indians World Series team was seventy-eight, significantly better than the normal life expectancy of men born in the 1890s.[4]

Carl Mays too enjoyed a long post-baseball life. Mays lived until 1971, cursing to the end the fate that he believed had denied him entrance into the Hall of Fame. His career credentials were at least arguable; he won 208 games with a .623 winning percentage and a lifetime 2.92 earned run average. Mays followed up his 26-victory 1920 season by winning 27 more in 1921, when he led the league in both appearances (49) and innings pitched (336.2).

Whatever Mays believed about the damage that the Chapman beaning did to his Hall of Fame prospects, others were less convinced. A few years after the pitcher's death, Fred Lieb, a well-known New York sportswriter who covered the Yankees during Mays's heyday, published a reminiscence that contained damning allegations against the pitcher. Acknowledging that he could not prove his assertions, Lieb reported that Yankees manager Miller Huggins believed Mays had thrown games during the 1921 World Series between the Yankees and the eventual world-champion New York Giants. Superficially any case against Mays based on his 1921 postseason efforts seems difficult to make. While it's true that he lost two of three decisions, his 1.73 ERA is an eloquent defense. The losses came in the fourth and seventh games by scores of 4–2 and 2–1, respectively.

The indictment against Mays focuses on the eighth inning of the fourth game. To that point the pitcher had been superb, following up a game 1 five-hit shutout with seven innings of two-hit shutout ball. The Yankees led 1–0 as Giants slugger Emil Meusel (Bob's brother) led off the eighth. As Lieb reported the story related to him by Huggins, Mays defied Huggins's instructions to throw Emil Meusel a fastball and instead delivered a slow curve. Meusel hit it off the wall for a triple. Two singles—one of them a bunt misplayed by Mays—and a double produced three runs. The Giants added a fourth run in the ninth and won 4–2. Later that evening, Lieb wrote, he was approached by a man who said he had seen Mrs. Mays signal her husband just before the controversial pitch to Meusel to confirm that gamblers had delivered some promised cash to her.

"Any ballplayers that played for me . . . I'd give them a helping hand," Huggins told Lieb. But he specifically exempted Mays from such generosity. If Mays were "in the gutter," Huggins said, "I'd kick [him]."[5] Lieb contended it was the suspicion of crookedness, widely known among Hall of Fame voters, and not his role in Chapman's death that kept Carl Mays from the Hall of Fame.

The most profound outcome of the 1920 season was its role as a triggering device in reformation of the game's governing structure. Once the Lasker plan surfaced, Johnson and his five American League loyalists argued that it would be folly to turn control of the game over to any panel of outsiders. That year's *Reach Guide*, a Johnson mouthpiece, asserted that however esteemed such men were, they "could not possibly have any practical or even theoretical knowledge of the professional game and the peculiar conditions that environed it."[6]

Johnson and his backers also correctly perceived any effort to revise baseball governance as a challenge to his status as the game's most powerful figure. "Most anybody on the inside of baseball knows that [a proposal for a new national commission] is a slap at Ban Johnson," contended Elbert Sanders in the decidedly pro-Johnson *Sporting News*.[7]

Confronted with the united support for the Lasker Plan of the National League plus three owners from his own league, Johnson initiated a delaying tactic. The time was not yet right, he contended. No proper assessment of the need could be made until the Black Sox grand jury finished its work.

Given that the Lasker Plan would have detached them from power over the game's governance as well, the willingness of National League club owners (plus American Leaguers Frazee, Ruppert, and Comiskey) to seriously consider it illustrates their antipathy toward Johnson, who was by then destined to be the big loser in any reallocation of governing power.

National League club owners quickly recommended the plan's adoption and passed a resolution calling for a joint meeting to work out the details of implementation. That meeting, held in Chicago on October 18, was attended by the eleven Lasker supporters but boycotted by the five Johnson loyalists. What ensued was a resolution abrogating the National Agreement and designating a subcommittee tasked with drafting a new agreement along the lines proposed by Lasker. The salary of the commission chairman was to be $25,000 ($280,000 in today's money). The other two members were to receive $10,000 each ($113,000 today). The terms of the agreement were declared to be not subject to amendment for twenty-five years. In other words the three designees (or their successors) would hold absolute power over the game's direction at least through 1945.

The signatory club owners plainly felt they were dealing from a position of strength, relating both to their numerical superiority and to a sense of public revulsion at the game's course. Atop their new agreement they layered three additional resolutions, the most important of which gave the five American League loyalists two weeks to agree to their terms or face the prospect that the eleven would band with an undesignated twelfth "owner" to form a new Major League. The twelfth owner was widely suspected to be from Detroit, an inference designed to dislodge Tigers owner Frank Navin from the Loyal Five and thereby break Johnson's coalition.

Johnson developed a counterproposal that would leave him in a position of at least some power. Resigned by that point to Landis's imminent accession, he asserted that if a single commissioner was needed, that person's role should be limited to resolving disputes between the leagues. In other words the commissioner would serve primarily as a "final arbiter."

Beyond that Johnson lawyered the proposal for a new league. Abrogation of the National Agreement, he argued, required the separate consent of both leagues, yet the majority of American League owners plainly had not consented. He also let it be known that he was prepared to challenge the right of the three renegades to disaffiliate from the American League, citing a twenty-year "voluntary association" agreement that had been ratified in 1910. Finally, he got help from various Minor League organizations, concerned as they were about being taken into the new association without their consent or representation. This last point was an obvious weakness of Lasker's proposal.

Three days before the November 1 deadline for a response from the five American League loyalists, Johnson convened a meeting of league owners and developed his formal counterproposal. It called for the creation of a nine-person committee—three members from each of the Major Leagues and three from the Minors—to craft "a feasible plan" of reorganization. The league's directors—Johnson loyalists Phil Ball, Frank Navin, Clark Griffith, and Ben Shibe—publicly dismissed the Lasker Plan as a basis for serious consideration. Bob Quinn, chief aide to Browns owner Phil Ball, the most loyal of Johnson's loyalists, spelled out the logic of his group's view to the *Sporting News* in terms regular Americans could understand. "He wouldn't any more favor an outsider bossing the job than he would think of engaging a pastry chef as chauffeur of his Buick touring car," Quinn said of Ball.[8]

Initially the renegades reacted by dismissing the Johnson loyalists' proposal as irrelevant. Heydler called an interleague meeting for November 8 to consider adoption of the Lasker Plan and announced that decisions would be based on a vote of teams rather than by league. Again the Johnson loyalists boycotted the session, which quickly proceeded to form a "New National League" consisting of the eight National League clubs as well as the Yankees, the Red Sox, the White Sox, and a twelfth team to be determined. Heydler was named president-secretary-treasurer, and the Minor Leagues—which were not represented at the session—were accorded consultative power in the drafting of the agreement that would govern the tribunal's formation. They were also to be allowed to appoint one of the three tribunal members.

The new league's magnates quickly nominated Landis for the chairmanship, at the same time declaring that the two remaining seats would be filled later. Then a delegation hurried off for Kansas City, where the national association was meeting, in the hope of winning the Minors' acquiescence to the new structure. Landis, who had not been formally approached ahead of time, instructed the league that he would "take the matter under advisement" and reply within a week.

Anticipating the New National League action, Johnson quickly issued a press release declaring his league's intention to put new teams in Chicago, New York, and Boston and challenge the New National League head-on. Then he raced for Kansas City and beat the National League delegation there. At the Minor Leagues meeting he pitched his own plan for a conference committee including equal representation for the Minors. Johnson asked Minor League officials not to align with the New National League and repeated his assertion that control of the game should "remain in the hands of men who had given their lives to its development." The next day Herrmann laid out his league's plans to those same Minor League officials, who responded as Johnson had requested they do, by "taking the matter under advisement."[9]

The result was an owners-only conference the next day in Chicago, from which emerged a compromise that replaced the three-person board with a single commissioner. In deference to the American League, that person was to be selected "by a majority vote of [the teams in] both leagues" rather than of the individual clubs. That deal effectively quashed the twelve-team New National League, forced the three American League renegades back into Johnson's sphere of influence, and ended the prospect of a baseball civil war. The sixteen club owners unanimously elected Landis to the commissioner's position.

Publicly and perhaps among the owners themselves, the extent of the new commissioner's power remained a subject of interpretation. Pirates owner Barney Dreyfuss, the first to propose the judge for the position, visualized a limited role. "The major league presidents will run things in their own leagues, and their power will end there," he said, echoing Johnson. "When it comes to inter-league disputes, that will be settled by Judge Landis."[10]

Landis would have none of that. He insisted that a provision calling on him to "recommend action" be amended to "take action."[11] Creation of the other two positions was never formally acted upon out of deference to Landis. The judge also left himself an out, electing to retain his seat on the federal bench. Having established his position as sole dictator and giving himself an option in the event owners didn't like it, Landis accepted the commissionership for a term of seven years.

Johnson understood the diminishment of his own power that had just taken place and accepted it with public grace. "I'm for Judge Landis," he said. "Baseball will be placed on the highest possible standard now, and there will be no more fights."[12] By early January 1921, the new National Agreement condensing Landis's responsibilities to writing had been given final form by representatives of the two Major Leagues and the Minors. He was charged with investigating "either upon complaint or his own initiative, any act or practice alleged or suspected to be detrimental to the best interests of base ball."[13]

15. Damon and Ring at the Series

The 1920 World Series between the Cleveland Indians and the Brooklyn Dodgers, which opened in Brooklyn on October 5, was covered by two of the best-known writers in the history of newspaper journalism.

Ring Lardner was thirty-three and fully fixed in the journalism consciousness when the Series opened. Born in Niles, Michigan, Lardner began his career as a teenager with the *South Bend Tribune*. He moved to the *South Bend Times* and from there to the *Chicago Inter-Ocean* in 1907. After a succession of stops in Boston and St. Louis, Lardner joined the staff of the *Chicago Tribune* in 1913, where he wrote and syndicated the famous In the Wake of the News column, eventually reaching more than one hundred newspapers.

In both his news columns and his subsequent short stories, beginning with "You Know Me Al" in 1916, Lardner often adopted a semiliterate, sometimes satirical vernacular, reinforced with deliberately misspelled words. But with the exposure of the Black Sox scandal, that approach gradually shifted from satirical to sarcastic, even embittered. Lardner had become a close acquaintance of many of the Chicago players. During the 1920 World Series, the impact of that still-recent experience evinced itself in Lardner's almost open disdain for the perceived importance of the events on the field. The Series' fifth game is today considered a classic because it featured the first World Series grand slam, the first home run by a pitcher, and the only unassisted triple play in World Series history. Yet consider Lardner's introduction to it: "Your correspondent walked out of this alleged baseball game in the 7th inning."[1]

Alfred Damon Runyon—the name was originally spelled "Runyan" but was later changed to "Runyon" through a typographical error—was nearing his fortieth birthday when the 1920 World Series opened. A fixture on the New York writing scene, he had ironically been born in Manhattan, Kansas, although his family—its roots already deep in the newspaper industry—moved to Colorado when Runyon was a young child. Runyon traveled to New York City in 1910 to take a job covering the Giants and professional boxing for the *New York American*. While Lardner produced material that was as much entertainment as information, Runyon's approach was debonair and rich in insight. He favored a "stream of consciousness" style, spinning the story via present-tense word pictures that allowed readers to see the game in their minds. His report on the Series' first game opens with just such an evocation. "Stanley Coveleskie, a burly Pole who is the victorious Cleveland pitcher, can be seen shoving through a knot of men and boys."[2]

The 1920 Series marked a turning point in the lives of the men, both of whom found themselves constrained by baseball, and both of whom turned to fiction. Fate brought the disillusioned Lardner into contact with a young F. Scott Fitzgerald, with whom he would become a close friend and drinking companion. Runyon continued to write for a time for the *American* and for his own syndicated column. But he did so only sporadically and eventually cemented his reputation with his renowned tales of midtown Manhattan's nightlife. Eventually both men succumbed to their vices. Lardner died of a heart attack brought on by the effects of recurring alcoholism at fifty-four in 1933. Runyon lived until 1946, when throat cancer—a product of his prolific smoking habit—did him in at age sixty-six.

What follows is a sample of classic sports journalism from the early 1920s, the story of that season's World Series as described by two of the profession's Hall of Famers.

Monday, October 4
By Damon Runyon

BROOKLYN—Charles Comiskey estimates the commercial value of the ballplayers who are now probably lost to him for good at $230,000. The value of their moral souls cannot be reckoned.

In the open market, Buck Weaver would probably have brought more money than any of the other players. Joe Jackson once sold for $30,000 but Jackson was about through as a ballplayer. Weaver was rated the top third baseman in the country.[3]

By Ring Lardner

BROOKLYN—Contrary to expectations, the Indians didn't get here today as Mgr. Speaker didn't want to take no chances of his boys being invited out to a theater by Abe Attell and etc. The Cleveland nine accompanied by a corpse of interpreters and guides will reach Brooklyn early in the morning. They will be no morning practice by the American League champs and they won't know what Ebbets Field looks like until they come out for the game.

After a hearty breakfast of Indian meal the Cleveland players will be took on a sight seen tour around Brooklyn. This is expected to take 10 minutes and will give the boys plenty of time to sleep it off before the game.[4]

Game 1, October 5

Cleveland	020	100	000—3
Brooklyn	000	000	100— 1

By Damon Runyon

BROOKLYN—Stanley Coveleskie, a burly Pole who is the victorious Cleveland pitcher, can be seen shoving through a knot of men and boys.

Let Coveleskie go back and thank the prematurely gray haired man who brings up the rear of the scattered Cleveland band.

This man is Tris Speaker, manager of the American League club from the Forest City. He is the man who is responsible for this moment of triumph for Stanley Coveleskie. A wonderful catch by Speaker gives this game to Stanley Coveleskie.

Speaker is the greatest outfielder in baseball. Perhaps he is the greatest outfielder that ever lives. A man has just so stated. Speaker comes from the town of Hubbard, Tex., which has little more population than one of those apartment houses yonder.

He is a pleasant-spoken young man, thirty-three or thirty-four years old, very unostentatious off the field, and can throw a lariat and spin a six-shooter around on his finger and do many other cowboy tricks.

You have to go to the animal kingdom to find similes for further description. He has the speed of a greyhound.

He has an eye like an antelope, which can see very far. His judgment on a fly ball corresponds in keenness to the sense of smell of a deer.[5]

By Ring Lardner

BROOKLYN—No doubt the experts will give you a idear about how this game was lose and win. Personly it looked to me like Brooklyn lose because it was the 1st time they ever played vs. a club that uses 6 outfielders in the game at the same time, 4 of witch is a manager. This is where the Indians has got a big advantage. Speaker don't only manage his club but he plays right center, left center and middle center field and shortstop while Robbie [Dodger manager Wilbert Robinson] don't do nothing only waddle out to the coachers box when he ain't takeing up 4 positions on the bench.

However my business is to tell what com off and not why. Well, it looked for a wile like they wouldn't be no game because when the Cleveland boys got over to Brooklyn and asked where was the ball pk. they couldn't find nobody that understood American dialect until finely they run across a bird that talks Stanley Coveleskie's tongue and Covey says to him, "Wheresky isky the ball parksky?" and the bird said, "I don't knowskie," so they hunted around till they found it.

In the 7th inning Coveleskie fouled one off and it lit on a home rooter's dome in the upper grandstand and a copper came up to recover the ball, but when he got there he seen it was lopsided and the bird responsible for its condition was allowed to take it home.

Amist those present in the press stand was Charley Herzog, who was nursing a few sliced knuckles where a man out in Joliet, Ill., tried to manicure him but the knife slipped. The fact that Charley dast play in an exhibition game in Joliet is pretty good evidence that he ain't like what it was charged that he was like. Joliet is the home of 1 of our best penitentiarys. The White Sox used to barnstorm down there, but for some reason or another they didn't schedule no game this year.[6]

Game 2, October 6

Cleveland	000 000 000—0
Brooklyn	101 010 000—3

By Ring Lardner

BROOKLYN—Along comes the 7th innings and Mr. Speaker sends John Gladstone Graney up to hit for Bagby in the pinch. "Well," says Gene, they should ought to call this the world cereal with [Dodger outfielder Zach] Wheat and Graney in it.

Gene asks who is pitching for Cleveland now and I tell him Uhle. So he says this looks like a good spot for a Swiss song number.

"Uhle, Uhle, U-ee-lee-o
Watch how we go through Alpine snow.
Uhle, Uhle, U-lee-lee-O
With a truly U-Uhle-lee-O."[7]

Game 3, October 7

Cleveland	000 100 000—1
Brooklyn	200 000 00x—2

By Damon Runyon

BROOKLYN—The Cleveland players are quitting the field in their steel-grey uniforms a bit downcast. They wear little bands of mourning on their left sleeves as a token of respect to Ray Chapman, their dead shortstop.

The memory of the brilliant Chapman comes back to-day strongly as one recalls a misplay in the first and decisive inning by the inexperienced Sewell.

Sewell will be a great ball player some day, but just now he lacks experience. Experience is a great asset in these big series.

Sewell can scarcely be blamed for a little nervousness. He is just out of college. He is filling the place of one of the greatest ballplayers of his time and taking part in a series on which hangs thousands of dollars and a big title.[8]

By Ring Lardner

BROOKLYN—Ping Bodie and a couple of friends come out to the pk. to see the game and Ping says:

"My name's Bodie; how much is 3 box seats?" and they told him $6.00 a smash, and Pink says:

"I wouldn't pay no $6.00 to see no ball game." Neither would I, Signor Pizzola.[9]

Game 4, October 9

| Brooklyn | 000 100 000—1 |
| Cleveland | 202 010 00x—5 |

By Damon Runyon

CLEVELAND—Stanley Coveleskie, the big Polack from the coal mines of Pennsylvania, is again too much for the Brooklyn Dodgers. Twenty-seven thousand Cleveland people are greatly delighted by this outcome.

They are cheering wildly for their victorious players.

Cleveland is now on even terms with Brooklyn in the series. Each team has won two games.

It is Coveleskie's second triumph. Coveleskie may win the entire series for Cleveland. It is not impossible. These Poles are powerful men. Coveleskie closes to-day against the Dodgers as strongly as he starts. He is a mighty pitcher.[10]

By Ring Lardner

CLEVELAND—The paper and the other Cleveland paper is full of stuff about the team witch they call the Tribe witch is a nickname for the Indians. We haven't been able to find out what Tribe these Indians belongs to but in the last 2 games they looked like one of the lost Tribes. However nobody is discouraged with the way the Serious has went so far especially the Brooklyn club. Heap big chief Speaker of the Tribe expects his warriors to start hitting again on the ground where they piled up most of their .302 average this summer and when the Cleveland boys is hitting they generally almost always scores more runs than vice versa. The Cleveland clubs trainer is the only one in the club that looks down in the mouth. He is sore because he went clear to the trouble of having the bats sent to Brooklyn when they wasnt used.

Even with the big school of fish that swum into Jim Dunn's ball pk to-day it looks like the winners share of the players pool in this serious won't be as much as the loosers got in 1919, not even half as much as some of the loosers got.[11]

Game 5, October 10

| Brooklyn | 000 000 001—1 |
| Cleveland | 400 310 00x—8 |

By Damon Runyon

CLEVELAND—Elmer Smith slugs the ball over the right field wall with the bases full in the first inning.

That definitely settles the matter of the fifth game of the world's series. It is the first home run made in the world's series with the bases full.

Big Jim Bagby, the Cleveland pitcher, comes along in the fourth inning after Burleigh Grimes purposely passes Steve O'Neill, the slugging Cleveland catcher, and hits another home run with two runners on base.

The twenty-six thousand people gathered here on this pleasant Sunday afternoon have little left of their voices after Elmer Smith's exploit to applaud Bagby's feat.

There is still occasion for further vocal exercise, however.

Little Pete Kilduff is the first Brooklyn Dodger to face Bagby in the Brooklyn's side of the fifth. He singles to left.

Otto Miller, the Brooklyn catcher, also singles to left. Then Clarence Mitchell, who replaces Burleigh Grimes in the fourth, hits a sharp liner at Wambsganss. The second baseman reaches out his gloved hand and spears the ball.

It is a great catch under any circumstances and, of course, puts out Mitchell. Kilduff leaves second as Mitchell hits the ball—the hit and run play being on foot. Kilduff is well on his way to third when Wambsganss runs over and steps on second.

This retires Kilduff. Wambsganss wheels and sees Miller on his way from first to second and, running down the base line with the ball, Wambsganss meets the catcher and tags him out also.

The crowd is fairly stunned for a moment, then realizing

the play sets up a clamor with the voices cracked by their efforts over the doings of Smith and Bagby.[12]

By Ring Lardner

CLEVELAND—Your correspondent walked out of this alleged baseball game in the 7th inning and you will half to ask some of the other boys how many hits the Robins got all told off Mr. Bagby without doing them no good.

This game was a conflict between Bagby's brains and Brooklyns brains. In fact it was a duel of masterminds. The Robins began using their noodle in the last ½ of the 1st inning. Jamieson and Wammbbssggannss hit singles and they was mens on 1st and 2nd with nobody out. It looked like this was a situation that hadnt never come up before the Brooklyn nine before. Any way a meeting was called in the midst of the diamond.

It was decided that when Mgr. Speaker bunted, Grimes was to set down on the grass and take a good rest. This piece of strategy worked like a charm, but the Robins then faced another situation namely the bases drunk and nobody out. Another conference was called to decide which was the quickest way to clear the bases and get a fresh start. The decision was to get Elmer Smith in the hole with 2 strikes and then pitch him a ball that he could hit over the fence.

In the 2nd and 3rd innings the Robins gave their brains a well earned vacation and they was fresh and ready for more action when the Indians come in for their 4th turn at bat. This time Doc Johnston got on 2nd base with 1 out and the League of Nations decided to walk Steve O'Neill and make a monkey out of Bagby. Three runs, 3 hits, no luck.

In the next inning Kilduff and Miller got base hits off Bagbys mastermind and Mitchell cleared the bases with a line drive to Wwammmbbssgannnss. A expert cuckoo sitting in the press box told me that it was the 1st time in world serious history that a man Wambsganss had ever made a triple play assisted by consonants only.[13]

Game 6, October 11

Brooklyn   000 000 000—0
Cleveland   000 001 00x—1

By Damon Runyon

CLEVELAND—Two are out in the sixth inning and Sherrod Smith, the Georgian, is pitching in masterful fashion. He is Brooklyn's last hope, the remnant of Robinson's great pitching staff.

Tris Speaker, the grey-haired but youthful manager of the Cleveland club, singles. Burns, the castoff who knows what it means to tour the big leagues with a baseball pillow to rest his head, so to speak, hits a two-bagger, scoring his manager.

This is the sum of the game.

Everybody knows it's the winning run as soon as Speaker arrives. Against Sherrod Smith's great left handed pitching another left-hander is pitching with even greater effectiveness. This is Walter Mails, nicknamed "Duster." He holds the Brooklyn club to three hits.[14]

By Ring Lardner

CLEVELAND—The Robins has now had 16 innings of Duster Mails and they hope they won't get no more of him. They will probably get that hope.

Willie Wambsganss and Elmer Smith was called up to the

plate before the game and presented with a couple of watches for what they done in Sundays game. Elmers alleged timepiece had his name engraved on it, but when the generous jeweler wanted the same thing done for Wamby the engraver busted him in the jaw and quit.

That is about all that happened today except Geo. Burns double in the sixth, witch isn't the same Geo. Burns that plays left field for the Giants.[15]

Game 7, October 12

Brooklyn	000 000 000—0
Cleveland	000 110 10x—3

By Damon Runyon

CLEVELAND—Three innings of the last game of the world's series pass and a gentleman viewing the unsteady Brooklyn Dodgers arises in the press stand and peevishly inquires:

"Well, who's going to kick this game away on Burleigh Grimes?"

Grimes presently answers the question. He kicks, or rather throws, it away on himself. The terms are synonymous in baseball.

Thus Cleveland, a most deserving and enthusiastic community, is the new seat of the baseball championship. It moves here from Cincinnati and the National League.

Everything is coming Ohio's way this year.

Stanley Coveleskie, the Pennsylvania coal miner, draws the curtain on the series of 1920. The bulky Pole pitches Cleveland to its fifth and his own third victory in the series. The Dodgers score but two runs out of his pitching in twenty-seven innings.

He is a big man in this town tonight.[16]

By Ring Lardner

CLEVELAND—Here and after the 12 of October will be known in Ohio as Cleveland Day instead of Columbus Day as Columbus is a whole lot smaller town than Cleveland and hasn't never done nothing to deserve the honors whereas the 12 of October is the date when Cleveland wins its 1st World serious.

Up to now Columbus Day has been celebrated mostly by wops. The ravioli of sunny Italy has been displayed in many a window. From now on in this well known state the day will be a Indian holiday and the flag run up will bear the insignia of the Speaker tribe witch consists of a figure of a left-handed guy scratching his gray head. But as Spoke wasn't the Lone Star on the team to-day it will be necessary to hang the flags up on a pole in honor of Coveleskie.

Well first and foremost leave us first get the story of the game off our reeking chest. The game showed the value of a pitching staff in the World serious. The experts that picked Brooklyn to cop pointed out that Robbie had 9 pitchers and they was all aces, or one more ace than they is in a pinochle deck when the White Sox ain't playing. Well, when it come down to picking his ace for this croocial brawl he picked Burly Grimes that hadn't pitched since Sunday. The other 8 aces was left in the card case with the trays. The deuces was out on the field, wild.

When it was announced that Cleveland's master slabber or slobber would be opposed by Robbie's ditto, President Dunn sent out for an extra order of cuspidors witch was parked in the vicinity of the pitchers mound. While the pitchers was warming up their salivary glands, Elmer Smith was called to the plate and presented with an automobile. Then Geo. Burns was called up and his admirers from Niles, Ohio, gave him a watch. Mgr. Speaker and President Dunn was presented with silver loving cups by the club chamber of commerce. The cups was empty when Spoke and Jim got them, but that condition was remedied to-night. Coveleskie and O'Neill was given watches by a local jeweler. All and all it begins to look hopeful for a Democrat victory in Ohio. The commonwealth has apparently went nuts.

Just about time for the pastime to start the grounds was infested by a delegation from the Plasterers, Bricklayers and Masons witch is in convention here this wk. The Plasterers expected to do a big business wile in Cleveland, but they found the gang pretty well plastered already.

The break of the game come in the 4th inning when Larry Gardner was on 3d base and Doc Johnston on 1st and 2 guys out. The Master Minds met in the middle of the diamond and had a long argument about witch as the surest and safest way to let Gardner score and settle the serious. They decided to leave Doc try a delay steal and Miller was to throw the ball back to Grimes and Grimes was to throw it wild to center-field. The strategy worked like a charm.[17]

Notes

1. Ralph Young's Big Moment

1. The best source for historical attendance data is http://www
.ballparksofbaseball.com.

2. See http://www.baseballchronology.com. The previous record
had been set by the New York Giants, who drew 910,000 fans to the
Polo Grounds in 1908. The Yankees' 1920 record was broken by the
New York Yankees, who drew 2,265,512 to Yankee Stadium in 1946.
The second-longest duration for an attendance record is ongoing;
the present mark was set by the Colorado Rockies (4,483,350) in
1993, and as of this writing has survived for sixteen seasons.

3. *Cleveland Plain Dealer*, Aug. 18, 1920.

4. Joe Wood, interview by Lawrence Ritter, Oct. 15, 1963, Lawrence
S. Ritter Audio Tapes, Joyce Sports Research Collection, Hesburgh
Library, University of Notre Dame.

5. Eugene C. Murdock, *Ban Johnson: Czar of Baseball* (Westport
CT: Greenwood Press, 1982), 159.

6. Comiskey's widely quoted "fish in the outfield" slap at Johnson
can be traced back to a biography by G. W. Axelson, at the time
a Chicago sportswriter, titled *Commy: The Life Story of Charles A.
Comiskey* (Chicago: Reilly & Lee, 1919), 132.

7. Murdock, *Ban Johnson*, 157.

8. Five players from those 1918 World Series teams were subsequently suspected of conspiring to fix one or more games. Only one,
Cubs first baseman Fred Merkle, had extensive playing time in that
series. Merkle batted .278 with one RBI in the Cubs' six-game loss
to the Red Sox. Following rumors of his involvement in the fixing
of a game in 1920, Merkel was allowed to quietly retire. In the 1918
World Series, teammates Claude Hendrix and Paul Carter were

informally declared persona non grata following the same rumors. The other two players were Red Sox pitchers Jean Dubuc, banned for advance knowledge of the 1919 World Series fix, and Dutch Leonard, who pitched several more seasons before being declared persona non grata by Judge Landis. The commissioner acted in 1927 after Leonard essentially implicated himself while accusing Cobb and Speaker of conspiring to fix games years earlier.

9. *New York Tribune*, Aug. 23, 1920.

2. A Babe in the City

1. *Sporting News*, Nov. 13, 1919.

2. Jim Reisler, *Babe Ruth: Launching the Legend* (New York: McGraw-Hill, 2004), 16.

3. Reisler, *Babe Ruth*, 1.

4. Reisler, *Babe Ruth*, 12.

5. Wood, interview.

6. *New York American*, July 19, 1920.

7. Ping Bodie obituary, *New York Times*, Dec. 19, 1961.

8. Reisler, *Babe Ruth*, 60.

9. *New York American*, Aug. 7, 1920.

10. *Sporting News*, Apr. 8, 1920.

3. Winter of Their Discontent

1. Murdock, *Ban Johnson*, 149.

2. Eliot Asinof, interview by Lawrence Ritter, Oct. 11, 1963, Lawrence S. Ritter Audio Tapes, Joyce Sports Research Collection, Hesburgh Library, University of Notre Dame.

3. Brian Stevens, *Deadball Stars of the American League* (Cooperstown NY: Society for American Baseball Research [SABR], 2006), 506.

4. Details of Cicotte's 1917 seasonal use can be found at http://www.retrosheet.org.

5. Asinof, interview.

6. Rumors of a possible 1918 World Series fix are discussed in greater detail in Sean Deveney, *The Original Curse: Did the Cubs Throw the 1918 World Series to Babe Ruth's Red Sox and Incite the Black Sox Scandal?* (New York: McGraw Hill, 2010).

7. Transcript of Eddie Cicotte's statement before the grand jury, Sept. 28, 1920. The transcript is available in the White Sox 1919

World Series baseball scandal collection at the Chicago History Museum.

8. Transcript of Cicotte's statement.

9. Transcript of Lefty Williams's statement before the grand jury, Sept. 29, 1920. The statement is available in the White Sox 1919 World Series baseball scandal collection at the Chicago History Museum. It can be accessed online at http://www. umkc.edu/faculty/projects/ftrials/blacksox/courtrdox.html.

10. Gandil is named as a participant and ringleader in the fix in the Jackson, Cicotte, and Williams confessions.

11. Risberg is also named as a ringleader in all the original confessions.

12. Felsch acknowledged his own guilt in published reports in September 1920 and was named as a participant in the fix by Jackson, Cicotte, and Williams.

13. Transcript of Joe Jackson's statement before the grand jury, Sept. 28, 1920. The statement is available in the White Sox 1919 World Series baseball scandal collection at the Chicago History Museum. It can be accessed online at http://www.umkc.edu/faculty/projects/ftrials/blacksox/courtrdox.html.

14. Eliot Asinof, *Eight Men Out* (New York: Holt, Rinehart & Winston, 1963), 123.

15. Leverett T. Smith, *The American Dream and the National Game,* (Bowling Green OH: Bowling Green University Popular Press, 1975), 133.

16. Asinof, *Eight Men Out*, 134.

17. Asinof, *Eight Men Out*, 129.

18. Gene Carney, a well-known researcher of the Black Sox era who died in 2009, wrote an article for the fall 2009 edition of the *Baseball Research Journal*, published by SABR, detailing his examination of the private investigators' report.

19. Grabiner's statement is also taken from the White Sox 1919 World Series baseball scandal collection at the Chicago History Museum.

20. Asinof, interview.

21. Asinof, *Eight Men Out*, 133.

22. Asinof, *Eight Men Out*, 135.

23. The circumstances of Jackson's 1920 signing were themselves controversial, although for reasons concerning the 1919 fix. In later

years Jackson, widely known to be illiterate, said he had demanded that Grabiner remove the standard ten-day waiver clause as a condition of signing. The story goes that Grabiner arrived unannounced in Savannah, Georgia, where Jackson lived, and presented him with the contract as they rode through the city's streets. The player asked for time to return home and allow his literate wife to read it in order to verify the clause's removal. But Grabiner insisted that he had to catch a train out of town immediately and falsely assured the ballplayer that the offending clause had been struck. Jackson signed.

24. Asinof, interview; Wood, interview; and Charley Jamieson, interview by Lawrence Ritter, Sept. 6, 1963, Lawrence S. Ritter Audio Tapes, Joyce Sports Research Collection, Hesburgh Library, University of Notre Dame.

25. Joe Jackson reported the conversation with Lefty Williams in his 1920 statement to the grand jury.

26. Transcript of Jackson's statement.

27. Wood, interview.

4. The Honeymoon

1. Chapman's statement of intent to play one more season is recorded in many places. It was specifically recalled by Harry Edwards, sportswriter for the *Cleveland Plain Dealer*, on Aug. 18, 1920.

2. Jamieson, interview.

5. Reactive Revolutionary

1. Murdock, *Ban Johnson*.

2. Undated statement to the press issued by Charles Comiskey, Comiskey Collection, Chicago History Museum.

3. Asinof, *Eight Men Out*, 77.

4. *Sporting News*, Feb. 19, 1920.

6. The Record

1. Information on this topic and numerous others related to the physics of baseball can be researched at the Web site of Alan Nathan, a professor of physics at the University of Illinois who has specialized in research related to the physics of baseball: http://webusers.npl.illinois.edu/~a-nathan/pob/index.html.

2. Jim Kaat, "The Mechanics of Baseball," *Popular Mechanics*, April 2003, 100–104.

3. Gregory Sawicki, Mont Hubbard, and William Stronge, "How to Hit Home Runs," *American Journal of Physics* 71, no. 11 (November 2003): 1152–62.

4. Research on the aerodynamics of baseball was conducted by the Glenn Research Center and is presented at http://www .baseball.grc.nasa.gov.

5. *New York Tribune*, July 18, 1920.

6. *New York Tribune*, July 18, 1920.

7. *Chicago Herald and Examiner*, July 25, 1920.

8. *Chicago Tribune*, July 18, 1920.

9. *New York Post*, July 20, 1920.

10. *New York Post*, July 20, 1920.

11. *New York World*, July 21, 1920.

12. *New York Sun*, July 21, 1920.

13. *Cleveland Press*, July 21, 1920.

14. *New York World*, July 25, 1920.

15. *New York Tribune*, July 26, 1920.

16. *New York Times*, July 27, 1920.

17. *New York World*, July 27, 1920.

7. The Last Three Weeks of Innocence and Purity

1. John McMurray, *Deadball Stars of the American League* (Cooperstown NY: Society for American Baseball Research), 627.

2. McMurray, *Deadball Stars*, 628.

3. Donald Gropman, *Say It Ain't So, Joe: The Story of Shoeless Joe Jackson* (Boston: Little, Brown, 1979).

4. *Chicago Tribune*, Aug. 1, 1920.

5. *New York American*, Aug. 2, 1920.

6. *New York Times*, July 29, 1920.

7. *New York Times*, July 29, 1920.

8. *New York Post*, July 30, 1920.

9. *Chicago Herald and Examiner*, Aug. 1, 1920.

10. *New York Sun*, Aug. 2, 1920.

11. *Chicago Tribune*, Aug. 4, 1920.

12. Ruth syndicated column, Aug. 4, 1920.

13. Rice syndicated column, Aug. 5, 1920.

14. *Chicago Tribune*, Aug. 5, 1920.

15. Ruth syndicated column, Aug. 5, 1920.

16. *New York Post*, Aug. 6, 1920.

17. *New York Sun*, Aug. 6, 1920.

18. *New York Tribune*, Aug. 8, 1920.

19. *New York American*, Aug. 9, 1920.

20. *Cleveland Press*, Aug. 5, 1920.

21. *Cleveland Press*, Aug. 5, 1920.

22. *New York American*, Aug. 10, 1920.

23. *New York American*, Aug. 15, 1920.

24. *New York American*, July 28, 1920.

8. Under Pallor

1. *New York American*, Aug. 17, 1920. It is appropriate at this point to interject a word in regard to Damon Runyon/Runyan. The famous writer was born in Manhattan, Kansas, as Damon Runyon. At some point early in his writing career, however, the name changed to Runyan, probably due to a typographical slip. Today it is referenced variously. The Runyon spelling is used in this book both because it was the original and also because it was the spelling most commonly used by the writer in 1920.

2. *New York Sun*, Aug. 18, 1920.

3. *New York Post*, Aug. 17, 1920.

4. *New York American*, Aug. 17, 1920.

5. Jamieson, interview.

6. *New York Sun*, Aug. 18, 1920.

7. *Cleveland Plain Dealer*, Aug. 18, 1920.

8. *Cleveland Plain Dealer*, Aug. 18, 1920.

9. Reisler, *Babe Ruth*, 186.

10. *New York American*, Aug. 18, 1920.

11. *New York Sun*, Aug. 18, 1920.

12. *New York Evening Post*, Aug. 17, 1920.

13. *Cleveland Plain Dealer*, Aug. 18, 1920.

14. *Cleveland Press*, Aug. 18, 1920.

15. *Chicago Tribune*, Aug. 18, 1920.

16. *Sporting News*, Aug. 26, 1920.

17. *New York Sun*, Aug. 18, 1920.

18. *New York Tribune*, Aug. 18, 1920.

19. *Sporting News*, Sept. 23, 1920.

20. *New York World*, Aug. 18, 1920.

21. Johnson's statement was released on Aug. 19, 1920, and was carried in all the major news media outlets in the interested cities.

22. *Cleveland Plain Dealer*, Aug. 19, 1920.

23. *Cleveland Plain Dealer*, Aug. 19, 1920.

24. *Cleveland Plain Dealer*, Aug. 19, 1920.

25. *New York American*, Aug. 19, 1920.

26. Wambsganss verified the Speaker-O'Neill fight during an interview with Mike Sowell in preparation for Sowell's book, *The Pitch That Killed* (New York: Macmillan, 1989).

27. *Cleveland Plain Dealer*, Aug. 21, 1920.

28. *Cleveland Plain Dealer*, Aug. 21, 1920.

9. Under Shadow

1. *New York World*, Aug. 19, 1920.

2. *Sporting News*, Aug. 26, 1920.

3. *New York Tribune*, Aug. 22, 1920.

4. *Sporting News*, Aug. 26, 1920.

5. *Sporting News*, Sept. 2, 1920.

6. *Sporting News*, Aug. 26, 1920.

7. *Cleveland Press*, Aug. 21, 1920.

8. *Cleveland Plain Dealer*, Aug. 24, 1920.

9. *New York Tribune*, Aug. 22, 1920.

10. *New York Times*, Aug. 22, 1920.

11. *New York Times*, Aug. 22, 1920.

12. *New York World*, Aug. 23, 1920.

13. *New York Times*, Aug. 23, 1920.

14. *New York Tribune*, Aug. 23, 1920.

15. *Chicago Herald and Examiner*, Aug. 24, 1920.

16. *New York Tribune*, Aug. 24, 1920.

17. *New York Post*, Aug. 24, 1920.

18. *Cleveland Press*, Aug. 24, 1920.

19. *Sporting News*, Aug. 26, 1920.

20. *Sporting News*, Sept. 2, 1920.

10. A Chigger in Conspiracy with Gamblers

1. The most complete and accurate set of ejection data is maintained by Project Retrosheet at http://www.retrosheet.org.

2. *Cleveland Plain Dealer*, Aug. 26, 1920.

3. *Sporting News*, Sept. 2, 1920.

4. *Cleveland Plain Dealer*, Aug. 28, 1920.

5. Timothy M. Gay, *Tris Speaker: The Rough-and-Tumble Life of a Baseball Legend* (Lincoln: University of Nebraska Press, 2005), 201.

6. *Cleveland Press*, Sept. 2, 1920.

7. *Cleveland Press*, Sept. 1, 1920.

8. *New York Times*, Aug. 27, 1920.

9. *Cleveland Press*, Sept. 2, 1920.

10. *Cleveland Press*, Aug. 30, 1920.

11. Ruth syndicated column, Aug. 29, 1920.

12. *Chicago Tribune*, Sept. 13, 1920.

13. *New York Tribune*, Aug. 26, 1920.

14. *Chicago Tribune*, Aug. 27, 1920.

15. *Chicago Herald and Examiner*, Aug. 27, 1920.

16. *New York Sun*, Aug. 29, 1920.

17. *New York American*, Sept. 2, 1920.

18. *Sporting News*, Oct. 7, 1920.

19. Asinof, *Eight Men Out*, 148.

11. A Phosphate at the Edelweiss

1. *Cleveland Plain Dealer*, Sept. 3, 1920. The fullest description of the Indians' singing habits is contained in Sowell, *Pitch That Killed*.

2. *Cleveland Plain Dealer*, Sept. 4, 1920.

3. *Chicago Tribune*, Sept. 5, 1920.

4. *Chicago Tribune*, Sept. 5, 1920.

5. *New York Tribune*, Sept. 5, 1920.

6. *Chicago Tribune*, Sept 8. 1920.

7. *Chicago Tribune*, Sept. 8, 1920.

8. *Cleveland Plain Dealer*, Sept. 8, 1920.

9. *Cleveland Plain Dealer*, Sept. 8, 1920.

10. *Chicago Daily News*, Sept. 9, 1920.

11. Ruth syndicated column, Sept. 10, 1920.

12. *Cleveland Press*, Sept. 18, 1920.

13. Ruth syndicated column, Sept. 14, 1920.

14. Jamieson, interview.

15. *Chicago Daily News*, Sept. 13, 1920.

16. *New York American*, Sept. 15, 1920.

17. Ruth syndicated column, Sept. 17, 1920.

18. *New York Times*, Sept. 18, 1920.

19. *Chicago Tribune*, Sept. 19, 1920.
20. *Chicago Tribune*, Sept. 19, 1920.

12. Eddie Chews, Chicago Stews

1. *Chicago Tribune*, Sept. 19, 1920.
2. *Chicago Tribune*, Sept. 19, 1920.
3. *Chicago Tribune*, Sept. 19, 1920.
4. *New York Times*, Sept. 19, 1920.
5. *New York American*, Sept. 19, 1920.
6. *New York American*, Sept. 25, 1920.
7. *New York Times*, Sept. 25, 1920.
8. *Chicago Tribune*, Sept. 20, 1920.
9. *Chicago Daily News*, Sept. 22, 1920.
10. *Cleveland Plain Dealer*, Sept. 22, 1920.
11. *Chicago Tribune*, Sept. 24, 1920.
12. *New York Tribune*, Sept. 27, 1920.
13. *Chicago Tribune*, Sept. 22, 1920.
14. *Chicago Tribune*, Sept. 22, 1920.
15. *Chicago Tribune*, Sept. 22, 1920.
16. *Chicago Tribune*, Sept. 23, 1920.
17. *New York American*, Sept. 23, 1920.
18. *Chicago Tribune*, Sept. 23, 1920.
19. *Sporting News*, Sept. 30, 1920.
20. *Chicago Tribune*, Sept. 23, 1920.
21. *Chicago Tribune*, Sept. 24, 1920.
22. Wood, interview.
23. *Chicago Tribune*, Sept. 24, 1920.
24. *Cleveland Plain Dealer*, Sept. 25, 1920.
25. *Chicago Herald and Examiner*, Sept. 25, 1920.
26. *Chicago Herald and Examiner*, Sept. 25, 1920.
27. *Chicago Herald and Examiner*, Sept. 25, 1920.

13. Losers Laugh, Winners Cry

1. *Sporting News*, Sept. 30, 1920.
2. *Chicago Herald and Examiner*, Sept. 26, 1920.
3. *Chicago Tribune*, Sept. 26, 1920.
4. *Chicago Tribune*, Sept. 26, 1920.
5. *Chicago Herald and Examiner*, Sept. 27, 1920.
6. *Cleveland Press*, Sept. 27, 1920.

7. *New York Post*, Sept. 27, 1920.

8. *Chicago Herald and Examiner*, Sept. 27, 1920.

9. *Chicago Herald and Examiner*, Sept. 27, 1920.

10. *New York Sun*, Sept. 27, 1920.

11. *Chicago Tribune*, Sept. 28, 1920.

12. *Chicago Tribune*, Sept. 28, 1920.

13. *Chicago Tribune*, Sept. 28, 1920.

14. *Chicago Tribune*, Sept. 28, 1920.

15. *Chicago Tribune*, Sept. 28, 1920.

16. Transcript of Jackson's statement.

17. Transcript of Jackson's statement.

18. *Chicago Tribune*, Sept. 28, 1920.

19. *Chicago Tribune*, Sept. 28, 1920.

20. *Chicago Tribune*, Sept. 28, 1920.

21. *New York Times*, Sept. 28, 1920.

22. *Chicago Tribune*, Sept. 28, 1920.

23. *Chicago Tribune*, Sept. 28, 1920.

24. *Chicago Daily News*, Sept. 29, 1920.

25. *Chicago Tribune*, Sept. 29, 1920.

26. *Chicago Tribune*, Sept. 28, 1920.

27. *New York Times*, Sept. 28, 1920.

28. *Cleveland Plain Dealer*, Sept. 29, 1920.

29. *New York World*, Sept. 29, 1920.

30. *Cleveland Press*, Sept. 28, 1920.

31. *Cleveland Plain Dealer*, Sept. 29, 1920.

32. *Chicago Daily News*, Sept. 28, 1920.

33. *Chicago Daily News*, Sept. 28, 1920.

34. *New York Sun*, Sept. 29, 1920.

35. *Chicago Tribune*, Sept. 29, 1920.

36. *Chicago Tribune*, Sept. 30, 1920.

37. Wood, interview.

38. *Chicago Tribune*, Oct. 3, 1920.

39. *Chicago Tribune*, Oct. 3, 1920.

40. *Chicago Herald and Examiner*, Oct. 3, 1920.

41. While largely forgotten today, the Lasker plan has been examined in many histories of the 1920s era, among them J. G. Taylor Spink's acclaimed biography of Commissioner K. M. Landis, *Judge Landis and Twenty-five Years of Baseball* (New York: Thomas & Crowell, 1947).

42. Spink, *Judge Landis*, 65.

43. Spink, *Judge Landis*, 65.

44. *Chicago Herald and Examiner*, Oct. 4, 1920.

45. *Cleveland Plain Dealer*, Oct. 3, 1920.

46. *Cleveland Plain Dealer*, Oct. 3, 1920.

14. Aftermath

1. *Sporting News*, Dec. 4, 1965.

2. *Lincoln (NE) Star*, May 12, 1922.

3. Sowell, *Pitch That Killed*.

4. For purposes of comparison, the average age at death of the 1920 White Sox player was seventy-one; for the 1920 Yankees it was seventy-four.

5. Fred Lieb, *Baseball as I Have Known It* (New York: Coward, Mccann & Geoghagen, 1977), 132.

6. *Reach Guide* (Chicago: A. G. Spalding, 1921).

7. *Sporting News*, Oct. 7, 1920.

8. *Sporting News*, Oct. 28, 1920.

9. *Sporting News*, Nov. 4, 1920.

10. *Sporting News*, Nov. 25, 1920.

11. *Sporting News*, Jan. 20, 1921.

12. *Sporting News*, Dec. 16, 1920.

13. Article 1, clause (a), New Major League Agreement, adopted 1921. The full text of this agreement can be found in the 1921 *Reach Guide*, 41–42.

15. Damon and Ring at the Series

1. *New York American*, Oct. 11, 1920.

2. *New York American*, Oct. 5, 1920.

3. *New York American*, Oct. 4, 1920.

4. *New York American*, Oct. 4, 1920.

5. *New York American*, Oct. 6, 1920.

6. *New York American*, Oct. 6, 1920.

7. *New York American*, Oct. 7, 1920.

8. *New York American*, Oct. 8, 1920.

9. *New York American*, Oct. 8, 1920.

10. *New York American*, Oct. 10, 1920.

11. *New York American*, Oct. 10, 1920.

12. *New York American*, Oct. 11, 1920.

13. *New York American,* Oct. 11, 1920.
14. *New York American,* Oct. 12, 1920.
15. *New York American,* Oct. 12, 1920.
16. *New York American,* Oct. 13, 1920.
17. *New York American,* Oct. 13, 1920.

Index

Abbaticchio, Ed, 18
Acosta, Jose, 189, 198, 199
Alexander, Grover Cleveland, 176, 177
American Journal of Physics, 71
American League: Ban Johnson and, 62–63; power imbalance in, 49–50; the reserve clause and, 62
American League owners: Ban Johnson and, 5–6, 63–64, 66–67; the Loyal Five, 66, 242, 243; and suspension of Black Sox conspirators, 226
Asinof, Eliot, 32, 37, 44, 169, 236
Attell, Abe, 197, 211
Austrian, Alfred, 40, 41, 225
Axelson, G. W., 261n6
Ayres, Yancey "Doc," 151, 173

Baer, Bugs, 148
Bagby, Jim: early career of, 54; games following Ray Chapman's death, 143, 144; longevity of, 239; 1920 season performances, 55, 58, 60, 78, 79, 89, 90, 113, 114, 116, 129, 156, 158, 160, 173, 175, 184, 186, 200, 206, 207, 226, 230; 1920 World Series performance, 238, 247, 254
Bagby, Jim, Jr., 54
Bailey, Gene, 108
Baker, John Franklin "Home Run Baker," 17, 20

Baker, Ottilie, 20
Ball, Phil, 66, 68, 243
Barber, Turner, 177
Barrow, Ed, 7, 12–13, 15, 79, 95
Barry, Jack, 6, 28, 95
baseball: American confidence in society and, 214–15; commissioner of, 234, 242–45; Cruisenberry-Loomis letter and, 195–96; free agents, 5; gloves, 206–7; National Agreement, 241, 242, 245; on-field fatalities and, 117–18; proposals to reorganize the governance of, 231–34, 240–45; response to the death of Ray Chapman, 3–4, 9–11, 125–28, 133–37, 145–47, 161–62; "review board" instituted by owners, 68; "syndicated," 62. *See also* baseball attendance; baseball gambling; bats; batters and batting; beanings
baseball attendance: Babe Ruth's impact on, 2–3, 15–16, 77, 80, 102–3, 111, 182; Chicago White Sox, 2, 102–3, 104, 106–7, 190, 192; Cleveland Indians, 96, 184, 205–6, 208; Detroit Tigers, 111; growth in, 2; modern records on, 261n2; New York Giants, 15, 261n2; New York Yankees, 80, 82, 88, 118, 147, 149–50, 165–66, 261n2

baseball gambling: allegations against 1920 White Sox, 9, 44, 45, 46–47, 100, 167–69, 189–90, 193–94, 204–5; Buck Herzog and, 202, 203; Cruisenberry-Loomis letter and, 193–94, 195–96; impact on baseball of, 1–2; Joe Jackson's grand jury testimony about, 222–23; Maclay Hoyne on, 231; 1918 World Series and, 8, 261n8, 262n6; 1920 Cubs and, 176–79, 202; 1920 Indians and, 112–13; 1920 grand jury investigation into, 178–79, 207–8; possible involvement of players in, 8. See also Black Sox scandal

Baseball Magazine, 93

Baseball Writers Association of America (BBWAA), 178

bases on balls, 101; Babe Ruth and, 105–6

bats: of Babe Ruth, 73–74; "bottle" bat, 73; and home runs, 70–71, 72–73; mass of, 73; speed of, 71, 72–73; stylistic experimentation with, 73; "sweet spot," 71; vibrational frequency of, 70–71

"Battering Babe" (song), 183

batters and batting: early twentieth-century averages, 73; home run physics, 69–76; NASA's "hit modeler," 71–72; swing arc, 71

Bayne, Bill, 77–78, 231

beanings: of Chick Fewster, 21, 121, 146; of Ray Chapman, 3–4, 9, 120–24; of Russ Corhan, 146

Bell, S. M., 201

Benton, Rube, 8, 203

Black Sox scandal: Ban Johnson and, 41, 67, 202, 203–4; Buck Weaver and, 40, 211, 217, 222, 224, 231, 237; Charles Comiskey and, 40, 41, 42, 67, 202, 204, 221; *Chicago Herald and Examiner*'s investigation into, 196–97; Chick Gandil and, 39,

42–43, 46, 211, 221, 222, 223, 236, 263n10; confessions of key conspirators, 45–46, 221–24, 227–28; crimes of conspirators, 225; Cruisenberry-Loomis letter and, 193–94, 195–96; early allegations and investigations into, 40–42; Eddie Cicotte and, 37, 38, 39, 211, 212, 220, 221–22, 236–37; effect of, on Ring Lardner, 246; Fred McMullin and, 40, 211, 217, 222; Happy Felsch and, 39, 211, 224, 228, 236, 263n12; Hughie Fullerton's inquiry into, 40, 41–42; Illinois state's attorney on, 225, 231; Joe Jackson and, 40, 45–46, 211, 222–24, 236, 237; Lefty Williams and, 38, 39, 45–46, 211, 222–23; *New York Sun*'s indictment of, 220–21; 1920 grand jury investigation into, 45–46, 202–4, 207–8, 217, 221–24, 227–28; origin of, 37; owner support for suspension of conspirators, 226; public opinion over, 228; Swede Risberg and, 39, 41, 211, 222, 263n11; and tainted World Series games and performances, 38–40

Bodie, Frank Stephen "Ping Bodie": acquired by the Yankees, 18–19; late-season injury in 1920, 182; 1920 season performances, 21, 23, 24, 25, 27, 81, 85, 86–87, 88, 90, 104, 111, 119, 123, 149, 151, 166, 181

Boston Braves, 65

Boston Knights of Columbus, 181

Boston Post, 15

Boston Red Sox: Amos Strunk's career with, 94–95; Babe Ruth's career with, 12–14, 95; 1918 dispute over postseason game profits, 66; sale of Babe Ruth to the Yankees, 12, 14–15; sale of Carl Mays to the Yankees, 7,

14–15; sale of Ray Caldwell to the Indians, 52; World Series of 1918 and, 8

Boston Red Sox (1920): and boycott discussion against Carl Mays, 4, 9, 125–26, 161, 162; games against the Indians, 59–60, 78–79, 112, 140–45, 200; games against the White Sox, 107–8, 166–69, 187–89; games against the Yankees, 22, 23–24, 26, 91, 180–81; the "New National League" and, 243; as noncontenders, 50

Brigham, Henry, 179, 196, 208

Brooklyn Dodgers: George Hildebrand with, 153; John Mails with, 159; in the 1920 World Series, 234, 238, 251–59

Brower, Frank, 139

Brunski, Milton, 165

Burns, Bill, 197

Burns, George: 1920 season performances, 112, 172, 185–86; 1920 World Series performance, 256; Ring Lardner on, 257; traded to the Athletics, 18

Burwell, Bill, 77

Bush, Bullet Joe, 145

Bush, Donie, 150, 161, 172, 219

Bush, Joe, 94, 166–67, 168, 181

Caldwell, Ray: acquired by the Indians, 52; games following Ray Chapman's death, 142, 143, 144; 1920 season performances, 84, 85, 113, 130, 156, 158, 173, 186, 230

Camp Jerome WI, 29

Carney, Gene, 263n18

Carter, Nick, 202

Carter, Paul, 261n8

Chapman, Kathleen Daly: Cuckoo Jamieson on, 60; death of, 238; marriage to Ray Chapman, 56; Ray Chapman's death and, 124–25, 128, 130, 131; World Series share given to, 235

Chapman, Rae Marie, 238

Chapman, Ray: baseball's response to death of, 3–4, 9–11, 125–28, 133–37, 145–47, 161–62; career with Cleveland Indians, 55–57, 264n1; death of wife and child of, 238; fatal beaning of, 3–4, 9, 120–24; funeral services for, 128, 130–32; marriage of, 56–57; Memorial Day held in Cleveland for, 171; the Pullman car Quartet and, 170

Chase, Hal, 8, 203, 211

Chesbro, Jack, 153–54

Chicago Cubs: 1918 dispute over postseason game profits, 66; 1918 World Series, 8, 261n8, 262n6; 1920 game fixing and, 176–79, 202

Chicago Daily News, 190, 201, 214, 215

Chicago Herald and Examiner, 103, 216, 219; accusations against Black Sox players by, 211–13; A. L. Hodges on Babe Ruth, 74–76; on gambling in baseball, 177, 231; investigation into Black Sox scandal, 196–97; on the Lasker Plan, 234

Chicago History Museum, 41

Chicago Inter-Ocean, 246

Chicago Tribune: Cruisenberry-Loomis letter in, 193–94; on gambling by 1920 Cubs, 177–78; Hughie Fullerton's inquiry into Black Sox scandal, 40, 41–42; I. E. Sanborn on Buck Weaver, 31; I. E. Sanborn on Happy Felsch, 100, 180; I. E. Sanborn on Lefty Williams, 200; reporting on Black Sox scandal by, 222, 225; reporting on Charles Comiskey's probe of St. Louis for corruption, 202; stories on Babe Ruth, 80–81, 105; stories on Carl Mays, 126, 136, 164

Chicago White Sox, 2, 28, 30;

Chicago White Sox (*cont.*)
acquisition of Eddie Collins, 28–29; acquisition of Joe Jackson, 35–36, 49, 263n23; contract conflicts within, 42; Eddie Cicotte and, 32–34; hatred of Charles Comiskey among, 28–29, 37; key acquisitions by, 28–29, 31–37; 1908 pennant race, 48; 1917 World Series and, 34; "Ping Bodie" and, 18; and player personalities, 30; "The Woodland Bards," 29. *See also* Black Sox scandal; Comiskey, Charles

Chicago White Sox (1920): allegations of gambling by, 9, 44, 45, 46–47, 100, 167–69, 189–90, 193–94, 204–5; Amos Strunk and, 97–98; Charles Comiskey's response to gambling allegations, 220; and Clean Sox, 224–25; confessions of Black Sox conspirators, 221–24, 227–28; and controversial call against Babe Ruth, 103–4; Cruisenberry-Loomis letter and, 193–94, 195–96; factions within, 8–9, 30, 97, 136; fan loyalty to, 216; final week of the season, 216; games against the Athletics, 44, 99–100, 137–38, 200–201; games against the Browns, 179, 187, 230, 231; games against the Indians, 44, 57, 58, 96–97, 98, 199–200, 205–7, 208–11, 212; games against the Red Sox, 107–8, 166–69, 187–89; games against the Senators, 108, 114, 138–40, 189; games against the Tigers, 44, 98–99, 115, 179–80, 217–19; games against the Yankees, 23, 80–83, 102–7, 161, 163, 164, 165–66, 187, 190–93; home attendance, 102–3, 104, 106–7, 190, 192; inconsistent early season play, 43–45; inconsistent late-season play, 47, 166–69, 179, 188–89; Joe Jackson's grand jury testimony about gambling, 222–23; longevity of players, 271n4; and "new batting order," 227; the "New National League" and, 243; plot to rob, 164–65; public opinion turns against, 228; replacement of Nemo Leibold, 95–96; response to Carl Mays and death of Ray Chapman, 10–11, 133, 136–37, 164. *See also* Black Sox scandal

chiggers, 163

Chill, Ollie, 90, 137, 138, 189

Chipman, William, 82, 102, 107, 121, 150

Cicotte, Eddie: affinity for living dangerously, 30; Black Sox scandal and, 37, 38, 39, 211, 212, 220, 221–22, 236–37; career with the White Sox, 32–34; contract conflict with Charles Comiskey, 42; factions within the 1920 White Sox and, 8; game fixing by the 1920 White Sox and, 167, 168–69, 205; 1920 season performances, 43, 44, 80, 99, 103, 114, 116, 138, 139, 165, 166–67, 179, 193, 201, 217–18; number of batter hits by, 135; the shine ball and, 54

Cincinnati OH, 234

Cincinnati Reds, 1, 38, 73

Clark, Bob, 145, 175

Clean Sox, 9, 224–25

Cleveland Indians: as the Cleveland Naps, 48; following the 1920 season, 238–39; and growth in attendance, 2; Jim Dunn's key acquisitions, 50–52; Joe Jackson's career with, 48–49, 98; key homegrown players, 52–57; 1908 pennant race, 48; purchased by Jim Dunn, 49; spitball pitchers on, 54–55

Cleveland Indians (1920): acquisition of Joey Sewell, 173; acquisition of John Mails, 159–60; anticipation of a World Series appearance, 201; boycott discussions against Carl Mays and, 9, 161–62; Cleveland celebrates the championship of, 234–35; early season performance, 57–60; fan organizations, 171; fatal beaning of Ray Chapman and, 3–4, 9, 120–24, 144, 131, 155–58, 170–71; gambling and, 112–13; games against the Athletics, 78, 112–13, 145, 154–57, 185–86; games against the Browns, 57, 60, 115, 174–75, 218, 219, 226; games against the Red Sox, 59–60, 78–79, 112, 140–45, 200; games against the Senators, 112, 160, 186; games against the Tigers, 171–73, 229–31; games against the White Sox, 44, 57, 58, 96–97, 98, 199–200, 205–7, 208–11, 212; games against the Yankees, 23, 25, 58, 59, 83–91, 113–15, 118–23, 128–30, 181–85; games following Ray Chapman's death, 140–45; home attendance, 96, 184, 205–6, 208; July road trip, 78–79; longevity of players, 239; public faith in baseball and, 215; the Pullman car Quartet, 170–71; Ray Chapman Memorial Day, 171; search for a fourth starter, 158–60; honoring Tris Speaker, 113; standings at the end of August, 160–61; and Tigers' informal agreement to "lay down" for, 229; World Series, 234, 238, 246–59. *See also* Chapman, Kathleen Daly; Chapman, Ray

Cleveland OH: celebrating the Indians' championship, 234–35; outrage directed at Carl Mays over Ray Chapman's death, 126

Cleveland Naps, 48

Cleveland Plain Dealer: on a Babe Ruth home run following Ray Chapman's death, 129; Henry Edwards on the Indians' singing, 170–71; on the Indians' chances of a World Series appearance, 201, 211; on the Indians winning the pennant, 226, 227, 234–35; urging baseball to boycott Carl Mays, 126

Cleveland Press: on Carl Mays and crisis in baseball, 126, 150, 161, 162; on Duster Mails, 160, 186; on Joey Sewell, 186; reporting on the Indians, 84, 112–13, 227; on Tris Speaker, 141

"closers," 85

Cobb, Ty: baseball's dislike of, 56; base hits record, 226; bases on balls and, 101; batting stats, 14; batting titles, 49; Carl Mays and, 8, 10, 134–35, 161; games following Ray Chapman's death, 147, 148–49, 150; 1920 season performances, 109, 172, 219; response to Ray Chapman's death, 125–26

Cohan, George M., 208

Collins, Eddie: accuses White Sox of fixing games, 169; affinity for "playing it straight," 30; Amos Strunk and, 98; beaned in Detroit, 98–99; Chick Gandil and, 29–30; and Clean Sox, 224; Charles Comiskey's acquisition of, 28–29; factions within the 1920 White Sox and, 9, 97; nicknamed "Cocky," 98; 1920 season performances, 43, 44, 45, 80, 85, 86, 98, 99, 116, 140, 163, 168, 188, 189, 191, 201, 207, 210–11, 219; superstitions of, 210

Collins, John Francis "Shano": early career with the White Sox, 35; factions within the 1920

Collins, John Francis (*cont.*)
    White Sox and, 9, 97; 1920 sea-
    son performances, 45, 95, 180,
    193, 227, 230
Collins, Rip: games following Ray
    Chapman's death, 147, 151; 1920
    season performances, 26, 77, 85,
    111, 187
Colorado Rockies, 71, 261n2
Comiskey, Charles: acquisition of
    Amos Strunk, 96; allegations
    of gambling by the 1920 White
    Sox and, 169, 204–5, 220; and
    Black Sox scandal, 40, 41, 42,
    67, 202, 204, 221; Buck Weav-
    er's 1920 audience with, 227;
    the Carl Mays crisis and, 11; and
    contract conflict with players,
    42; Damon Runyon on, 248;
    development of the American
    League and, 63; Eddie Cicotte
    and, 32–34; key acquisitions
    for the White Sox, 28–29,
    31–37; and relationship with
    Ban Johnson, 2, 5–6, 11, 63, 64,
    204–5, 261n6; reorganization of
    baseball's governance and, 232,
    241; supporting suspension of
    Black Sox conspirators, 226; the
    White Sox's hatred of, 28–29, 37
Comiskey Park attendance, 2,
    102–3, 104, 106–7, 190, 192
Connolly, Tommy, 103, 104, 106,
    129, 134
Coogan's Bluff, 88
Corhan, Russ, 146
Corridon, Frank, 153, 154
Courtney, Harry, 80, 139, 160, 189
Coveleski, Harry, 54
Coveleski, Stan: Damon Runyon
    on, 249, 252–53, 257; games fol-
    lowing Ray Chapman's death,
    144; longevity of, 239; 1920 sea-
    son performances, 57, 58, 59, 86,
    97, 112, 113, 115, 116, 119, 120, 123,
    141, 154, 158, 172, 183, 185, 186,
    200, 226; 1920 World Series

performance, 238, 252–53, 257;
    as a spitball pitcher, 54–55
Cox, James, 130
Cruisenberry, James, 80–81,
    193–94, 202
Cruisenberry-Loomis letter,
    193–94, 195–96
curve balls, 71

Daley, George, 227
Daly, Kathleen. *See* Chapman,
    Kathleen Daly
Daniel, Dan, 127
Dauss, Hooks, 98, 109, 173, 218–19
Davis, Dixie, 101–2, 166, 179, 219
Davis, Frank "Dixie," 197
defensive replacements, 85
Detroit Free Press, 236
Detroit Tigers: boycott discussion
    against Carl Mays and, 4, 9,
    10, 125–26, 161; games against
    the Indians, 171–73, 229–31;
    games against the White Sox,
    44, 98–99, 115, 179–80, 217–19;
    games against the Yankees, 25,
    108–12, 145–52, 186–87; hidden-
    ball trick against the Yankees,
    111; informal agreement to "lay
    down" for the Indians, 229;
    1908 pennant race, 48; 1920
    attendance, 111; as noncontend-
    ers in 1920, 50
Deveney, Sean, 262n3
Dinneen, Bill, 134, 189
Dixon, Donald, 113
Dreyfuss, Barney, 232, 244–45
Dryden, Charles, 211–13
Dubuc, Jean, 8, 262n8
Dugan, Joe, 22, 78, 155, 156, 201
Dunn, Jim: acquisition of Joey
    Sewell, 173; Babe Ruth and, 113;
    Ban Johnson and, 66; entering
    the American League, 63; key
    acquisitions of, 50–52; purchase
    of the Indians, 49; at Ray Chap-
    man's funeral, 131; September
    series against White Sox and,
    208

Dunn Field, 96, 184, 205–6, 208
Dykes, Jimmy, 155, 185

The Edelweiss (Chicago), 192
Edwards, Henry, 170–71, 234–35, 264n1
Ehmke, Howard, 109, 148, 187
Eight Men Out (Asinof), 32, 44, 169, 236
ejections, 154
Ellerbe, Frank, 139
Erickson, Eric, 80, 139
Evans, Billy, 134, 208–9
Evans, Joe: acquired by the Indians, 53; games following Ray Chapman's death, 141, 144; longevity of, 239; 1920 season performances, 85, 174, 184, 200, 206, 207, 226; the Pullman car Quartet and, 170

Faber, Urban Clarence "Red": affinity for "playing it straight," 30; career with the White Sox, 34–35, 37; factions within the 1920 White Sox and, 9, 97; and friendship with Buck Weaver, 35; 1920 season performances, 44, 80, 82, 105–6, 108, 116, 137, 139–40, 166, 179–80, 189, 191, 208, 209, 230
Faeth, Tony, 87, 159
Falk, Bibb, 227
Falls, Joe, 236, 237
fan organizations, 171
fans: anger toward Black Sox conspirators, 228; Babe Ruth and, 199; Buck Herzog's fight with, 228; and Carl Mays's fight with Bryan Hayes, 6, 22; criticism of Lefty Williams, 96–97; harassment of Joe Jackson, 96–97, 206, 212
fastballs, 71
Federal League, 17, 28, 35
Felsch, Happy: Black Sox scandal and, 39, 211, 224, 228, 236,

263n12; on Camp Jerome, 28; dugout brawl with Dickie Kerr, 189; factions within the 1920 White Sox and, 9; leaves the 1920 season, 219; on near-strike by White Sox, 37; 1920 season performances, 43, 44, 99, 108, 139, 140, 169, 180, 188, 189, 191, 193, 201, 207
Fenway Park, 181
Fewster, Charles "Chick," 21, 121, 125, 146
films. *See* movies
Finley, Charles O., 28
Fitzgerald, F. Scott, 247
Fitzgerald, W. S., 130
fixed games. *See* baseball gambling; Black Sox scandal
Fohl, Leo, 52
Ford, Russ, 146
Foster, Eddie, 79, 108, 143, 200
fraud, 225
Frazee, Harry: the Carl Mays crisis and, 7; and dealings with the Yankees, 14–15, 19; joining the National Commission, 68; purchasing Elmer Myers, 158; questioning Ban Johnson's leadership, 63–64; Red Sox players sold by, 7, 14–15, 52; reorganization of baseball's governance and, 241; supporting suspension of Black Sox conspirators, 226
free agents, 5
Fullerton, Hughie, 40, 41–42

gambling. *See* baseball gambling
Gandil, Chick: affinity for living dangerously, 30, 36–37; Black Sox scandal and, 39, 42–43, 46, 211, 221, 222, 223, 236, 263n10; Charles Comiskey's acquisition of, 29; contract conflict with Charles Comiskey, 42; Eddie Cicotte's grand jury testimony against, 222; Eddie Collins and,

Gandil, Chick (*cont.*)
29–30; factions within the 1920
White Sox and, 8; with the
Indians, 50; Joe Jackson's grand
jury testimony against, 223;
replaced by Shano Collins, 95
Gardner, Larry: acquired by the
Indians, 51; games following
Ray Chapman's death, 142, 145;
1919 gambling conspiracy and,
86; 1920 season performances,
84, 85, 87, 88, 90, 119, 120, 122,
123, 155, 173, 175, 185, 186, 200,
229; Ray Chapman's marriage
and, 57; and slump following
Ray Chapman's death, 157
Gedeon, Joe, 41, 202
Gehrig, Lou, 17
Gharrity, Patsy, 139
Gleason, Kid: confessions of key
Black Sox conspirators and,
221, 224; denies game fixing by
the 1920 White Sox, 205; "new
batting order" after suspension
of Black Sox conspirators, 227;
1920 season, 43, 140, 169, 200–
201, 206, 207, 208, 212, 230;
on playing against Carl Mays,
136; telling White Sox about
robbery plot, 165; working with
Ray Schalk, 32
Gleich, Frank, 26
Glenn Research Center, 265n4
The Glory of Their Times (Ritter), 4
Grabiner, Harry, 41, 42, 264n23
grand slams, 238, 247, 254
Graney, Jack: on Carl Mays, 3;
games following Ray Chap-
man's death, 141, 142, 143,
145; longevity of, 239; 1920
season performances, 59, 129,
175; offensive shortcomings
of, 51; the Pullman car Quartet and, 170; Ray Chapman's
fatal beaning and, 122, 124;
Ray Chapman's wedding and,
56; and slump following Ray

Chapman's death, 157; Tris
Speaker and, 131, 142
Griffin, Ivy, 185
Griffith, Clark, 66, 67, 243
Griffith Stadium, 115
Grimes, Burleigh, 257
Groh, Heinie, 73

Hanlon, Ned, 153
Hanna, William, 82–83, 104, 109,
121, 125
Hannah, James Harrison "Truck,"
17–18
Harper, Harry, 108
Harris, Bucky, 139
Harriss, Slim, 154–55
Haverstraw NJ, 148, 163
Hayes, Bryan, 6, 22
Headin' Home (film), 148, 164
Heilmann, Harry, 109
Hendrix, Claude, 176, 177, 202,
261n8
Hendryx, Tim, 142, 144, 200
Henry, John, 121
Herrmann, Garry: meeting with
the Minor Leagues, 244; and
the National Commission, 42,
64, 65, 66, 67, 232
Herzog, Buck, 8, 177, 202, 203, 228
Heydler, John, 66, 67, 178, 232,
233, 243
hidden-ball trick, 111
Hildebrand, George, 106, 108,
153–54, 155–56
hit batters: Chick Fewster, 21, 121,
146; Eddie Collins, 98–99; number hit by Carl Mays, 135; Ray
Chapman, 3–4, 9, 120–24; Russ
Corhan, 146. *See also* beanings
"hit modeler," 71–72
Hodge, Clarence "Shovel," 180,
230
Hodges, A. L., 74–76
Hofmann, Fred "Bootnose," 18, 26
home runs: Babe Ruth and, 13,
16, 23–24, 59, 76–78, 80–82, 89,
91, 102, 105, 107, 109, 111, 115,

116, 130, 163, 181, 182, 183, 184, 187, 190, 198–99; Elmer Smith's World Series grand slam, 238, 254, 255; Happy Flesch and, 43; Jim Bagby's World Series home run, 238, 247, 254; Perry Werden and, 181; and the physics of hitting, 69–76

Hooper, Harry, 7, 19, 66

Hoyne, Maclay, 41, 225, 231

Hoyt, Waite, 22, 140, 141, 188

Hubbard, Mont, 71, 72

Huggins, Miller, 15, 104, 239–40

Huston, Tillinghast L'Hommideau: and Ban Johnson, 6, 63–64; and Carl Mays, 135, 147, 181; drunken celebration in Windsor, Ontario, 109–11; and Harry Frazee, 14–15, 19; players acquired by, prior to 1915 season, 16–21; and rumored train accident involving Ruth, 183

instructional films, 164

In the Wake of the News (column), 105, 204, 246

Italian Americans, 18

Jackson, Joe: acquired by the White Sox, 35–36, 49, 263n23; affinity for living dangerously, 30; Amos Strunk and, 98; Black Sox scandal and, 40, 45–46, 211, 222–24, 236, 237; and Chick Gandil, 36–37; contract conflict with Charles Comiskey, 42; Damon Runyon on, 248; dugout brawl with Dickie Kerr, 189; factions within the 1920 White Sox and, 9; and harassment by Indians fans, 96–97, 206, 212; with the Indians, 48–49, 98; and military deferment during World War I, 36, 97; 1920 season performances, 43, 44, 45, 46, 80, 98, 99, 104, 107, 108,

116, 137, 163, 168, 169, 180, 188, 191, 201, 207, 212, 217, 219; and Swede Risberg, 36–37, 224

James, Bill, 8

Jamieson, Charlie "Cuckoo": acquired by the Indians, 51; games following Ray Chapman's death, 140–41, 142, 143, 145; 1920 season performances, 59, 79, 119, 123, 129, 219, 229; suspects game fixing by the White Sox, 189

Jennings, Hughie, 10

Johnson, Ban: accusations against the 1920 White Sox, 204; and the American League, 62–63; Black Sox scandal and, 41, 67, 202, 203–4; and Charles Comiskey, 2, 5–6, 11, 63, 64, 204–5, 261n6; diminishment of the power of, 245; Jacob Ruppert and, 6, 7, 63–64; and the National Commission, 64–68; and the National League, 61–63; 1919 postseason money dispute with the Yankees, 67; personality of, 4, 61; reorganization of baseball's governance and, 240–45; at Ray Chapman's funeral, 131; and relationship with owners, 5–6, 63–64, 68, 241; responding to Ray Chapman's beaning, 4–5, 6–7, 9, 11, 126, 128, 134, 135, 165

Johnson, Walter, 24, 50, 80, 108, 138, 146

Johnston, Jimmy, 53

Johnston, Wheeler "Doc": career with the Indians, 53; on Carl Mays, 3; 1920 season performances, 57–58, 59, 87, 89, 120, 123, 129, 141, 155, 172, 173, 183, 200, 206, 207; the Pullman car Quartet and, 170; and slump following Ray Chapman's death, 157

Jones, Fielder, 5

Jones, Sam "Sad Sam," 7, 91, 107–8, 166, 168, 188

Joss, Addie, 48, 49

Jourdan, Ted, 43, 45, 227

Judge, Joe, 139, 189

Keefe, Dave, 99, 156, 186

Kelly, Mark, 103

Kerr, Dickie: acquired by the White Sox, 37; affinity for "playing it straight," 30; Clean Sox celebration after teammates confess to game fixing, 224; contract conflict with Charles Comiskey, 42; dugout brawl with Joe Jackson and Happy Felsch, 189; factions within the 1920 White Sox and, 9, 97; the 1919 World Series gambling conspiracy and, 38; 1920 season performances, 43, 44, 81, 99, 107, 108, 114, 137, 138, 140, 163, 167, 169, 179, 188, 189, 190, 206–7, 218, 231

Kessel and Baumann, 148

Kiefer, Joe, 230

Kilduff, Pete, 254

Kilgallen, Jim, 237

Knights of Columbus, 181

Kofoed, J. C., 93

Lajoie, Napoleon, 48, 49, 131

Landis, Kenesaw M., 42; as baseball commissioner, 244–45; declaring Dutch Leonard persona non grata, 262n8; New National League and, 243; reorganization of baseball's governance and, 232, 233, 234

Lanyon, James, 171

Lapp, Jack, 28

Lardner, Ring: career of, 246; death of, 248; fiction writing and, 247; reporting on the 1920 World Series, 246–47, 248–59; writing style of, 246

Lasker, Albert, 231–33, 234

Lasker Plan, 231–34, 240, 241, 243, 270n41

league presidents: "review board" instituted by owners, 68

Leibold, Nemo: affinity for "playing it straight," 30; Charles Comiskey's acquisition of, 35; Clean Sox celebration after teammates confess to game fixing, 224; factions within the 1920 White Sox and, 9; 1920 season performances, 43, 45, 80, 95, 98, 99, 227; replaced by Amos Strunk, 95–96

Leonard, Dutch, 7, 19, 172, 180, 262n8

Lewis, Duffy: acquired by the Yankees, 19; 1920 season performances, 23, 85, 123, 129, 166, 182; at Ray Chapman's funeral, 131

Lieb, Fred, 239–40

Loomis, Fred, 194

Loomis letter. See Cruisenberry-Loomis letter

Lord, Bris, 48–49

Louisville Slugger, 73–74

Loyal Five, 66, 242, 243

Lunte, Harry: games following Ray Chapman's death, 171, 173–74; 1920 season performances, 123, 129, 141, 144, 156, 157

Lynn, Byrd, 25

Mack, Connie: Amos Strunk and, 94, 95, 96; Ban Johnson and, 66; breakup of the Athletics, 28, 94; the Carl Mays crisis and, 6, 161–62; and fan-ended game at Shibe Park, 138; and sale of Bob Shawkey, 17; Scott Perry incident and, 65; trading Joe Jackson to the Indians, 98

Magee, Lee, 8

Mails, John Walter "Duster": acquired by the Indians, 159–60; attitude of, 160; debut with the Indians, 160; nicknames, 159, 160; 1920 season performances, 174, 185, 186, 200, 208–11, 219, 229; 1920 World Series performance, 256

Maloney, Louis, 165

Mann, Les, 66, 203

Mannix, Daniel, 82

Mathewson, Christy, 34, 40

Mays, Carl: acquired by the Yankees, 14–15; allegations of crookedness against, 239–40; appearances following Ray Chapman's death, 149–51, 165, 166, 180, 181, 187, 191, 198; assault on Bryan Hayes, 6, 22; Ban Johnson and, 5, 6–7; baseball's dislike of, 7–8, 56; career stats of, 239; fatal beaning of Ray Chapman by, 3, 9, 120–24; and fight with Swede Risberg, 106; Hall of Fame prospects of, 239; legal interview following Ray Chapman's death, 125; 1920 season performances, 22, 23, 25, 27, 58, 84, 91, 102, 106, 114, 116, 119, 120; number of batters hit by, 135; as one of few southern baseball players, 56; with the Red Sox, 6–7, 14–15; traffic violations of, 91–92; Ty Cobb and, 8, 10, 134–35, 161

McBride, George, 161

McClellan, Harvey, 227

McDonald, Charles, 178, 223, 225

McDonough, Joseph, 224

McGeehan, W. O.: on Babe Ruth's suing of movie producers, 164; defending Carl Mays, 10, 127, 135–36, 149; on gambling in baseball, 178, 202; on the Polo Grounds, 89

McGraw, John, 232

McInnis, Stuffy, 7, 91, 108, 142, 188

McMullin, Fred: affinity for living dangerously, 30; Black Sox scandal and, 40, 211, 217, 222;

factions within the 1920 White Sox and, 9; gambling and, 44; 1920 season performances, 98–99

McNally, Mike, 91

McNichol, Walter, 131

McNutt, William Slavens, 129

Meadows, Lee, 176

Menosky, Mike, 125, 142, 188–89

Merkle, Fred, 177, 202, 261n8

Merrigan, T. M., 124

Meusel, Emil "Irish," 20, 240

Meusel, Robert William "Long Bob": joins the Yankees, 20–21; 1920 season performances, 81, 84, 86, 87–88, 89, 90, 104, 109, 151, 180, 182, 191

Milan, Clyde, 139

Miller, Orlando F., 115

Miller, Otto, 254

Minor Leagues, 242, 243–44

Mitchell, Clarence, 254

Mitchell, Fred, 176

Mogridge, George, 17, 23, 90, 163, 193

Moran, Pat, 40

Moriarity, George, 156

Morton, Guy: games following Ray Chapman's death, 141, 144; 1920 season performances, 79, 87, 112, 114, 158, 160, 161, 175; at Ray Chapman's fatal beaning, 122

movies: Babe Ruth and, 148, 162, 163–64

Murdock, Eugene, 4

Murphy, Eddie, 28, 188, 224

Myers, Elmer, 51, 86, 158

Nallin, Dick, 78, 129, 147, 149

Nathan, Alan, 264n6

National Aeronautics and Space Administration (NASA), 71–72

National Agreement, 241, 242, 245

National Commission: and Ban Johnson, 64–68; the Carl Mays crisis and, 66–67; demise of,

National Commission (*cont.*) 178, 232; on free agents, 5; Garry Herrmann and, 42, 64, 65, 66, 67, 232; proposals to replace, 232–33

National League: Ban Johnson's war with, 61–63; the reserve clause and, 62; "syndicated" baseball and, 62

National League owners, 241

Navin, Frank, 66, 242, 243

Navin Field, 111

"New National League," 243–44

New York American, 21, 73–74, 111, 115, 121, 198

New York Giants: attendance records, 15, 261n2; 1913 world tour of, 34; 1921 World Series, 239–40; Urban Faber and, 34

New York Post, 82, 102, 121, 150, 164, 220

New York State Supreme Court, 67

New York Sun: Dan Daniel's defense of Carl Mays, 127; Happy Felsch's interview with, 228; indictment of the Black Sox, 220–21; on Ray Chapman's death, 121; stories by William Hanna, 82–83, 104, 109, 121

New York Times, 91, 101, 149, 191, 198

New York Tribune: Grantland Rice on Carl Mays, 149; on Tillinghast Huston, 111; W. O. McGeehan on Babe Ruth suing movie producers, 164; W. O. McGeehan on Carl Mays, 10, 127, 135–36, 149; W. O. McGeehan on gambling in baseball, 178, 202; W. O. McGeehan on the Polo Grounds, 89

New York World, 41–42, 82, 127, 149, 227

New York Yankees: attendance records, 261n2; building of Yankee Stadium, 6; the Chick Fewster beaning and, 21; and the Jack Quinn controversy, 5–6; 1919 postseason money dispute, 67; 1921 World Series, 239–40; owners of, 6; players acquired prior to the 1915 season, 16–21; purchase of Babe Ruth from the Red Sox, 12, 14–15; purchase of Carl Mays from the Red Sox, 14–15

New York Yankees (1920): Babe Ruth's impact on baseball attendance, 2–3, 15–16, 77, 80, 102–3, 111, 182; Babe Ruth's late-season slump, 162; Babe Ruth's pursuit of the home run record, 76–78, 80–82; Carl Mays and the fatal beaning of Ray Chapman, 6–7, 10, 11, 120–24; as contenders, 50; drunken celebration in Windsor, Ontario, 109–11; early season woes, 21–23; exhibition game against the Pirates, 182; games against the Athletics, 22–23, 26, 181; games against the Browns, 23, 25, 100–102, 166, 197–98; games against the Indians, 23, 25, 58, 59, 83–91, 113–15, 118–23, 128–30, 181–85; games against the Red Sox, 22, 23–24, 26, 91, 180–81; games against the Senators, 24–25, 115, 198–99; games against the Tigers, 25, 108–12, 145–52, 186–87; games against the White Sox, 23, 80–83, 102–7, 161, 163, 164, 165–66, 187, 190–93; home attendance, 80, 82, 88, 118, 147, 149–50, 165–66; late-season injury to Ping Bodie, 182; longevity of players, 271n4; the "New National League" and, 243; players at Ray Chapman's funeral, 131; resurgence in May and June, 23–27; rumored train accident involving, 183; St. Mary's Boys

Band and, 182–83; strike over third-place shares, 22; the Tigers' use of the hidden-ball trick against, 111

Niehaus, Dick, 79, 159

Nunamaker, Les, 141, 172

Oakland Athletics, 28

O'Leary, Charlie, 26

O'Leary, James, 167, 168–69

O'Neill, Jim, 139

O'Neill, Steve: career with the Indians, 55; and Daly-Chapman wedding, 56; games following Ray Chapman's death, 141, 142, 143; 1920 season performances, 59, 85, 87, 120, 122, 172, 206, 218; the Pullman car Quartet and, 170; Ray Chapman's death and, 124; and Speaker-Graney fist-fight, 131, 267n26

Over the Fence (instructional film), 164

Owens, Brick, 111, 138, 169, 210

owners: as check on powers of league presidents, 68; proposals for reorganization of baseball management and, 231–34; proposals to reorganize baseball's governance and, 241–45; relationship with Ban Johnson, 5–6, 63–64, 68, 241; "syndicated" baseball and, 62. *See also* American League owners

Pacific Coast League, 154

Paulette, Gene, 8

Peckinpaugh, Roger: career with the Yankees, 18; 1920 season performances, 27, 85, 86, 88, 89–90, 91, 120, 165; 1920 team strike and, 22

Pennock, Herb: Connie Mack's unloading of, 28; 1920 season performances, 23, 140, 141, 167, 169, 200

Perkins, Cy, 186

Perry, Scott, 65, 138, 201

Pershing, John H., 233

Pezzolo, Francesco Stephano. *See* Bodie, Frank Stephen "Ping Bodie"

Pfeffer, Jeff, 21, 121, 146

Phair, George, 213

Philadelphia Athletics: Amos Strunk's career with, 93–94, 95; Connie Mack's breakup of, 28, 94; decline of, 50; growth in attendance, 2; Joe Jackson–Bris Lord trade, 48–49; and sale of Bob Shawkey, 17; and Scott Perry incident, 65; and trade for Braggo Roth, 51; and trade of Francesco Pezzolo (Ping Bodie), 18

Philadelphia Athletics (1920): boycott discussion against Carl Mays and, 161–62; games against the Indians, 78, 112–13, 145, 154–57, 185–86; games against the White Sox, 44, 99–100, 137–38, 200–201; games against the Yankees, 22–23, 26, 181

Philadelphia Phillies, 20, 176–77

Pick, Charlie, 203

Pinelli, Babe, 111, 135, 172

Ping Bodie. *See* Bodie, Frank Stephen "Ping Bodie"

Pipp, Wally: career with the Yankees, 16–17; 1920 season performances, 77, 81, 84, 85, 87, 90, 91, 114, 119, 123, 129, 165, 184, 185, 187; at Ray Chapman's funeral, 131

pitchers: "closers," 85; home runs by, 247; "spitball," 153–54; World Series home runs by, 238, 247, 254

pitches: hitting a home run and, 70; shine ball, 54; spitball, 54–55

The Pitch That Killed (Sewell), 131

Pittsburgh Pirates, 53, 65, 159, 182

Polo Grounds: attendance records,

Polo Grounds (*cont.*)
261n2; 1920 attendance, 3, 80, 82, 88, 118, 147, 149–50, 165–66; press area, 121; sense of intimacy in, 120; W. O. McGeehan on, 89

Popular Mechanics, 70

Pratt, Del: acquired by the Yankees, 18; 1920 season performances, 87, 97, 115, 123, 149, 151, 184, 187; 1920 team strike and, 22; Project Retrosheet, 267n1

Pullman car Quartet, 170–71

Quinn, Jack "Picus": free agent controversy over, 5–6; 1920 season performances, 23, 24, 27, 89, 166, 183, 190

Quinn, John, 180

Quinn, Robert, 131, 243

Ray Chapman Memorial Day, 171

Reach Guide, 240

Reichow, Oscar, 136–37, 201

Replogle, Hartley: Black Sox investigation and, 178, 179, 202–3; Joe Jackson's grand jury testimony and, 222, 223; Maclay Hoyne and, 225; rumors of game fixing by the 1920 White Sox and, 219

reserve clause, 62

"review board," 68

Rice, Grantland, 106, 146, 150

Risberg, Swede: affinity for living dangerously, 30, 36–37; Black Sox scandal and, 39, 41, 211, 222, 263n11; contract conflict with Charles Comiskey, 42; death of, 238; Eddie Cicotte's grand jury testimony against, 222; factions within the 1920 White Sox and, 9; and fight with Carl Mays, 106; Joe Jackson's fear of, 224; 1920 season performances, 43, 45, 80, 99, 105, 106, 108, 139, 166, 168, 169, 180, 188, 191, 201, 206, 207, 209, 217

Ritter, Lawrence, 4

Robinson, Arthur, 21, 73–74, 100–101, 111, 115

Rommel, Eddie, 99, 137, 186, 201

Roth, Braggo, 51

Rothstein, Arnold, 196–97, 203–4

Rowland, Pants, 34

Royal Canadian Mounted Police, 110

Ruel, Herold "Muddy": acquired by the Yankees, 17; 1920 season performances, 86, 87, 88, 89, 90, 91, 111, 119, 120, 123, 129, 151, 165, 182; on Ray Chapman's death, 127

Runyon, Damon: on Babe Ruth, 198, 199; career of, 247–48; on Carl Mays, 150; death of, 248; on gambling in baseball, 204; on the 1920 World Series, 248, 249–50, 251–53, 254, 256, 257; on Ray Chapman's fatal beaning, 121, 125; Runyon/Runyan spelling, 247, 266n1; writing style of, 247

Ruppert, Jacob: Ban Johnson and, 6, 7, 63–64; defending Carl Mays, 7, 147; and Harry Frazee, 14–15, 19; and players acquired prior to the 1915 season, 16–21; reorganization of baseball's governance and, 241; on the "review board," 68; St. Mary's Boys Band and, 182–83; supporting suspension of Black Sox conspirators, 226; on Yankees attendance in 1920, 88

Ruth, Babe: appearances at The Edelweiss, 192; bases on balls and, 101, 105–6; on batting with Louisville Slugger, 73–74; career with the Red Sox, 12–14, 95; controversial call against at Comiskey Park, 103–4; drunk driving and, 26–27; fan presentations to, 113–14; games following Ray Chapman's death, 147–48, 149, 150; Harry Frazee and, 14; home runs and, 13, 16, 23–24, 59, 74–78, 80–82, 89, 91, 102, 105, 107, 109, 111, 115, 116, 130, 163, 181, 182, 183, 184, 187, 190, 198–99; impact on baseball attendance, 2–3, 15–16, 77, 80, 102–3, 111, 182; injuries, 22–23, 74, 114–15, 163; movies and, 148, 162, 163–64; New York fans and, 199; 1920 late-season slump, 162; 1920 season performances, 21, 22–27, 50, 76–78, 86, 87, 88, 89, 90, 91, 101–2, 103–4, 105, 106–7, 109, 111, 114–15, 116, 123, 128–29, 130, 180, 181, 183, 184, 190–92; offensive stats, 12, 13; personality of, 16; pitching appearance in 1920, 24–25; pitching stats, 12, 13; and the power of positive thinking, 115; public appeal of, 16; public faith in baseball and, 215; rumored train accident involving, 183; sold to the Yankees by the Red Sox, 12, 14–15; St. Mary's Industrial School of Baltimore and, 182; visiting wounded World War I veterans, 115

Ryan, James, 165

Salsinger, H. G., 134–35

Sanborn, Irving E.: on Babe Ruth, 105, 107; on Buck Weaver, 31; on Carl Mays, 164; on Happy Felsch, 100, 180; and investigation into gambling by the 1920 Cubs, 178; on Lefty Williams, 200

Sanders, Elbert, 205, 241

San Francisco Seals, 18, 19

Sawicki, Gregory S., 71, 72

Schalk, Ray: accusations against the 1920 White Sox, 100, 167, 168, 169; affinity for "playing it straight," 30; career with the White Sox, 31–32; Clean Sox celebration after teammates confess to game fixing, 224; factions within the 1920 White Sox and, 9, 97; fan turnout in support of, 229; *New York Sun*'s indictment of, 221; 1920 season performances, 43, 165, 188, 206, 209

Schang, Wally, 7, 94, 188

Schupp, Ferdie, 56

Scott, Everett, 79, 144

Scullen, William, 132

Sewell, Joey: acquired by the Indians, 173; Damon Runyon on, 252; longevity of, 239; 1920 season performances, 184, 185, 209, 218

Sewell, Mike, 131

Shanks, Howie, 139

Shawkey, Bob "Bob the Gob": acquired by the Yankees, 17; Connie Mack's unloading of, 28; 1920 season performances, 23, 27, 87, 88, 111, 114, 116, 130, 151, 166, 181, 184, 187, 192–93; 1920 team strike and, 22

Sheckard, Jimmy, 101

Sheridan, John, 127

Shibe, Ben, 63, 66, 243

Shibe Park, 138

shine ball, 54

Shocker, Urban, 101, 102, 166

Shore, Ernie, 19, 131

singing. *See* Pullman car Quartet

Sisler, George, 27, 45, 65, 126, 219, 226

slugging percentage: trends in the early twentieth century, 73

Smith, Earl, 174–75, 179, 230

Smith, Elmer: acquired by the Indians, 51; games following Ray Chapman's death, 142, 143, 145; longevity of, 239; 1920 season performances, 59–60, 89, 113, 114, 119, 130, 155, 173, 174–75,

Smith, Elmer (*cont.*)
200; 1920 World Series grand slam, 238, 254, 255; Ring Lardner on, 256–57
Smith, Sherrod, 256
Somers, Charles, 35, 49, 63
South Bend Times, 246
South Bend Tribune, 246
southerners in baseball, 56
Sowell, Mike, 267n26
Speaker, Tris: acquired by the Indians, 49; and Carl Mays, 3, 7, 9, 124; Damon Runyon on, 249–50; effect of Ray Chapman's death on, 155–56, 157–58; games following Ray Chapman's death, 141–45; and George Hildebrand, 155–56; honoring of, 113; impact on the Indians of, 50; injuries, 59; Jack Graney and, 131, 142, 267n26; and John Mails, 160; 1920 season, 27, 58, 59, 60, 78, 79, 84, 85, 86, 87, 89, 97, 114, 116, 119, 172, 173, 175, 183, 184, 185, 186, 200, 208, 209, 218, 226, 231; 1920 World Series performance, 256; as on-field manager, 52; at Ray Chapman's death and funeral, 124–25, 128, 131; Ray Chapman's wedding and, 56–57; with the Red Sox, 19; search for a fourth starter in 1920, 158–60; Smoky Joe Wood and, 51
Spink, C. C., 215
Spink, J. G. Taylor, 270n41
Spink family, 68
spitball pitchers, 54–55, 153–54
Sporting News: Ban Johnson and, 67, 205, 241; on Carl Mays's fatal beaning of Ray Chapman, 126, 127; on Carl Mays's return to the mound following Ray Chapman's death, 150–51; Elbert Sanders on Charles Comiskey and Ban Johnson, 205; on George Hildebrand and

the spitball, 153; on the 1920 Yankees' strike, 22; on public opinion against the White Sox, 215; on reform of baseball governance, 67; the Spink family and, 68
Sportsman Park, 226
sports writers: on Carl Mays's return to mound following Ray Chapman's death, 149, 150–51; descriptions of Ray Chapman's fatal beaning, 121; responses to Ray Chapman's fatal beaning, 126, 127. *See also individual writers and newspapers*
St. John's Cathedral, 130
St. Lawrence Hospital, 124
St. Louis Browns: August–September road trip, 175–76; the Carl Mays crisis and, 9; games against the Indians, 57, 60, 115, 174–75, 218, 219, 226; games against the Tigers, 230, 231; games against the White Sox, 179, 187; games against the Yankees, 23, 25, 100–102, 166, 197–98; George Sisler and, 65; as noncontenders, 50
St. Mary's Boys Band, 182–83, 187, 197–98
St. Mary's Industrial School of Baltimore, 182–83
Stanage, Oscar, 172, 180
Stick to the Finish club, 171
stolen bases, 163
Stricklett, Elmer, 153, 154
strikes: by the 1918 Cubs and Red Sox, 66; by the 1920 Yankees, 22
Stringer, Percy Harold, 110
Stronge, William J., 71, 72
Strunk, Amos: career with the Athletics and Red Sox, 93–95; Clean Sox celebration after teammates confess to game fixing, 224; dislike of Carl Mays, 7; Eddie Collins and, 98; injuries and, 94; Joe Jackson and, 98;

nicknamed "The Mercury of the American League," 93; 1920 season performances, 97–98, 107–8, 165, 189, 209; traded to the White Sox, 96

Sturm, Theodore, 130

Styles, Lena, 138

Sullivan, Alex, 127

Sullivan, Joseph J. "Sport," 30

"syndicated" baseball, 62

Taft, William Howard, 68, 233

Tener, John, 65, 66

Tennes, Mont, 208

Tenney, Ross: on Carl Mays and the crisis in baseball, 126, 150, 161, 162; on Duster Mails, 160, 186; on Indians vs. Red Sox, 84; on Indians' odds of winning the pennant, 112–13; on Indians winning the pennant, 227; on Joey Sewell, 186; on Tris Speaker, 141

Terry, Zeb, 36

"That Old Gang of Mine," 170

Thomas, Pinch, 141

Thormahlen, Herbert "Hank," 23, 181, 184, 185, 191

Tobin, Johnny, 174–75

triple play, unassisted, 238, 247, 254–55, 256

triple steal, 163

Uhle, George, 78, 79, 158, 175, 218

Veach, Bobby, 56, 151

Veeck, William, 176, 178, 203, 232

vibrational frequency of baseball bats, 70–71

Vick, Sammy, 25, 165, 181

Vila, Joe, 22, 136

Vitt, Oscar "Ossie," 108, 143, 169, 188

Wagner, Honus, 63

Walker, Clarence "Tilly," 13, 156, 186

walks. *See* bases on balls

Walsh, Ed, 146

Walters, Roxy, 79

Wambsganss, Bill "Wamby": early career with the Indians, 52–53; longevity of, 239; 1920 season performances, 58, 79, 85, 86, 89, 90, 113, 120, 141, 172, 207; Ring Lardner on, 256–57; and slump following Ray Chapman's death, 157; on the Speaker-O'Neill fight, 131, 267n26; unassisted triple play in the World Series, 238, 254–55, 256

Ward, Aaron: early career with the Yankees, 20; 1920 season performances, 77, 87, 90, 104, 105, 166, 191

Washington Senators: games against the Indians, 112, 160, 186; games against the White Sox, 108, 114, 138–40, 189; games against the Yankees, 24–25, 115, 198–99; as noncontenders in 1920, 50; proposed boycott against Carl Mays and, 9, 161; suspicion of game fixing by the White Sox, 189

Weaver, Buck "The Ginger Kid": affinity for living dangerously, 30; Black Sox scandal and, 40, 211, 217, 222, 224, 231, 237; career with the White Sox, 31; contract conflict with Charles Comiskey, 42; Damon Runyon on, 248; factions within the 1920 White Sox and, 9; and friendship with Urban Faber, 35; 1920 audience with Comiskey, 227; 1920 season performances, 43, 44, 45, 80, 99, 104, 116, 139, 140, 163, 188, 189, 193, 210, 219

Weilman, Carl, 102

Welch, Frank, 78

Werden, Perry, 181

Western League, 181

Wilkinson, Roy, 43

Williams, Lefty: accused of fixing games, 167, 168; affinity for living dangerously, 30; Black Sox scandal and, 38, 39, 45–46, 211, 222–23; Charles Comiskey's acquisition of, 35; criticized by Indian fans, 96–97; factions within the 1920 White Sox and, 8, 97; grand jury confession of game fixing in 1919, 227–28; Joe Jackson's grand jury testimony against, 222–23; 1920 season performances, 44, 81, 97, 99, 105, 108, 116, 137, 139, 166, 179, 200–201, 212

Windsor, Ontario, 110–11

Woltz, Larry, 216, 219

"The Wonderful Wop." See Bodie, Frank Stephen "Ping Bodie"

Wood, Smoky Joe: acquired by the Indians, 50–51; as acting manager following Ray Chapman's death, 140–41; on Babe Ruth, 16; on Carl Mays, 4; game fixing by the 1920 White Sox and, 205; games following Ray Chapman's death, 140–41, 142, 143; and George Hildebrand, 155–56; longevity of, 239; 1920 season performances, 47, 85, 90; Ray Chapman's death and, 128; Ray Chapman's wedding and, 57; on the Tigers' informal agreement to "lay down" for the Indians, 229

Wood, Wilbur, 156–57

"The Woodland Bards," 29

Woodruff, Harvey, 105, 126, 204

World Series of 1917, 34

World Series of 1918, 8, 66, 261n8, 262n3

World Series of 1919: Black Sox scandal and, 37–42. See also Black Sox scandal

World Series of 1920: contestants in, 234; Game 1, 249–50; Game 2, 251; Game 3, 251–52; Game 4, 252–53; Game 5, 247, 253–56; Game 6, 256–57; Game 7, 257–59; Indians victories in, 238; reports by Ring Lardner and Damon Runyon on, 246–59

World Series of 1921, 239–40

Yankee Stadium, 6, 261n2

Young, Ralph, 1, 11, 111, 150, 172

Zachary, Tom, 138–39, 186

Zimmerman, Heinie, 8

Zinn, Jimmy, 182